D0264636

Sauces

by
THE EDITORS OF TIME-LIFE BOOKS

TIME-LIFE BOOKS·AMSTERDAM

TIME-LIFE BOOKS
EUROPEAN EDITOR: John Paul Porter
Design Director: Louis Klein
Photography Director: Pamela Marke
Planning Director: Alan Lothian
Chief of Research: Jackie Matthews
Chief Sub-Editor: Ilse Gray

THE GOOD COOK
Series Editor: Ellen Galford
Series Co-ordinator: Deborah Litton

Editorial Staff for *Sauces*
Text Editor: Jane Havell
Anthology Editor: Anne Jackson
Staff Writers: Alexandra Carlier, Sally Crawford,
Thom Henvey
Researcher: Margaret Hall
Designer: Cherry Doyle
Sub-Editors: Charles Boyle, Kate Cann, Frances
Dixon, Sally Rowland
Anthology Researchers: Stephanie Lee, Debra Raad
Anthology Assistant: Aquila Kegan
Proofreader: Judith Heaton
Editorial Assistant: Molly Sutherland

EDITORIAL PRODUCTION FOR THE SERIES
Chief: Ellen Brush
Quality Control: Douglas Whitworth
Traffic Co-ordinators: Jane Lillicrap, Linda Mallett
Picture Co-ordinator: Ros Smith
Art Department: Janet Matthew
Editorial Department: Lesley Kinahan, Debra
Lelliott, Sylvia Osborne

© 1982 Time-Life Books B.V.
All rights reserved. First printing in English.
No part of this book may be reproduced in any form or by
any electronic or mechanical means, including information
storage and retrieval devices or systems, without prior
written permission from the publisher, except that brief
passages may be quoted for review.

ISBN 7054 0613 X
TIME-LIFE is a trademark of Time Incorporated U.S.A.

PLANET EARTH
PEOPLES OF THE WILD
THE EPIC OF FLIGHT
THE SEAFARERS
WORLD WAR II
THE GOOD COOK
THE TIME-LIFE ENCYCLOPAEDIA OF GARDENING
HUMAN BEHAVIOUR
THE GREAT CITIES
THE ART OF SEWING
THE OLD WEST
THE WORLD'S WILD PLACES
THE EMERGENCE OF MAN
LIFE LIBRARY OF PHOTOGRAPHY
THIS FABULOUS CENTURY
TIME-LIFE LIBRARY OF ART
FOODS OF THE WORLD
GREAT AGES OF MAN
LIFE SCIENCE LIBRARY
LIFE NATURE LIBRARY
YOUNG READERS LIBRARY
LIFE WORLD LIBRARY
THE TIME-LIFE BOOK OF BOATING
TECHNIQUES OF PHOTOGRAPHY
LIFE AT WAR
LIFE GOES TO THE MOVIES
BEST OF LIFE

Cover: A serving ladle is lifted from a sauceboat of melted
butter sauce (*page 26*). Made by gradually whisking cubes
of cold butter into hot water, this smooth, light sauce is an
excellent accompaniment to boiled or steamed vegetables.

THE CHIEF CONSULTANT:
Richard Olney, an American, has lived and worked since 1951
in France, where he is a highly regarded authority on food and
wine. He is the author of *The French Menu Cookbook* and the
award-winning *Simple French Food,* and has contributed to
numerous gastronomic magazines in France and the United
States, including the influential journals *Cuisine et Vins de
France* and *La Revue du Vin de France.* He has directed
cooking courses in France and the United States and is a
member of several distinguished gastronomic and oenologi-
cal societies, including *L'Académie Internationale du Vin, La
Confrérie des Chevaliers du Tastevin* and *La Commanderie
du Bontemps de Médoc et des Graves.*

THE STUDIO CONSULTANT:
David Schwartz, an American from North Carolina, prepared many of the dishes for th
photographs in this volume. He has run restaurants both in London and in Bosto
Massachusetts, and is the author of a book on chocolate.

THE PHOTOGRAPHER:
Tom Belshaw was born near London and started his working career in films. He no
has his own studio in London. He specializes in food and still-life photograph
undertaking both editorial and advertising assignments.

THE INTERNATIONAL CONSULTANTS:
Great Britain: *Jane Grigson* was born in Gloucester and brought up in the north
England. She is a graduate of Cambridge University. Her first book on food, *Charc
terie and French Pork Cookery,* was published in 1967; since then, she has published
number of cookery books, including *Good Things, English Food* and *Jane Grigsor
Vegetable Book.* She became cookery correspondent for the colour magazine of th
London *Observer* in 1968. *Alan Davidson* is the author of *Fish and Fish Dishes of Lao
Mediterranean Seafood* and *North Atlantic Seafood.* He is the founder of Prospe
Books, which specializes in scholarly publications on food and cookery. **Franc**
Michel Lemonnier was born in Normandy. He began contributing to the magazir
Cuisine et Vins de France in 1960, and also writes for several other important Frenc
food and wine periodicals. The co-founder ,and vice-president of the society *L
Amitiés Gastronomiques Internationales,* he is a frequent lecturer on wine and
member of most of the vinicultural confraternities and academies in France. **German**
Jochen Kuchenbecker trained as a chef, but worked for 10 years as a food photogra
pher in many European countries before opening his own restaurant in Hamburg. *Ann
Brakemeier,* who also lives in Hamburg, has published articles on food and cooking
many German periodicals. She is the co-author of three cookery books. **Italy:** *Massim
Alberini* divides his time between Milan and Venice. He is a well-known food writer ar
journalist, with a particular interest in culinary history. Among his 14 books are *Storia a
Pranzo all'Italiana, 4000 Anni a Tavola* and *100 Ricette Storiche.* **The Netherland**
Hugh Jans, a resident of Amsterdam, has been translating cookery books and article
for more than 25 years. He has also published several books of his own, including *Bist
Koken* and *Sla, Slaatjes, Snacks,* and his recipes are published in many Dutc
magazines. **The United States:** *Carol Cutler,* who lives in Washington, DC, is the auth
of three cookery books, including the award-winning *The Six-Minute Soufflé and Oth
Culinary Delights. Judith Olney* received her culinary training in England and Franc
and has written two cookery books.

Valuable help was given in the preparation of this volume by the following members
Time-Life Books: *Maria Vincenza Aloisi, Joséphine du Brusle* (Paris); *Janny Hovinç*
(Amsterdam); *Berta Julia* (Barcelona); *Elisabeth Kraemer* (Bonn); *Ann Natanson, Mi*
Murphy (Rome); *Bona Schmid* (Milan).

CONTENTS

Finishing Touches

The accomplished sauce cook is often called the magician of the kitchen. But, like the magician's sleight of hand, the art of sauce-making owes more to the intelligent application of basic skills than it does to the intervention of unseen spirits. There is no mystique to a good sauce. Some sauces are as swift to make as they are simple, consisting of little more than a few spoonfuls of melted butter, or the juices captured from a roast. Others are more ambitious, demanding a long list of ingredients and hours of simmering, but repaying these efforts with a remarkable concentration of flavours. Whatever elements it contains, the sauce's purpose is always to enhance the food it accompanies, contributing the sum of its own flavour, colour and texture to the whole.

The word "sauce" comes from the Latin *salsus,* meaning "flavoured with salt"—and with good reason, for Roman sauces were salty indeed, almost invariably seasoned with the potent condiment known as *liquamen,* produced from heavily salted and fermented fish. This ubiquitous seasoning was used much as salt anchovies are in Mediterranean cookery today, to add savour to virtually every kind of food.

In the development of sauces, as in all branches of cookery, practicality has gone hand in hand with aesthetics. Marinades, for example, were probably first employed for their preservative and tenderizing powers, but it was soon discovered that steeping meat in wine, vinegar or verjuice—the juice of unripe grapes or other sour fruits—would also improve its flavour. Then, as now, resourceful cooks transformed these liquids into sauces, to moisten a stew or accompany roasted meats. Other sauces were originally devised as means of modifying strong flavours, or tempering the saltiness of preserved meats: creamy purées made from beans or peas served this purpose admirably, and still do.

The halcyon days of sauce-making came in France, during the 17th and 18th centuries, when master-cooks were courted and coveted by prospective employers, when courtiers—and the king himself—dabbled in the kitchen, when cookery was accepted by philosophers as both an art and a science. François Pierre La Varenne, sometimes called the father of classical French cuisine, published his magisterial *Le Cuisinier François* in 1651 and introduced the invaluable fat and flour thickening known as the roux. Talented cooks concocted new sauces for royal banquets and other great occasions, and named their prize creations for their patrons. Thus the Marquis de Béchamel achieved immortality through a white sauce (*page 28*) and the memory of the Prince de Soubise lives on by virtue of an onion purée (*page 34*).

Perhaps the most important legacy of this gastronomic golden age was a small group of basic sauces, sometimes called the "mother sauces", from which hundreds of variations spring: stock-based brown sauce and velouté; milk or cream-based béchamel; hollandaise and other preparations derived from egg yolks. Another basic sauce came somewhat later: it took a century or two after the tomato's arrival from the New World before cooks relinquished the belief that its scarlet flesh was deadly poison, and realized how readily it broke down to a piquant purée.

Sauce cookery has had its fads and fashions: types of thickening and specific ingredients fall into and out of favour, are taken up with the fervour of a religious conversion, then abandoned in search of new sensations (although rarely so eccentric as that proposed in 1920 by the Italian Futurist writer Marinetti, who suggested saucing meat with *eau de Cologne*). But the principles behind the making of good, honest sauces have changed relatively little, even if the equipment and ingredients available to the modern cook are beyond the wildest dreams of La Varenne.

Although every cuisine has its characteristic sauces, the French influence has been paramount in European cookery, and this predominance is reflected in the contents of this volume. The introductory pages include a guide to some useful herbs and spices, and a compendium of flavourings and garnishes—including a versatile chopped mushroom mixture that La Varenne himself invented for the Marquis D'Uxelles. The sauces demonstrated in Chapter 1 are simple mixtures of harmonious ingredients: olive oil and wine vinegar stirred into a vinaigrette; herbs, garlic and nuts pounded into fragrant pastes in a mortar; melted butter sharpened into a creamy *beurre blanc* by the addition of a little reduced wine and vinegar; and colourful fruit and vegetable purées. The art of making stocks and stock-based sauces of consummate flavour and perfect clarity is the subject of the second chapter, while Chapter 3 demonstrates techniques for preparing the classic egg-based sauces: gleaming mayonnaise that rises miraculously in minutes from the judicious blending of oil and beaten egg yolks; delicate hollandaise and its colourful derivatives such as *maltaise,* béarnaise and *choron*; savoury and sweet sabayons; and the ingenious *bâtarde,* swiftly prepared from beaten egg yolks and hot water thickened with a roux.

The final chapter explores meat, fish and vegetable preparations that virtually create their own integral sauces while they cook. The principle of wasting nothing of the food's flavour is applied to a range of sautéed, roasted, poached and braised dishes, including an elaborate meat stew complete with garnishes (*page 82*). These illustrated techniques are followed by an anthology of some 200 sauce recipes, ancient and modern, putting into practice the principles presented in the first half of the book.

Fragrances from the Herb Garden

Herbs make an invaluable contribution to the art of cookery; the 12 illustrated below are among the most useful to the sauce-maker. Each herb has a distinct character and can stand alone—the flavour of basil, for example, is essential to *pesto* (*page 22*) and that of tarragon to béarnaise (*page 62*), while mint makes an excellent flavouring for salad dressings. Rosemary may be used to perfume roast meat that is destined to be served with a very plain sauce.

The more common function for herbs, however, is to provide an unassertive background to a sauce's main flavour.

Sauces with lengthy cooking times are best flavoured with the bundle of herbs and aromatics known as a bouquet garni (*opposite page, below*). Apart from the components of a bouquet garni, most fresh herbs are at their best if given only minimal cooking or none at all. A few herbs, chopped or torn, make excellent garnishes for completed savoury sauces; for plain sauces, such as *bâtarde* or white sauce, such additions often provide an essential edge of flavour.

The delicate herbs that make up the mixture known as *fines herbes*—chives, chervil, parsley and also, if you like, tarragon—should only be added to a sauce at the last minute: their fragrance and flavour are destroyed by cooking.

Bouquet garnis and garnishes are not the only ways to introduce herbs into a sauce. You can also whisk a herb-flavoured butter (*page 12*) into a completed sauce for flavour and enrichment.

Certain herbs—oregano, thyme and winter savory among them—are particularly useful in dried form. A combination of the three—augmented, if you like, with a little marjoram—makes a versatile blend that may be used whenever mixed dried herbs are called for.

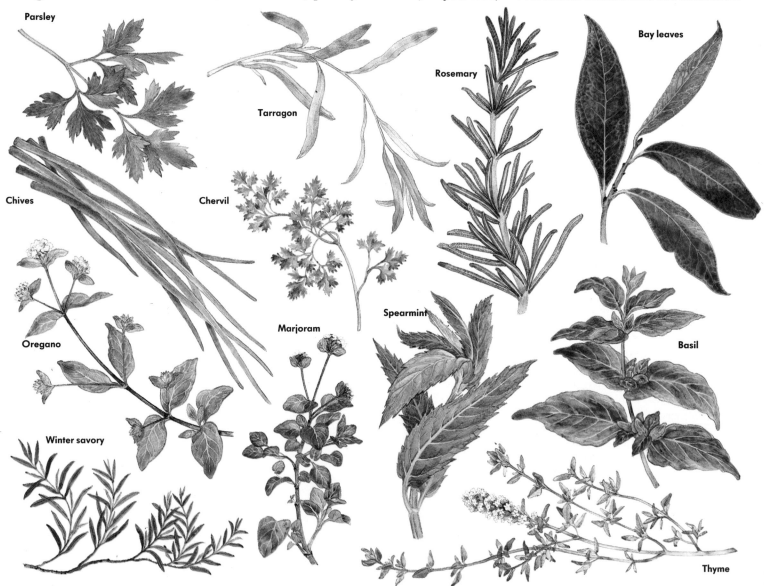

Parsley

Tarragon

Rosemary

Bay leaves

Chives

Chervil

Oregano

Marjoram

Spearmint

Basil

Winter savory

Thyme

A Sampler of Spices

For most sauces, spices are as essential a seasoning as salt. Peppercorns (*right*)—the dried berries of the pepper vine—are the most familiar; black peppercorns retain their skins and are more pungent than white ones. A mixture of 10 parts peppercorns to one part aromatic allspice berries (*far right*) makes an unusual blend for grinding in a pepper mill.

The spices shown in the centre row have more specific uses. Saffron lends colour and a delicate, slightly bitter flavour to fish or poultry sauces. Juniper berries, slightly pine-flavoured, are traditionally used in sauces for game. Fiery cayenne pepper is a natural partner for pungent sauces, especially for those that accompany fish.

Sweet, aromatic nutmeg and more delicate mace, nutmeg's outer covering, together with the spicy buds of the clove tree (*right, bottom row*) are very versatile. Used alone or in combination, they flavour sauces as diverse as bread sauce, vegetable purées and meat sauces.

Black peppercorns — **White peppercorns** — **Allspice berries**

Powdered saffron — **Juniper berries** — **Cayenne pepper**

Blades of mace — **Nutmeg** — **Cloves**

Assembling an Aromatic Bouquet

The most convenient flavouring for all stocks, and for sauces that are created as part of a whole dish, is the bouquet garni: herbs and aromatics bound into a neat package with string so that they can be easily added to and removed from the pot. The aromatic ingredients—celery and leek greens—also serve as a wrapping for the herbs, preventing them from falling apart and dispersing in the liquid during lengthy cooking.

The herbal mainstays of a bouquet garni are parsley, bay leaf and thyme, shown on the right. The bay leaf and thyme can be either fresh or dried. Parsley, however, should always be fresh; for the strongest flavour, you should include the plant's aromatic stems and, if possible, the washed root. Flat-leaf parsley is fuller in flavour than the curly variety. To vary a classic bouquet garni, you can include other herbs—notably rosemary, tarragon or savory—or even a small piece of orange or lemon rind.

1 Assembling the ingredients. Cut off the green top from a washed leek (*above*). Have ready flat-leaf parsley, a bay leaf, thyme, a celery stick, and some kitchen string or twine for tying.

2 Tying the bundle. Wrap the greens and celery round the herbs. Wind string tightly round the bundle along most of its length, and tie the string in a firm knot. Make a loop with the loose ends so that the bundle is easy to handle.

Subtle Effects from Diverse Additions

The wide range of flavouring elements shown here and overleaf can all be used to enhance sauces. Roasting juices (*right*), for instance, cleansed of fat, form a convenient, meaty essence to enrich a simple sauce such as Valentinoise (*page 20*) or to intensify the flavour of other sauces, for example those based on a meat stock.

Vegetables contribute colour and texture as well as flavour. Peeled and seeded chunks of tomato (*opposite page, left*), can be cooked briefly to make a fresh purée or somewhat longer to make a more concentrated one (*page 30*). A purée of tomatoes or sweet peppers (*opposite page, right*) will combine smoothly with a vinaigrette (*page 16*), suffuse a white sauce or a velouté with flavour and colour, or augment another vegetable purée (*page 34*).

Vegetables are also used to lend aromatic support without themselves becoming part of the finished sauce. *Mirepoix (below)*—made from finely chopped onions, celery and carrots—is added to the cooking liquid of a braise. At the end of cooking, when the flavours of the vegetables have been extracted, the solids are strained out and the liquid is used as the base of a sauce. Red wine, simmered with a *mirepoix* until the alcohol evaporates and the liquid reduces (*page 10, bottom*),

makes a potent concentrate for a fish, meat or game sauce.

The mixture of chopped mushrooms, onions, parsley and lemon juice known as *duxelles (opposite page, below)* forms both a flavouring and a garnish. Cooked in butter, it makes an ideal supplement to any mild-tasting sauce, such as a white sauce or fish velouté.

Another treatment for mushrooms is shown on page 11. Stewing whole mushrooms in butter, water and lemon juice to keep them white produces both a delicious garnish and a highly flavoured liquid. Prawns and mussels also provide both garnish and liquid (*page 10, top and centre*) when they are cooked in wine or a court-bouillon.

Truffles are warmed in butter (*page 11, left*); flavoured with a little brandy, they produce one of the most exquisite and penetrating of garnishes. The truffle peelings, pounded to a paste, also act as a powerful flavouring.

Bone marrow (*page 11, bottom*) makes a delicate garnish for any meat-based sauce. Choose beef marrow bones and boil them in salted water so that the marrow can be easily shaken free. The marrow needs only to be chilled and diced, then briefly poached just before serving.

Pan Juices from a Roast

1 **Pouring off roasting juices.** Remove meat from its roasting dish. Using a towel to protect your hands, pour the juices into a small bowl (*above*).

2 **Removing the surface fat.** Cool the juices, then refrigerate them until the fat rises to the surface and solidifies. Use a metal spoon to scrape the fat off (*above*); discard it.

A Mirepoix of Finely Diced Vegetables

1 **Dicing.** Cut onions into small dice. Cut carrots lengthwise, then cut the slices into small dice (*above*). Dice a stick of celery in the same way.

2 **Cooking.** Melt butter in a pan. Add the diced vegetables, mixed dried herbs (*page 6*) and salt. Then cook the mixture over a low heat for about 30 minutes, stirring occasionally.

3 **Storing.** Transfer the *mirepoix* to a bowl, packing it down well. When it is cool, cover it with plastic film, pressing the film against the surface, and store it in a refrigerator until needed.

Preliminary Treatment for Tomatoes

1 **Loosening skins.** Cut out the cores of large tomatoes; leave small tomatoes uncored. Cut a cross in the base of each tomato and plunge it into boiling water for 10 seconds, then put it into cold water.

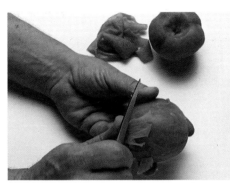

2 **Skinning.** Starting at the base where you have cut the cross, grip a section of skin between your thumb and the blade of a knife and strip it off (*above*). Repeat to strip off the rest of the skin.

3 **Seeding.** Halve each tomato crosswise to expose the seeds. Use your fingertips to dislodge the seed clusters (above), then shake each tomato half to rid it of any remaining seeds.

4 **Chopping coarsely.** Pile up the tomato halves together on a chopping board. Use a large, heavy knife to chop them into coarse pieces (*above*).

Puréeing Sweet Peppers

1 **Peeling.** Roast sweet peppers in a hot oven, or grill them; cover them with a damp towel to loosen the skins. Pull away the stems and the seeds; strip off the skins (*above*).

2 **Puréeing the flesh.** Remove stray seeds from the pepper flesh. Then use a pestle to purée the flesh of the peppers through a sieve set over a bowl (*above*).

Duxelles: a Marriage of Mushrooms and Onions

1 **Chopping mushrooms.** Using a heavy knife, slice mushrooms thinly (*above*) together with any stalks that may be left from other preparations. Pile the slices together and chop them finely.

2 **Cooking duxelles.** Finely chop onions. Gently cook them in butter until they are soft. Add the mushrooms (*above*) and salt; raise the heat and cook, stirring, until the mushrooms' liquid has evaporated.

3 **Adding herbs.** Finely chop parsley and add it to the mixture in the pan (*above*). Grind in pepper, add lemon juice and continue cooking for a few seconds.

Poaching and Peeling Prawns

1 Cooking the prawns. Prepare white wine court-bouillon (*recipe, page 159*); pour it over fresh Dublin Bay prawns (*above*). Bring the liquid to the boil, then reduce the heat and simmer for 7 to 8 minutes.

2 Removing the meat. Drain the prawns in a colander, reserving the cooking liquor as a flavouring. Pull the head off each prawn, then use scissors to snip through the underside of the shell from head to tail (*above, left*). Grasp the flesh and pull it free (*above, right*). Reserve the shells to pound and sieve for a flavouring.

Steaming Shellfish in White Wine

1 Preparing mussels. Soak mussels and scrape them clean; discard their fibrous "beards". Put them in a heavy pan with chopped onions, garlic, thyme, parsley, a bay leaf and a splash of white wine.

2 Steaming. Cook the mussels, covered, over a high heat for 3 to 5 minutes, until the shells open. Strain the mussels over a bowl and remove the flesh from the opened shells (*above*).

3 Straining the liquor. Strain the liquid into another bowl through a sieve lined with several layers of dampened muslin. Then moisten the mussels with some of the liquor; reserve the rest as a flavouring.

Reducing Red Wine to Intensify Flavour

1 Flavouring red wine. Pour red wine into a non-reactive pan. Add some cooked *mirepoix* (*page 8*) to flavour the wine—here, 2 heaped tablespoons of *mirepoix* are added to every bottle of wine.

2 Skimming. Bring the wine to the boil; reduce the heat and move the pan to the side, then simmer, removing scum as it rises on the cooler side (*above*). Reduce the wine by about two-thirds.

3 Straining. Strain the reduced red wine into a bowl through a nylon sieve lined with several layers of dampened muslin. Press out the liquid firmly, then discard the solids. Cool and cover the wine.

Capturing the Essence of Truffles

1 **Peeling truffles.** Scrub truffles in cold water, using a small brush. Hold the truffles over a mortar and peel them thinly with a vegetable peeler (*above*).

2 **Pounding the peelings.** Use a pestle to pound the peelings to a paste (*above*). Use the paste for additional flavour when truffles are to be used as a garnish.

3 **Cutting shapes.** Use a sharp knife to slice the truffles thinly. Leave the slices whole or cut them into whatever shape you like. Here, they are chopped evenly into dice.

4 **Cooking.** Rub a heavy pan with garlic and butter it thickly. Put in the truffle dice and moisten them with brandy (*above*). Warm the truffles, covered, for 10 to 15 minutes over a very low heat.

Keeping Mushrooms White

1 **Adding lemon juice.** Trim the stalks from small white button mushrooms. Put the caps in a pan with salt, pepper, a knob of butter, a little water and lemon juice (*above*).

2 **Simmering.** Heat the mushrooms, covered, until the liquid comes to a foaming boil (*above*). Let them cool. Before use, drain them over a bowl; reserve the juices for flavouring.

Extracting the Goodness of a Marrow Bone

1 **Simmering the bones.** Add sections of beef marrow bone to a pan of boiling salted water. Bring the water back to the boil, reduce the heat and then simmer, uncovered, for 10 minutes.

2 **Extracting the marrow.** Take out the bones. When they are cool enough to handle, hold each bone broad end down and give it a sharp shake—the marrow will slide out in a single piece.

3 **Dicing and cooking.** Chill the marrow to firm it, then cut it into small dice. Before using, poach the dice in salted water (*above*) for 1 to 2 minutes or until they are transparent, then drain them.

Flavoured Butters for Finishing Touches

A simple way to finish many hot sauces, giving them body and sheen, is to whisk in cubes of butter. To give extra flavour and colour, you can flavour the butter itself beforehand (*recipes, page 163*).

Most flavourings will need some preparation to reduce them to a purée fine enough to combine smoothly with the butter. The herbs for a green butter, for example, are chopped, blanched to intensify their colour, then pounded to a paste with blanched shallots (*right*). Salt anchovies are soaked and filleted; they are then easily pounded to a purée (*below*). More effort is needed to make a purée from crayfish (*opposite page*), but the flavour of the resulting butter fully justifies the work involved.

Use fresh, soft, unsalted butter: either stand it at room temperature for an hour or so, or beat it with a rolling pin to make it malleable. Never soften butter over heat as this would make it oily. Flavoured butters should be used as soon as possible, but they may be kept, covered, in the refrigerator for two to three days.

A flavoured butter finish is most appropriate for delicate sauces that already contain some butter—sauces thickened with a roux, for instance, such as a white sauce (*page 28*) or a velouté (*pages 49-51*). Hot vegetable sauces (*page 32*) particularly welcome flavoured butters—a herb butter would be a good choice.

Nuances of Flavour from Herbs and Shallots

1 Blanching herbs. Prepare *fines herbes* (*page 6*) and plunge them into a pan of boiling salted water (*above*) for about 2 minutes. Drain, rinse them in cold water and squeeze them dry.

2 Adding shallots. Put the blanched herbs in a mortar. Finely chop shallots; simmer them in boiling water for 2 minutes. Drain well and, if necessary, squeeze them dry; add them to the herbs (*above*).

3 Pounding the ingredients. Sprinkle a little coarse salt into the mortar, then pound the herbs and shallots until they form a paste. Add softened butter and pound again (*above*) to blend all the ingredients thoroughly.

4 Sieving the herb butter. Using a plastic scraper, press the butter, a spoonful at a time, through a drum sieve (*above*), scraping it from the underside of the sieve into a dish. Discard any fibres that are caught in the mesh.

Piquancy from Pounded Anchovies

1 Filleting. Soak salt anchovies in cold water for 5 minutes; rub off any salt that remains. Split each anchovy lengthwise; remove the backbone and separate the fillets. Dry them on kitchen paper.

2 Pounding. Place the anchovy fillets in a mortar and pound them to a smooth paste. Add softened butter and pound again (*above*) until the ingredients are smoothly blended.

3 Sieving. Using a plastic scraper, press the butter, a little at a time, through a drum sieve. Invert the sieve to scrape the butter from its underside (*above*). Put the butter in a dish; cover and chill.

The Delicacy of Freshwater Crayfish

1 **Shelling crayfish.** Poach live crayfish in a white wine court-bouillon (*recipe, page 159*) for 5 to 10 minutes; let them cool. Twist the tail of each crayfish to snap it apart from the head. Put the heads in a mortar. Shell the tails (*above*), reserving the meat; add the shells to the mortar.

2 **Pounding.** Pound the shells and heads, initially with a wide pestle. When the solids begin to break up, use a narrower pestle (*above*). Continue to pound until the solids are reduced to a creamy paste containing fragments of shell— a process that will take up to 30 minutes.

3 **Grinding the paste.** Fit a coarse disc in a food mill and set it over a large bowl. To remove fragments of shell from the paste, pass the mixture through the food mill (*above*), discarding any fragments that are left behind.

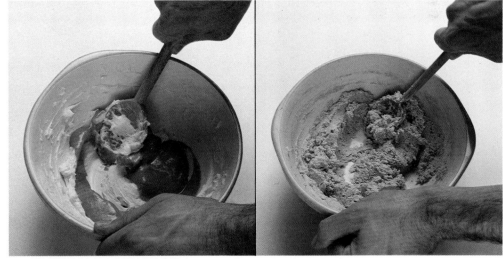

4 **Sieving the purée.** Set a drum sieve over a large plate. To eliminate all traces of debris and shell from the purée, and to ensure that it is smooth, press the purée, a little at a time, through the drum sieve, using a plastic scraper (*above*). Scrape the purée from the underside of the drum sieve on to the plate.

5 **Blending the purée with butter.** Put softened butter into a large mixing bowl and beat it with a wooden spoon until it is smooth and light-textured. Add the slightly liquid crayfish purée and beat it into the butter (*above, left*) until the two elements are uniformly blended (*above, right*). Cover the butter and chill it well before using it.

1
Simple Sauces
A Panoply of Accompaniments

Simple mixtures, cold and hot

Pounding solids into sauces

Managing melted butter

A fundamental roux-based sauce

Purées from fruit and vegetables

Melting chocolate

Turning sugar to liquid flavouring

The chief purpose of sauces is to act as a foil by introducing flavours and textures that throw the main components of a dish into sharper relief. The simplest sauces are blends of raw or cooked ingredients. The category includes such diverse examples as vinaigrette, sauces based on butter or bread or a butter and flour roux, vegetable sauces, fruit sauces and sweet sauces exclusively for desserts.

Many of these sauces, notably vinaigrette (*page 16, above*), require no cooking. The marrying of opposites—oil and vinegar—gives vinaigrette and its many derivatives their character, and the same principles of judiciously balancing ingredients based on oils or fats with those that are acid is applied in a cream and lemon sauce (*page 16, below*).

Other blended sauces are made by pounding solid ingredients together and binding them with oil. One of the best known is *pesto* (*page 22*), a pungent compound of garlic, pine-nuts, basil and cheese that endows a dish of plain pasta with an abundance of exciting flavours. Garlic is also an important feature of the French sauce known as *aïoli* that is traditionally served with salt cod. The blend shown on page 24 contains potatoes, which introduce a mild, starchy element to complement the delicacy of the preserved fish. Starch—in the form of bread—also provides the basis of a smooth sauce suitable for partnering rich game (*page 19*).

Butter can be a sauce in itself, and when it is whisked over very low heat with wine, vinegar and shallots to make *beurre blanc* (*page 26*) it provides an impeccable accompaniment—creamy yet piquant—for dishes that are delicate in flavour, such as poached white fish. By contrast, the basic white sauce made from milk thickened by cooking with a flour and butter roux (*page 29*) is neutral in itself—a quality that makes it an excellent foundation for flavourings. Tomato sauce is another standard preparation that lends itself to variation—and tomatoes are only one of many vegetables that can be turned into sauces by puréeing (*pages 30-35*).

With their blend of sweetness and acidity, sauces based on puréed fruit (*page 36*) complement both savoury dishes and—with additional sweetening—desserts. For sauces that are designed specifically for desserts, sugar and chocolate prove especially versatile ingredients (*page 38*).

A vegetable sauce made from puréed carrots is poured into a warm sauceboat. Cooked gently with butter, sugar and a little water, the carrots were finished over a high heat to glaze them, then they and their syrupy glaze were puréed in a food processor. Reheated to serving temperature, the purée was mixed with cream and finished with butter (*page 32*).

Vinaigrette and Its Variants

Vinaigrette, a simple mixture of seasoned vinegar and olive oil (*right; recipe, page 157*), is the classic dressing for green salads and vegetables such as asparagus or French beans. With the addition of extra flavourings, or the substitution of different ingredients (*right, below, and page 18*), vinaigrette becomes the foundation for a family of derivative sauces that complement fruit, meat, fish and shellfish.

Any vinaigrette is only as good as the ingredients that compose it. Use good wine vinegar—red has a more robust flavour than white—and the finest olive oil you can buy. Stir the mixture vigorously just before serving: left to stand, the oil and vinegar soon separate. Normal proportions are about one part vinegar to four parts oil, but the ratio will vary to suit the food the sauce accompanies or to take account of other flavourings in the dressing. Slightly bitter salad greens, such as chicory, endive and rocket, call for more vinegar than does a sweet lettuce. Less vinegar is required if you incorporate piquant flavourings—puréed raw tomatoes, for example (*page 18, top*).

Flavourings for a vinaigrette can be as simple as a dash of mustard, a few spoonfuls of chopped fresh herbs or pounded garlic, or as complex as the five different ingredients that go to make the Italian green sauce, *salsa verde* (*page 18, centre*).

If you use mustard or strong spices, such as paprika, which would mask the fruity flavour and delicate aroma of olive oil, choose instead a flavourless oil, such as peanut or sunflower oil.

As well as adding flavourings, you can substitute other ingredients for the basic oil or vinegar, creating yet more permutations. Lemon juice can replace vinegar, for example, and a favourite dressing for a salad of pungent dandelion leaves calls for hot bacon fat rather than oil.

One traditional salad dressing (*right*) uses cream and lemon juice to provide the essential elements of fat and acid. Here, the lemon juice is flavoured with mint, then double cream is stirred in; the juice's acidity causes the cream to thicken dramatically. On page 18, a thinner version of the same sauce is made with single cream, then flavoured and coloured with a purée of sweet red peppers.

Oil and Vinegar: the Classic Combination

1 **Blending ingredients.** Put salt and freshly ground pepper in a bowl. Add red wine vinegar, stirring until the salt has dissolved (*above, left*). Pour in olive oil, stirring vigorously (*above, right*): use about four parts of oil to one of vinegar. If you are not using the vinaigrette immediately, stir it up again just before serving.

A Rich Alliance of Cream and Lemon

1 **Flavouring with mint.** Squeeze a lemon and pour the juice into a bowl. Add fresh mint leaves and crush them lightly with a pestle (*above*). Allow the bruised mint to macerate in the juice for at least 15 minutes to release its flavour, then strain the liquid and discard the mint leaves.

2 **Pouring in cream.** Measure out double cream—about 30 cl (½ pint) for each lemon used. Pour the cream into the lemon juice in a thin stream, stirring constantly (*above*). As it is stirred, the mixture will thicken.

2 **Dressing a salad.** Pour the vinaigrette over a salad—here, composed of lamb's lettuce, oakleaf lettuce, curly endive, cress, chervil and chopped herbs. Using your hands, toss the salad thoroughly until the leaves are evenly coated (*inset*).□

3 **Testing consistency.** Continue stirring until the mixture holds firm peaks when the spoon is lifted (*above*). Use the finished sauce at once: it will continue to thicken more if allowed to stand. Here, it is served with fresh figs, peeled, slit and opened out into quarters, then garnished with strips of Parma ham and fresh whole mint leaves (*right*).□

Intensity of Hue from Ripe Tomatoes

1 Flavouring. Dissolve salt in lemon juice or—as here—in wine vinegar. Prepare tomatoes (*page 9*); press them through a fine-meshed sieve set over a bowl. Add the purée to the vinegar and stir (*above*).

2 Adding oil. Pour in olive oil gradually, stirring the mixture until it is smoothly blended. To counteract the tomatoes' acidity, use slightly more oil than for a plain vinaigrette.

3 Serving the sauce. Just before serving, stir the sauce thoroughly again. Here, it is spooned over an hors-d'oeuvre of calf's brains poached in a court-bouillon, then cooled and sliced.□

A Pungent Salsa Verde

1 Pounding. Soak, fillet, rinse and dry salt anchovies (*page 12*). In a mortar, pound the anchovies with peeled garlic cloves and coarse salt (*above*) until the mixture forms a smooth paste.

2 Adding herbs. Stir in lemon juice or vinegar and then oil. Add finely chopped herbs—parsley, chives, tarragon, basil, chervil (*above*)—chopped capers and chopped, drained, parboiled spinach.

3 Serving the sauce. Serve the sauce with a dish of mixed poached meats—here, boned shin of beef, pickled ox tongue, chicken and pork sausage.□

Tinting Cream Sauce with Pepper Purée

1 Adding red pepper purée. Put salt and pepper in a bowl and add lemon juice, stirring until all the salt is dissolved. Stir in a sweet red pepper purée (*page 9*).

2 Blending in cream. Stir single cream into the sweet pepper and lemon mixture as for lemon and cream sauce (*page 16*). Continue adding cream until the sauce has the colour and consistency desired.

3 Serving the sauce. Serve the sweet red pepper, lemon and cream sauce with salads, poached fish or—as here—fresh prawns, poached in a court-bouillon, cooled and peeled.□

A Medley of Mixtures

A surprising range of ingredients can thicken or lend body to simple mixtures, hot and cold. Bread, fruit jelly and butter are the main constituents of the three sauces shown here and on page 20.

Crumbled white bread has long been used as a classic thickener for hot sauces. The sauce on the right (*recipe, page 164*) employs day-old bread as the main ingredient, both for its flavour and its thickening qualities. The bread is simmered with milk and aromatics over gentle heat until the bread absorbs the liquid.

The quantity of bread used—100 g (3 to 4 oz) to every 60 cl (1 pint) of milk—gives the sauce a distinctive soft, thick consistency. Smoothness is achieved by whisking the mixture; for extra richness, you can add cream and whisk in some butter. A little fresh grated horseradish will add a touch of sharpness to the finished sauce. Hot bread sauce is a traditional accompaniment for game or poultry.

Valentinoise (*page 20, above; recipe, page 86*) is something of a curiosity: a sauce for grilled meats that becomes a sauce only when it is served. Valentinoise begins as a colourful assemblage of finely chopped vegetables and herbs, drenched with lemon juice and mixed with cold butter. Meat, sizzling hot from the grill, is laid on top; the butter melts and, when the meat is carved, its juices mingle with all the other elements, creating an aromatic sauce bound lightly by the butter.

The same principle holds good for different ingredients: you could add *duxelles* (*page 9*), *mirepoix* (*page 8*) or cooked mushrooms (*page 11*) to the mixture, for example; experiment with a variety of herbs (*page 6*); or substitute fortified wine for the lemon juice.

A tangy fruit jelly such as redcurrant or cranberry makes a delicious base for sauces to accompany rich meats. The Cumberland sauce also shown on page 20 (*recipe, page 98*) is a mixture of redcurrant jelly, port, shallots and the rinds and juice of oranges and lemons. Sharper flavourings can include mustard, ginger and cayenne pepper. The jelly is first melted so that it can be easily mixed with the other ingredients; in addition to its role as a flavouring, it gives body to the sauce.

1 Adding bread. Remove the crusts from day-old white bread; tear the bread into pieces. In a pan, put milk, an onion stuck with one or two cloves, a blade of mace, a bay leaf and salt. Bring the milk to the boil, then turn down the heat and add the bread (*above*).

2 Removing the flavourings. Over a low heat, simmer the bread, milk and flavourings for about 20 minutes, or until the bread has disintegrated. Remove the onion, mace and bay leaf from the pan (*above*) and discard them.

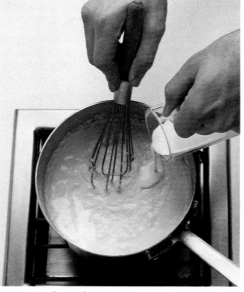

3 Finishing the sauce. Whisk the sauce to give it a smooth consistency. If it is not thick enough, stir in white breadcrumbs and cook for a few minutes longer. To finish the sauce, whisk in double cream, then remove the pan from the heat.

4 Serving the sauce. Transfer the sauce from the pan to a warmed bowl or sauceboat. Serve the hot bread sauce with meat dishes such as roast chicken, turkey or—as here—roast partridge.□

Valentinoise: a Colourful Amalgam

1 **Assembling the ingredients.** Remove the fat from roasting juices (*page 8*). Cut butter into cubes. Squeeze the juice from a lemon. Skin and seed tomatoes (*page 9*), and chop the tomatoes finely. Finely chop parsley and shallots. Warm a large serving platter. Scatter the shallots and parsley over the platter, then add the tomatoes (*above*).

2 **Seasoning.** Spoon the cleansed roasting juices over the chopped vegetables on the platter, scatter the butter cubes on top and pour on the lemon juice. To season the sauce, grind black pepper over the surface (*above*).

3 **Mixing the ingredients.** Use a fork to mash the butter into the rest of the ingredients, working the mixture until it is loosely amalgamated (*above*). With the fork, spread the mixture evenly over the surface of the platter.

Cumberland: the Meeting of Sweet and Sour

1 **Blanching rind.** Using a sharp knife, pare the rind from an orange and a lemon, leaving the bitter white pith on the fruit. Cut the rind into *julienne*. To remove any bitterness, parboil the rind for a minute or two (*above*), then drain it. Chop shallots finely and parboil them in the same way.

2 **Assembling the ingredients.** Melt redcurrant jelly in a bowl set over a pan of boiling water; remove the pan and bowl from the heat. Add the rind and shallots (*above*). Squeeze the juice from the orange and lemon and measure out port and white wine vinegar.

4 **Serving the dish.** Grill steak—here, a 5 cm (2 inch) thick slice of rump. Place the hot steak on the platter (*above*). Carve the steak in slices on the bias, and allow its juices to run out and mingle with the sauce. Serve the dish at once (*right*).□

3 **Finishing the sauce.** Stir in the juice of the orange and lemon, the port and the vinegar (*above*). Transfer the finished mixture to a sauceboat and serve the sauce over slices of cold meat or game (*right*)—in this case, roast haunch of venison.□

Pastes Pounded in a Mortar

When they are pounded in a mortar, foods as diverse as garlic, nuts, bread and cooked potatoes are reduced to a fine paste. Flavoured and bound with olive oil, the pastes form sauces that are ideal accompaniments to both hot and cold dishes. Pounding ingredients by hand with a pestle is a lengthy process but a worthwhile one: it gives you control over the texture of the paste at all stages. A food processor, though quicker and easier to use, often gives uneven results, puréeing some ingredients too finely and leaving others in distinct lumps.

To achieve a perfectly blended sauce, it is important to crush the most resistant ingredients first to ensure a paste fine enough to combine properly with soft or liquid elements. For the classic Italian *pesto* shown on the right (*recipe, page 92*), garlic and pine-nuts are reduced to a paste into which fresh basil leaves are then incorporated. To finish the sauce, oil and grated cheese are added alternately and gradually, so that the paste absorbs them evenly. The robust flavour of *pesto* is a delicious contrast to the delicacy of pasta and enhances any green vegetable.

The garlic-flavoured sauce overleaf (*page 24, above; recipe, page 124*) gets its thickening from the pounded flesh of newly boiled potatoes. The purée of potatoes and garlic becomes a rich, creamy sauce when oil is gradually stirred into it. You can, if you like, add an egg yolk to the potato purée; yolks absorb oil easily and help to make the sauce really smooth. The sauce—a traditional accompaniment for poached salt cod—is best made with a waxy variety of potato, whose slightly elastic flesh combines easily with the oil.

The unusual almond sauce also shown on page 24 (*recipe, page 90*) has a coarser texture than either the *pesto* or the garlic sauce since the solid ingredients—bread cubes, garlic and blanched almonds—are first fried to make them crisp. They are then pounded together with a tomato purée before being bound with oil. This pungent and colourful sauce complements strongly flavoured seafood, especially crustaceans, octopus and squid.

Pesto: the Powerful Presence of Fresh Basil

1 Pounding garlic. Rinse fresh basil leaves; weigh out pine-nuts. Finely grate firm, hard cheese—in this case, a mixture of *pecorino* and Parmesan. In a mortar, pound garlic cloves together with coarse salt (*above*)—the salt will help grind the garlic down to a smooth paste.

2 Adding pine-nuts. Drop the pine-nuts, a few at a time, into the mortar. Use the pestle to crush the nuts before adding more. Then pound the crushed nuts to reduce them to a coarse paste. Continue to pound, stirring occasionally with the pestle, until the pine-nuts are smoothly blended with the garlic.

5 Testing the consistency. Continue to add more cheese, tasting the sauce occasionally until you have a blend of flavours to your taste. Add enough oil to give the sauce a pouring consistency. Stir the sauce thoroughly with the pestle so that the oil and cheese are well worked in. The mixture should be a smooth, homogeneous paste (*above*).

6 Thinning the paste. Cook and drain pasta—egg noodles are used in this demonstration—reserving the cooking liquid. Transfer the pasta to a warmed serving bowl. Stir into the paste enough of the pasta's cooking liquid to make the sauce thin enough to pour easily.

3 **Adding basil.** Remove the stalks from the basil leaves and discard them. Add the leaves to the mortar. Use the pestle to pound the leaves to a pulp and stir them into the rest of the mixture.

4 **Adding grated cheese and oil.** To enable you to control the flow of oil, cut a lengthwise groove down either side of the bottle's cork. Alternately add about a spoonful of the grated cheese (*above, left*) and a thin trickle of olive oil (*above, right*), pounding each addition into the mixture before adding the next.

7 **Serving the sauce.** Ladle the sauce over the pasta in the serving bowl (*above*). Then toss the pasta until the sauce coats each strand evenly, and serve the pasta immediately on warmed plates.☐

A Creamy Fusion of Garlic and Potatoes

1 **Combining garlic and potatoes.** Boil potatoes until they are tender, drain and peel them. In a mortar, pound garlic cloves together with coarse salt to make a paste. Add the potatoes to the mortar while they are still warm. Pound them with the garlic and coarse salt (*above*) until they form a smooth paste.

2 **Stirring in oil.** Squeeze a lemon. Add olive oil to the mortar in a thin stream, stirring the paste continuously with the pestle (*above*). If the mixture becomes unmanageably thick, stir in a little lemon juice or tepid water to thin it.

3 **Finishing the sauce.** Continue to add oil, stirring it in until the mixture becomes glossy and is almost too thick to stir. To give the sauce further flavour, pour in the lemon juice (*above*).

Romesco: Savour and Substance from Sautéed Nuts

1 **Sautéing.** Remove the crusts from thick slices of stale white bread; cut the bread into cubes. Blanch almonds. Skin, seed and coarsely chop tomatoes (*page 9*). Heat oil in a frying pan and sauté the bread cubes on all sides until they are golden. Put the croûtons in a mortar. Sauté the almonds and garlic (*above*), and add them to the mortar.

2 **Pounding.** Sauté the tomatoes rapidly over a high heat for a few minutes until they are reduced to a coarse pulp. Add the tomatoes to the mortar. Pound the mixture vigorously to break down the croûtons, almonds and garlic to a fairly smooth, even-coloured paste (*above*).

3 **Adding flavourings.** To give the paste more flavour and thin it a little, pour in dry sherry in a thin stream (*above*), stirring with the pestle. Then stir in salt, black pepper and cayenne pepper. Taste and adjust the seasoning if necessary.

4 **Serving the sauce.** Use the pestle to stir in the lemon juice (*left*); taste the sauce and, if necessary, squeeze another lemon and add more juice as desired. Serve the sauce from the mortar, spooning it to the side of the main dish (*above*)—here, boiled salt cod accompanied by whelks, green haricots, a small violet artichoke, new potatoes and young carrots.□

4 **Blending in oil.** Add olive oil in a thin stream, stirring all the time with the pestle to incorporate it. As you stir in the oil, the mixture will gradually become lighter in colour (*above*).

5 **Finishing the sauce.** Continue to add oil until the mixture is glossy. The finished sauce should be soft enough to retain an impression when the pestle is drawn through it (*above*).

6 **Serving the sauce.** Spoon the sauce directly from the mortar to the side of the main dish—in this demonstration, it accompanies pieces of boiled squid, the pouch cut across into rings and the tentacles left whole.□

Melted Butter, Whisked with Vinegar

When butter is whisked gradually into a small amount of liquid over heat, the mixture thickens—or "mounts"—to form a light, foamy sauce. For the piquant sauce known as *beurre blanc*—a classic accompaniment to poached fish—the liquid is a sharply flavoured reduction of wine, vinegar and finely chopped shallots (*right; recipe, page 165*). For a mild sauce, lighter in texture and flavoured solely by the fresh, creamy butter itself, the only ingredient you add is water (*box, right, below*). Such a sauce is suitable for serving with hot, plainly cooked vegetables.

To make the *beurre blanc*, use any good dry white wine and a good quality white wine vinegar. You can vary the intensity of the sauce's flavour by adjusting the amount of butter from 250 to 400 g (8 to 14 oz) for every 20 cl (7 fl oz) of liquid.

To make perfectly smooth mounted butter sauce, you must take care in combining the fat and the liquid. If the butter is overheated, it will make the sauce oily. Therefore, when you begin to whisk the butter in, the liquid must be warm, rather than hot. A fireproof mat is an invaluable aid because it diffuses the heat evenly over the base of the pan. Cut the butter into small cubes—it is easiest to cut cold butter straight from the refrigerator—and add it in amounts of about 30 g (1 oz) at a time. Each addition should be whisked in thoroughly before you add the next.

Butter sauces are warm rather than hot and they should be served without delay since they solidify as they cool. If any sauce remains, you can refrigerate it for use later as a flavouring. Cooled and set, *beurre blanc* makes an unusual finish for other sauces, instead of conventional flavoured butters such as those shown on pages 12-13. Both leftover *beurre blanc* and plain butter sauce can also be cut into cubes and allowed to melt over grilled fish or meat, or hot vegetables.

1 Chopping shallots. Pour dry white wine and white wine vinegar into a heavy, non-reactive pan. Peel shallots and cut them in half lengthwise. Make fine slices through each half parallel to the cut surface; cut lengthwise across the slices to make strips, then across the strips to make fine dice (*above*).

2 Reducing the liquid. Add the shallots to the pan. Cook the mixture over a medium heat. When it boils, lower the heat to maintain a simmer and continue to cook the mixture until the reduced liquid barely coats the shallots.

A Variation Made with Water

1 Combining butter and water. Cut cold butter into cubes. In a heavy pan, bring water almost to the boil; add seasoning. Over a very low heat—using, if you like, a fireproof mat—add the butter to the pan, a few cubes at a time (*above*), whisking in each addition before adding more. As butter is whisked in, the mixture will lighten and become frothy.

2 Serving the sauce. Transfer the sauce to a warmed sauceboat or serve it directly from the pan. Pour the butter sauce immediately over the main dish—in this case, spears of boiled broccoli.

3 **Adding butter.** Remove the pan from the heat; season the mixture with salt and pepper and let it cool for a few seconds. Meanwhile, put a fireproof mat over a low heat to warm, and cut cold butter into cubes. Put the pan on the mat and add the butter a handful at a time (*above*). Whisk until each addition has almost disappeared before adding more.

4 **Whisking.** Continue to add the butter, a handful at a time, whisking constantly. As more butter is added, the sauce will thicken slightly until finally it has the consistency of single cream (*above*).

5 **Serving the sauce.** Transfer the sauce immediately to a warmed sauceboat (*left*): take care that the sauceboat is not too hot or it would make the sauce oily. Alternatively, serve the sauce from the pan. Pour the sauce over fish—here, a section of poached halibut (*below*).□

White Sauce: a Versatile Foundation

One of the most useful thickening agents in the whole repertoire of sauce-making is a roux—butter and flour blended to a smooth paste over gentle heat. The white sauce shown here (*right; recipe, page 160*) is perhaps the most fundamental roux-based sauce, consisting simply of the paste itself, milk and a little cream.

The blandness of a plain white sauce makes it an ideal base. Here, for example, it provides the foundation for two more elaborate sauces: a sauce flavoured with crayfish butter to serve with fish (*right, below*) and a cheese sauce for vegetables (*opposite page, below*).

To make the roux, the butter is first melted so that the flour will combine with it smoothly and evenly. The resulting paste is cooked for only a minute or two—until it begins to bubble—before milk is whisked in. Longer cooking at this stage would not only lessen the flour's thickening power but discolour the roux and hence the finished sauce. After the milk is added, the mixture should be whisked until it comes to the boil to prevent flour lumps from forming, and then simmered gently for at least 45 minutes. This long cooking improves both the texture and the flavour of the sauce: the liquid reduces and thickens and any taste of raw flour is eliminated. After sieving, the sauce is seasoned and thinned with cream until it has the consistency you want.

Special flavourings and colourings for a white sauce are usually added at this stage. You can stir in grated cheese, finely chopped herbs or capers, or a spoonful of prepared mustard, or you can whisk in a few pieces of a flavoured butter—the butters shown on pages 12-13 are all suitable. Alternatively, the milk used for the sauce can be first infused with aromatics such as carrot, onion and a bouquet garni.

The versatility of a white sauce does not end with the variety of flavourings it can accept. The sauce itself can be used as a cooking medium. Thinned with extra cream to allow for further reduction in the oven's heat, the sauce can be poured over prepared fish or vegetables and the whole dish cooked to make a golden gratin.

A Basic Blend Enriched with Cream

1 Adding milk. Melt butter in a heavy pan. When it foams, shake an approximately equal amount of flour evenly over its surface. With a whisk, stir the flour rapidly into the butter. Cook the resulting paste for a minute or so, then slowly pour in cold milk, whisking all the time (*above*).

2 Cooking the sauce. Increase the heat and, to prevent the formation of lumps, whisk the sauce until it boils. Season with a little salt. Reduce the heat to very low and simmer the sauce gently for at least 45 minutes. To keep the sauce from sticking to the pan, stir it from time to time with a wooden spoon or a whisk (*above*) scraping the pan's bottom and sides.

Nantua: Finishing with Crayfish Butter

1 Adding flavoured butter. Prepare and chill crayfish butter (*page 13*). Break the butter into rough pieces. Make a white sauce (*Steps 1 to 4, above*); remove the pan from the heat and stand it on a trivet. Add the crayfish butter, a handful at a time, stirring continuously (*above*).

2 Serving the sauce. When the mixture is evenly blended, pour the sauce into a warmed sauceboat. Serve this sauce with any poached, delicately flavoured fish, such as turbot, brill, sole or—as here—monkfish fillets. You can also use it to make a gratin of crayfish tails. □

3 **Sieving the sauce.** To remove any lumps that may have formed during cooking, place a sieve over another pan, and strain the sauce through (*above*). Then return the strained sauce to the heat.

4 **Finishing with cream.** To enrich the sauce and thin it to the right consistency, whisk in double cream (*above*). Add white pepper to taste, and, if you like, a little freshly grated nutmeg. Serve at once over vegetables, or finish the sauce with additional flavouring.□

Mornay: Sharpening with Cheese

1 **Adding grated cheese.** Finely grate hard cheese—in this case, equal amounts of Gruyère and Parmesan. Make a white sauce (*Steps 1 to 4, above*), using extra cream to give it a thin consistency. Off the heat, add the grated cheese to the sauce (*above*) and stir until it is melted.

2 **Pouring on the sauce.** Arrange prepared vegetables—here, boiled cardoons—in a gratin dish. Ladle the *sauce mornay* evenly over the vegetables (*above*), then sprinkle more grated cheese on top.

3 **Serving the gratin.** Put the gratin dish in an oven preheated to 190°C (375°F or Mark 5). After 15 to 20 minutes, when the sauce is slightly reduced and thickened and the surface of the gratin is pale golden, remove from the oven. Serve the gratin straight from the dish (*above*).□

Vibrant Colour from Sun-Ripened Tomatoes

Ripe tomatoes simmered with aromatics, garlic and herbs form delicious sauces that are simple to prepare. The fresh-flavoured, coarse-textured sauce (*right*), and the more piquant, smoother purée (*right, below; recipe, page 164*) shown here are both excellent with pasta and other farinaceous dishes, such as rice; they will also lend a touch of sharpness to deep-fried foods. In addition, either preparation can be used to contribute colour and flavour to other sauces.

The differences between the sauces demonstrated here are largely the result of their different cooking times. Skinned, seeded and chopped, then cooked rapidly to evaporate excess liquid, tomatoes are quickly reduced to a coarse pulp that retains their fresh savour. Longer, slower cooking, followed by sieving and reduction, produces a dense, smooth purée with a more intense, concentrated flavour.

Since part of the attraction of a tomato sauce lies in its dramatic colour, choose tomatoes that are firm, ripe and deep red. If these are unavailable, you can make the sauce with canned tomatoes, or use canned tomatoes to deepen the colour of a sauce made with out-of-season fruit.

Many herbs and aromatics combine well with tomatoes, and it is worth experimenting to find the ones you like best. Try thyme, oregano, tarragon or a last-minute addition of fresh basil. Onions, shallots or celery will add extra piquancy: chop them finely and sauté them until soft before you add the tomatoes.

Brief Cooking to Retain Freshness

1 **Skinning tomatoes.** Using a small, sharp knife, cut round the core of each tomato (*above*); remove both core and stalk together. Skin and seed the tomatoes and chop the flesh coarsely (*page 9*).

2 **Adding flavourings.** Pour a little olive oil into a pan to prevent the ingredients from sticking. Put the tomatoes in the pan with flavourings—here, a sprig of thyme and two lightly crushed garlic cloves are added for 1 kg (2 lb) of tomatoes. Season with salt and a little pepper.

Slow Simmering to Concentrate Flavour

1 **Preparing the ingredients.** Finely chop onions and garlic cloves. Sauté them in olive oil in a heavy pan over a low heat until the onions are soft but not coloured. Coarsely chop large tomatoes or quarter small ones. Add them to the pan with a bay leaf and a few sprigs of thyme (*above*). Season the mixture with salt.

2 **Cooking the mixture.** Cook the tomato mixture, uncovered, over medium heat, stirring occasionally and crushing the tomatoes with a wooden spoon to help them to disintegrate (*above*). After about 30 minutes, most of the moisture released by the tomatoes will have evaporated and they will have become a thick pulp.

3 **Judging the consistency.** Over a high heat, sauté the tomatoes, uncovered, until most of the liquid has evaporated and the tomatoes attain a smooth, thick consistency (*above*).

4 **Serving the sauce.** Remove and discard the garlic and thyme; taste for seasoning and add salt and pepper if required. Here, the sauce is served with round-grain rice—boiled and then steamed—and garnished with finely chopped parsley.☐

3 **Making a purée.** Remove the mixture from the heat and discard the thyme and bay leaf. Place a sieve over a deep bowl. Using a wooden pestle, press the mixture through the sieve (*above*). Discard the skins and seeds that remain in the sieve. Return the purée to the pan and cook it over a low heat, stirring frequently.

4 **Reducing the sauce.** Cook the sauce for another 30 minutes, or until it has reduced to a smooth purée (*above*). Taste the purée and adjust the seasoning as required. Transfer it to a warmed sauceboat; here, it is served with deep-fried prawns (*inset*).☐

Vegetable Purées: the Garden's Delights

Puréed root and leaf vegetables diluted with cream, wine or stock furnish a range of light sauces admirably suited to accompany any roasted or grilled meat.

Root vegetables—such as turnips, celeriac or carrots—need lengthy cooking to soften them. The carrots used here (*right; recipe, page 164*) are simmered for about 45 minutes in a little water and butter, with sugar added to emphasize their natural sweetness. Most leaf vegetables—lettuce or spinach, for example—need only brief boiling. When they are cooked, the vegetables—roots or leaves—can be puréed in a food processor or food mill, or pressed through a coarse sieve.

Tender young sorrel leaves (*below*) call for different treatment. Stewed in butter, they melt into a purée. Older sorrel leaves should be rubbed through a fine drum sieve to remove any tough fibres.

Whether wine, stock or cream is used to convert a vegetable purée into a sauce, you can enrich it further by adding butter. Whisk it in, a few cubes at a time, after removing the sauce from the heat.

Glazed Carrots Transformed in a Processor

1 **Preparing carrots.** Peel and trim carrots. Leave young carrots whole. Remove the cores from older carrots and discard them; cut the carrots into pieces. Put the carrots in a saucepan; for every 500 g (1 lb), add 30 g (1 oz) of butter and up to a tablespoon of sugar. Add salt and cover the carrots half way with water (*above*).

2 **Puréeing.** Bring the water to the boil, then reduce the heat to low. Partially cover the pan and simmer the carrots, shaking the pan occasionally, for up to 45 minutes or until they are tender. Reduce the liquid, uncovered, over high heat until a syrupy glaze coats the carrots. Transfer the carrots and glaze to a food processor (*above*) and purée them.

Sorrel Sieved for Extra Smoothness

1 **Preparing sorrel.** Pick over sorrel leaves, discarding any that are blemished. Wash and drain the sorrel, then fold each leaf in half and tear out the central stem. Roll a few leaves together and, with a sharp knife, slice them across (*above*).

2 **Cooking the sorrel.** Melt a little butter in an enamel or other non-reactive pan and toss in the sorrel (*above*). Stew the sorrel gently, stirring occasionally to prevent it from sticking to the pan. When the sorrel has melted to a loose purée—after 10 to 20 minutes, depending on the age of the leaves—remove it from the heat.

3 **Sieving the sorrel.** A little at a time, spoon the purée into a fine-meshed drum sieve set over a plate. With a flexible plastic scraper, force the sorrel purée through the sieve (*above*). Discard any fibres that remain in the sieve.

3 **Thinning the purée.** Return the purée to the pan and stir it continuously over a high heat until it is heated through. Whisk in enough double cream (*above*) to give the sauce a pouring consistency.

4 **Serving the sauce.** Remove the purée from the heat and whisk in a handful of butter cubes (*above*). Pour the sauce into a warmed sauceboat and serve it immediately; in this case, the sauce accompanies slices of roast veal (*inset*).□

4 **Adding cream.** Put the sieved purée into a clean pan and return it to a low heat. Pour in double cream, stirring with a wooden spoon (*above*) until the cream is blended smoothly into the purée.

5 **Serving.** Continue adding cream until the purée has a pouring consistency; in this case, about 30 cl (10 fl oz) of cream was added for every 500 g (1 lb) of sorrel. Pour the sauce into a warmed sauceboat; here, it is served with grilled calf's sweetbreads.□

Harmonious Partnerships

Some vegetables automatically turn into sauces just by being puréed, but others need to be combined with ingredients that thicken or dilute the purée to produce the right consistency. Onions, for example, baked until they are soft, make a juicy purée that lacks body. However, adding approximately the same volume of white sauce binds the purée into a full-bodied sauce known as soubise (*right; recipe, page 160*). A more substantial thickener such as cooked rice or potato may be used instead of white sauce; cream or butter can provide extra enrichment.

Pulses, on the other hand, make stiff purées that need considerable thinning to transform them into sauces. For a white bean sauce (*below*), pre-soaked beans are cooked with aromatic vegetables, puréed and thinned to a sauce consistency with a little of their cooking liquid, and then coloured and flavoured with tomato purée (*page 30*). A sweet red pepper purée could replace the tomato purée; a purée of flageolet beans might be enhanced with one of fresh green beans.

An Onion Purée Bound with White Sauce

1 **Peeling baked onions.** In a preheated 190°C (375°F or Mark 5) oven, bake large unpeeled onions until a skewer will penetrate the onions easily—for 1 to 2 hours, depending on size. When the onions are cool enough to handle, use a small, sharp knife to remove the skins and any discoloured parts (*above*).

2 **Puréeing the onions.** Place the peeled onions in a sieve set over a bowl. With a wooden pestle, and using a circular motion, press the onion flesh through the sieve into the bowl (*above*). Discard any membrane left in the sieve.

A Mellow Mixture of Beans and Tomatoes

1 **Adding aromatics.** Cover dried beans— here, white haricots—with cold water in a heavy pan and bring them to the boil, covered. Turn off the heat and leave them to soak for 1 hour. Drain the beans, return them to the rinsed pan and cover with fresh water. Add an onion stuck with cloves, unpeeled garlic cloves, carrots and a bouquet garni (*page 7*).

2 **Puréeing the beans.** Boil the beans for 10 minutes, then cover and simmer them for 1 to 2 hours or until a bean can be easily crushed between your fingers. Drain the beans, reserving their cooking liquid. Place a sieve over another bowl. A few ladlefuls at a time, transfer the beans to the sieve and use a wooden pestle to press the flesh through (*above*).

3 **Moistening the beans.** As you purée the beans, moisten them with a little of their reserved cooking liquid (*above*) so that they can pass through the sieve easily. Discard the bean skins that remain in the sieve after each batch.

3 **Combining the purée with sauce.** Make a white sauce (*page 28*). Transfer the onion purée to a saucepan. Using a wooden spoon, stir in the sauce (*above*); continue adding the sauce and keep stirring until the mixture is evenly blended and its consistency is to your liking.

4 **Finishing the sauce.** Place the pan over a low heat and rapidly heat the sauce through, stirring continuously. To finish and enrich the sauce, stir in double cream (*above*) or add cubes of butter.

5 **Serving the sauce.** Transfer the finished sauce to a warmed sauceboat. Serve the sauce with grilled or roasted meat—here, it accompanies a serving of roast saddle of lamb (*above*).☐

4 **Adding tomato purée.** Prepare a tomato purée (*page 30*). Whisk it into the bean purée, a little at a time (*above*), until the sauce has attained the desired colour and consistency.

5 **Finishing the sauce.** Transfer the sauce to a pan. Over a high heat, bring the sauce to the boil, stirring continuously. Remove the pan from the heat and whisk in a few cubes of cold butter (*above*).

6 **Serving the sauce.** Transfer the bean and tomato sauce to a warmed sauceboat. In this case, it is then ladled to the side of the plate, as an accompaniment to grilled pork loin chops (*above*).☐

Capturing the Sweetness of Seasonal Fruits

Fruit sauces are simple to make and almost infinitely variable. Most begin as a purée, which—if liquid enough to pour—needs no further addition. A stiff purée may be diluted with a little sugar syrup, water or cream.

Different fruits require different techniques of puréeing. Firm but smooth-textured apples (*right*) and pears, cooked in a little water, form purées on their own. Plums, peaches and apricots (*opposite page, below*) have a somewhat coarser structure. They should first be poached in sugar syrup, and then pressed through a sieve. Use a nylon sieve, since metal may taint the fruit's flavour. Sweet, soft berry fruits—raspberries (*below*), strawberries or redcurrants, for instance—can be converted into liquid purées simply by sieving. Any pips or skins will be left in the sieve and should be discarded. Very hard or fibrous fruits—such as pineapples—are most easily puréed in a food processor.

All fruits have an element of sweetness, but their flavours can be easily modified. Vinegar, onion or freshly ground pepper will lend a sharp edge to a sauce to be served with a savoury dish. Dessert sauces usually include sugar or honey, perhaps mixed with a liqueur or spirit. Rum, for example, makes an excellent flavouring for a hot apricot sauce. Grated citrus rind and spices such as cloves or nutmeg will add piquancy to any fruit sauce, savoury or sweet.

Fruit preserved by canning or bottling, or dried fruit that has first been soaked, may be puréed in the same way as fresh fruit. And the liquid used to poach raw fruit can be thickened by reduction over heat to make a light, translucent sauce.

Fruit sauces with a touch of tartness—a purée of cooked gooseberries, for example—are traditional accompaniments for meat and game dishes. But sweeter sauces—such as those made from apples, apricots or berry fruits—need not be restricted to desserts. Apple sauce is usually served with rich meats that are themselves slightly sweet, such as pork, duck or goose. Apricot sauce also makes an unusual and fragrant sauce for pork.

Apples Stewed to a Sauce

1 **Preparing apples.** Add lemon juice to a bowl of water. Cut apples—in this case, russets—into quarters. Peel and core each quarter (*above*); to prevent them from discolouring, place the quarters immediately in the acidulated water.

Berries Sieved and Sweetened

1 **Puréeing berries.** Pick over soft berry fruit—here, raspberries—removing any leaves or stalks. Place a fine-meshed nylon sieve over a deep bowl; with a pestle, press the berries through the sieve to make a liquid purée (*above*).

2 **Sweetening the purée.** Sprinkle a little castor sugar over the purée (*above*). Stir in the sugar and taste the purée for sweetness. If necessary, stir in a little more castor sugar.

3 **Serving the sauce.** Pour the sauce into a serving jug. If you are serving the sauce with a cold dessert, chill it first in the refrigerator. Here, the chilled raspberry sauce is poured over vanilla ice cream and peaches poached in sugar syrup—a dish known as Peach Melba (*above*). □

2 **Cooking the apples.** Place the apple quarters in a pan with a little fresh water. If you like, add sugar, depending on the natural sweetness of the fruit. Cook the apples gently, stirring them from time to time (*above*), until they are reduced to a purée. Remove them from the heat.

3 **Enriching the sauce.** Stir cubes of cold butter, a few at a time, into the hot apple purée (*above*). The proportions used here are about 30 g (1 oz) of butter to every 500 g (1 lb) of apples. Serve the sauce with meat—in this case, with roast loin of pork (*inset*).□

Apricots Poached and Puréed

1 **Poaching apricots.** Make a light sugar syrup (*recipe, page 164*). Halve ripe apricots and remove the stones. Poach the fruit in the syrup until it is soft—about 5 minutes. Place a nylon sieve over a deep bowl. Transfer the apricots to the sieve (*above*), reserving the syrup. With a pestle, press the apricots through the sieve, discarding the skins that remain.

2 **Thinning the purée.** Stir enough of the poaching liquid into the purée to give it a pouring consistency (*above*). Transfer the sauce to a serving jug. Reserve the remaining poaching liquid for use in other preparations.

3 **Serving the sauce.** Serve the sauce with roast pork or with a dessert. The sauce can be used hot or cold; here, it is poured cold over a moulded tapioca soufflé pudding (*above; recipe, page 153*).□

A Trio of Dessert Sauces

Sauces based on sugar syrups and on melted chocolate are mainstays for enhancing desserts. At its simplest, a syrup sauce is nothing more than sugar and water boiled together. The proportions of water and sugar, and the temperature to which the syrup is boiled, determine the sauce's consistency. The sauce on the right (*recipe, page 154*) contains butter and cream, and is known as butterscotch; because the addition of extra flavourings can cause a syrup to turn grainy, the mixture includes some liquid glucose, which inhibits crystallization.

If a syrup is cooked until all the water evaporates, the molten sugar that remains turns rapidly into caramel—a useful foundation that can be diluted with water to make a pouring sauce (*below*).

To give chocolate a pouring consistency, it is melted with a little water or cream over low heat—overheating would scorch it, impairing its flavour and texture. In this case (*opposite page, below*), it is melted with water, then combined with butter for further enrichment.

Butterscotch: a Deep Golden Coating from a Sugar Syrup

1 **Dissolving sugar in water.** To warm a sugar thermometer, put it in a jug of very hot water. Put sugar, water and butter in a heavy pan. Add liquid glucose. Set the pan over a medium heat and stir the ingredients (*above*) until the sugar has dissolved. Do not let the mixture boil until the sugar has completely dissolved; if necessary, reduce the heat.

2 **Boiling the syrup.** When all the sugar has dissolved, stop stirring. Put the warmed sugar thermometer in the pan, bring the syrup to the boil (*above*) and continue to boil until it reaches 116°C (240°F)—the soft-ball stage. Take the pan off the heat and dip it in cold water to arrest cooking.

Caramel: an Amber Pool of Molten Sugar

1 **Diluting caramel.** Put 15 cl (¼ pint) of water in a heavy pan and add 500 g (1 lb) of sugar. Stir gently over a medium heat until the sugar has dissolved. Bring the syrup to the boil and boil it, without stirring, until it turns reddish-amber. Dip the pan in cold water. Let the caramel cool a little; pour in cold water (*above*).

2 **Dissolving the caramel.** Return the pan to the heat and stir the water and caramel together until the caramel is smoothly dissolved. Once diluted, the caramel will not harden even when quite cold.

3 **Serving caramel sauce.** Refrigerated in a stoppered bottle, the sauce will keep for weeks. Serve caramel sauce hot or cold, with a hot or cold dessert. Here, it is served hot with bread pudding. □

3 **Testing the syrup.** Place a teaspoonful of syrup in a bowl of iced water. Mould the cooled syrup into a ball in the water, then lift it out. Squeeze the ball gently between your finger and thumb. If it holds its shape under the water but rapidly flattens when taken out (*above*), the syrup has reached the correct stage.

4 **Stirring in cream.** If the sugar syrup is too liquid, return it to the heat and test it again when the temperature has risen by a few degrees. Once the syrup has reached the soft-ball stage, let it cool slightly. Pour in double cream (*above*) and stir until the syrup and cream are blended.

5 **Serving the sauce.** Serve the sauce hot or cold; in this case, it is served hot with ice cream (*above*). The butterscotch sauce can be kept, covered, in the refrigerator for up to two weeks.□

Chocolate: a Dark Delight

1 **Melting chocolate.** Break plain eating chocolate into pieces and put them in a bowl with a little cold water. Place the bowl in a pan of hot water over a medium heat. Stir the chocolate until all the pieces have melted smoothly.

2 **Incorporating butter.** Cut cold butter into cubes—use about 60 g (2 oz) of butter for every 250 g (8 oz) of chocolate. Remove the pan from the heat and stir a few cubes into the chocolate (*above*). When the butter is blended in, add more. Continue until all the butter is stirred in and the mixture is smooth.

3 **Serving the chocolate sauce.** Serve the chocolate sauce immediately, while it is still hot: it sets as it cools. Here, the sauce is poured over a cold dessert—choux pastries filled with ice cream.□

2
Sauces from Stocks
Coaxing Flavours
from a Simmering Pot

Rich in flavour, a veal stock (*page 42*)—ready for use in any one of hundreds of sauces—is ladled into a pan. To make the stock, meat and bones were simmered in water for several hours to release their flavours; the liquid was then strained and cooled so that fat could rise to the surface and be removed.

Stock is one of the principal elements of all good cooking and the foundation for a wide repertoire of superb sauces. Although it is invested with a certain mystique, stock-making is simplicity itself: the appropriate ingredients—meat or fish combined with aromatic vegetables—are given long, gentle cooking, and the resulting broth is carefully cleansed to produce a clear, richly flavoured essence.

Since an important purpose of a stock-based sauce is to complement the flavours of a finished dish, the stock ingredients may be supplemented or even wholly supplied by trimmings from the meat that the sauce will accompany. Most kinds of meat, poultry and game are suitable elements in a stock, provided that they contain enough gelatine to give body to the liquid. Often, however, a sauce has to be prepared quite independently of the main dish, and in these cases a basic veal stock (*opposite*) will supply an excellent foundation. Rich in body yet unassertive in flavour, veal stock marries well with other meats. For a more robustly flavoured dark-coloured meat stock, veal can be combined with other meats or game and all the ingredients seared in the oven before any liquid is added. The counterpart of veal stock for fish and shellfish dishes is called "fumet" and is made with fish carcasses (*page 42*).

In sauce-making, stocks are points of departure rather than ends in themselves. With sufficient reduction by boiling, a meat stock yields a meat glaze or *glace de viande* (*page 44, above*)—a concentrated essence that can be introduced into any meat sauce to give it added depth of flavour. Another savoury concentrate, *coulis* (*page 44, below*), is a kind of double stock: browned meats are simmered in previously made veal stock and the resulting savoury liquid is concentrated by reduction.

Thickening with a roux of flour and butter is the usual means by which a basic stock is turned into a sauce. A very dark roux yields brown sauce (*page 46*); a light-coloured roux yields the classic velouté. Brown sauce is profitably combined with garnishes, flavourings and thickeners; some game dishes, for example, are traditionally served with a sauce thickened with blood. A basic velouté can also be varied with enrichments as simple as cream or butter (*page 49*), or as elaborate as a purée of sea urchin corals (*page 54*). And both velouté and brown sauce can be reduced and chilled to form *chaud-froid* (*page 52*)—a sauce used to coat cold dishes.

Extracting the Essence of Meat and Fish

A basic stock, made by simmering meat or fish, bones and aromatic vegetables in water, provides the liquid for numerous savoury sauces. Excellent meat stocks are made with beef, lamb, pork and game but a veal stock (*right; recipe, page 158*), with its unassertive flavour, full body and light colour, is the most versatile.

The meats for a stock may include trimmings and carcasses. Shin of veal is used here, with shin of beef for extra flavour. Meat and bones rich in natural gelatine—pork rinds, calf's feet and pig's trotters, or the veal knuckle bone and chicken trimmings that are used here—give the stock body and smoothness.

The meat and bones, covered in cold water, are brought very slowly to the boil. As the water heats, albuminous proteins are drawn out of the meat and coagulate, forming a grey scum that rises to the surface of the water. To obtain a clear stock, this scum must be patiently skimmed off (*Step 2, right*). Herbs and aromatic vegetables are then added. To draw out the maximum flavour and gelatine, the stock must be simmered for at least 5 hours. Chilling the strained stock after cooking allows the fat to rise to the surface, where it forms a solid layer that is easily removed (*Step 5*).

The best ingredients for a fish fumet (*below; recipe, page 159*) are white fish with a delicate flavour, such as sole and whiting, and those that provide gelatine, such as brill, turbot and monkfish. Their delicacy dictates a shorter cooking time than for meat stocks.

A basic meat stock can continue to be simmered for a lengthy period until it eventually forms a small amount of glaze, powerfully concentrated in flavour (*page 44, above*). Known as *glace de viande*, it is used in small quantities to add flavour and body to stock-based sauces.

Veal stock also provides the cooking liquid for making *coulis*, a luxurious meat essence (*page 44, below; recipe, page 158*). Veal and ham are browned, then braised in stock; strained, reduced and cleansed, the liquid makes a smooth reduction with a voluptuous depth of flavour.

Basic Steps to a Veal Stock

1 **Preparing the meats.** Place meat and bones—here, shin of veal sections, a veal knuckle bone, beef shin, chicken necks and wings—on a wire rack set in the bottom of a large pan: the rack will help to prevent the large meats from sticking to the pan. Add enough water to cover the meats by about 5 cm (2 inches).

Fish Fumet: a Delicate Distillation

1 **Assembling ingredients.** Prepare some aromatics—here, carrots, onions, leeks and celery are sliced and combined with thyme, parsley and bay leaves. Put them in a large pan. Rinse fish free of blood and remove the bitter-tasting gills from fish heads. Brill and sole carcasses are used here, together with a salmon head for extra flavour. Cut the fish into pieces.

2 **Adding water.** To prevent the pieces of fish sticking to the bottom of the pan, place them on the bed of aromatics. Add red or white wine and enough water to cover the fish. Season lightly with coarse salt. Put the pan over a low heat and bring the liquid to a simmer, skimming off any scum that rises to the surface. Cover, and simmer for about 30 minutes.

3 **Completing the fumet.** Strain the fumet into a bowl through a colander lined with dampened muslin. The fumet can be used at once, or you can store it in a refrigerator for a few days, bringing it to the boil and cleansing it every two days in the same way as the meat stock (*Step 7, opposite page*). It will keep in a freezer for up to three months. □

2 **Removing scum.** Put the pan on a low heat. With a skimming spoon, skim off the grey scum that appears on the surface of the liquid as the temperature rises. To retard boiling, add a little cold water: if the liquid comes to the boil too quickly, the scum disperses. Continue skimming until no more scum rises.

3 **Adding aromatics.** Add whole carrots and onions—one stuck with cloves—a whole, unpeeled head of garlic and a bouquet garni (*page 7*). Add a little salt, unless you intend to reduce the stock—in that case, do not add salt. Bring the stock to the boil, then reduce the heat until the liquid barely simmers.

4 **Straining.** Place the lid of the pan slightly ajar and simmer for at least 5 hours, occasionally skimming off any fat that rises to the surface. Strain the stock through a colander into a large bowl (*above*). Discard the solids, then strain the stock again through a colander lined with dampened muslin.

5 **Cleansing the stock.** Let the stock cool, then refrigerate it, uncovered, until it has set to a jelly—about 8 hours or overnight. As the stock cools, the fat rises to the surface and sets in a solid layer. Scrape off the fat from the surface with a spoon (*above*) and discard it.

6 **Removing the last traces of fat.** Press kitchen paper gently on to the surface of the jellied stock: the paper will absorb and remove any small specks of fat that may still remain.

7 **Using the stock.** To melt the jellied stock, spoon it into a small pan and put it over a very low heat. Stir the jelly until it liquefies. Leftover stock can be kept, uncovered, for up to two weeks in a refrigerator; every two days it must be brought to the boil, then simmered and cleansed for 15 minutes. The stock can also be stored for up to six months in a freezer. □

Meat Glaze: a Dramatic Reduction

1 Skimming the stock. Put cleansed veal stock (*page 42*) in a pan that is just large enough to hold it. Bring it to the boil; then set the pan half off the heat and leave to boil gently. Impurities will repeatedly form a skin that collects on the cooler side of the pan. When the skin has thickened, pull it to the side of the pan with the edge of a metal spoon and remove it (*above*).

2 Transferring the stock. Leave the stock to reduce gently, skimming off the skin every time it thickens, for about 1 hour, or until the stock has reduced by about a third. So that you can continue skimming the stock more easily, pour the reduced liquid through a fine-meshed sieve into a smaller pan (*above*).

3 Removing impurities. Return the clean pan of stock to the heat, setting the pan half off the heat as before. Continue to simmer the stock and to skim off any impurities that form a skin (*above*).

Coulis: Doubling the Flavour

1 Browning ingredients. Heat olive oil in a large pan. Add veal and ham—in this case, boned veal shin with a knuckle of Parma ham—and coarsely chopped carrots and onions. Cover the pan and cook the ingredients over a low heat, turning them occasionally, for about 45 minutes, until their juices have reduced and have begun to caramelize.

2 Pouring on wine. Add a little white wine (*above*), then scrape the bottom of the pan vigorously with a wooden spoon or spatula, loosening all the caramelized deposits so that they dissolve in the wine. Turn up the heat and reduce the wine completely. When the juices begin to caramelize again, add more wine, and scrape and reduce as before.

3 Removing scum. Pour in veal stock (*page 42*) until the *coulis* ingredients are well covered. Bring to a simmer and skim off the scum that rises to the surface (*above*). When no more scum appears, add a bouquet garni (*page 7*) and set a lid slightly ajar on the pan. Simmer the *coulis* for about 4 hours.

4 **Straining the stock.** When the stock has again reduced by about one-third, remove the pan from the heat. Pour the reduced stock through a fine-meshed sieve into a smaller pan (*above*). Set the pan half off the heat and continue to simmer and skim the stock as before.

5 **Completing the reduction.** When the stock has again reduced by a third and has become thick and syrupy (*above*)—after about 3 hours in all—pour it into a bowl. Cool the liquid, then refrigerate it. It will set to a solid, rubbery jelly (*inset*) that will keep almost indefinitely in a refrigerator.□

4 **Removing meat and vegetables.** Take the meats out of the pan; they can be eaten at once or served later. Transfer the bouquet garni to a sieve set over a pan just large enough to hold the liquid; press out the juices from the bouquet garni, then discard it. Pour the *coulis* into the sieve (*above*); press the juices from the vegetables and discard them.

5 **Straining the coulis.** Set the pan of liquid half off the heat and simmer gently, skimming off the skin of impurities that forms repeatedly on the cooler side of the pan. When the liquid has reduced to about half its volume, remove the pan from the heat. Pour the reduced liquid through a *chinois*—a very fine-meshed sieve—into a bowl (*above*).

6 **Cooling the coulis.** To prevent a skin from forming, stir the liquid continuously as it cools. Here, the *coulis* is set in a bowl of iced water so that it will cool quickly. Refrigerate the *coulis* overnight until it sets to a firm jelly; it will keep indefinitely provided it is brought to the boil and cleansed every few days in the same way as veal stock (*page 43, Step 7*).□

A Savoury Concentrate from Deglazed Meats

The richly flavoured variation on basic stock that is known as brown sauce or *demi-glace* (*right; recipe, page 160*) provides a classic foundation for many other sauces to serve with meat and game. To complement the dish, the strained, reduced and cleansed brown sauce is always combined with a garnish or blended with other flavourings before it is served.

Browning the meats and vegetables for the sauce in oil intensifies their flavour and deepens the colour of the finished product. Flour is then added to the pan, mingling with the fat to form a roux. Further cooking in a hot oven causes the flour to darken: the resulting brown roux also colours the sauce as well as thickening it. During this preliminary cooking of the ingredients, juices are drawn out from the meats and caramelize in the bottom of the pan as savoury deposits, which are then dissolved in wine.

Once these steps are complete, the brown sauce can be made with plain water, as for a veal stock (*page 42*). But to achieve a much greater depth of flavour, veal stock can be chosen for the cooking medium, as in the demonstration here. A game brown sauce can be prepared in the same way, using game carcasses with game or veal stock.

The meats and vegetables are cooked in the stock for up to 6 hours to draw out the maximum flavour and gelatine from the ingredients. When the strained sauce has been cleansed and reduced, it can be used at once or it may be stored in the same way as veal stock.

Strips of ham, stewed mushrooms or tiny onions, or tomato purée (*page 30, below*) are just a few of the many garnishes and flavourings that combine well with a brown sauce. To complement the game pâté on page 48, for example, a game brown sauce is garnished with truffles warmed in brandy; such a sauce is called *périgueux*. To enhance grilled steaks, a *bordelaise* is chosen—a basic brown sauce combined with a reduction of red wine and aromatics, then flavoured with a little meat glaze (*page 44, above*) and garnished with diced bone marrow.

1 Coating with oil. Parboil pork rind for 2 to 3 minutes, rinse it and chop it coarsely. Cut shin of beef and veal into chunks; put them in a roasting pan with pieces of veal knuckle, chicken wings and the rind. Add coarsely chopped carrot, onion, leek and celery, crushed garlic cloves, thyme and bay leaves. Sprinkle with oil and toss with your hands (*above*).

2 Adding flour. Put the pan in a preheated 230°C (450°F or Mark 8) oven. After about 15 minutes, remove the pan and turn the ingredients with a spatula so that they will brown evenly. Return the pan to the oven for a further 15 minutes, or until all the ingredients are well browned. Sprinkle on flour (*above*) and stir it well into the mixture with the spatula.

5 Removing the meat and bones. Take the pan off the heat. Set a sieve over a large bowl and put a few ladlefuls of the cooked meat into the sieve (*above, left*). Pick out any bones and discard them. To extract the meat juices, press the meat with a wooden pestle (*above, right*). Discard the pressed meat and extract the juices from the rest of the meat in the same way. Strain the cooking liquid from the pan into the bowl; remove the sieve and let the liquid cool slightly, then skim off any fat on the surface of the liquid.

3 **Deglazing.** Return the pan to the oven for about 10 minutes, until the flour has browned. Then set the pan on a medium heat. Add enough wine to moisten all the ingredients and dissolve the meat juices that have caramelized (*above, left*). Using the spatula, scrape free the deposits on the bottom of the pan (*above, right*). Increase the heat, bring the liquid to the boil and cook rapidly for about 10 minutes, or until almost all the liquid has evaporated.

4 **Adding stock.** Melt veal stock (*page 42*). Transfer the contents of the roasting pan to a large saucepan. Add enough stock to cover all the ingredients generously (*above*). Bring the liquid to the boil; reduce the heat and set a lid slightly ajar on the pan. Simmer very gently for at least 3 hours, preferably for 5 to 6 hours.

6 **Straining the sauce.** Strain the liquid, a ladleful at a time, through a *chinois*—a conical sieve with a very fine mesh—held over a pan. Move a small ladle up and down, very gently, in the liquid to help it pass through the mesh, but take care not to press any solids through the mesh. Discard the solids.

7 **Cleansing the sauce.** Place the pan over a medium heat. Bring the liquid to the boil; set the pan half off the heat and leave the sauce to reduce. Repeatedly pull to one side and discard the skin of impurities that collects on the cooler side of the pan (*above*). When the sauce has reduced to the desired consistency, taste and add salt if necessary, then remove the pan from the heat.☐

Périgueux: a Game Sauce with Truffles

1 Making a game sauce. Prepare a brown sauce (*page 46*) using game carcasses and trimmings instead of beef and veal. Here, hare and partridge carcasses are used and the ingredients are simmered in game stock. When the cleansed sauce has reduced to the desired consistency, remove the pan from the heat.

2 Garnishing the sauce. Scrub and peel truffles; pound the peelings; dice the truffles finely and warm them with a dash of brandy (*page 11*). Add the truffles and puréed peelings to the sauce (*above*).

3 Serving the sauce. Stir the truffles and peelings into the sauce, then transfer it immediately to a warmed sauceboat for serving. Here, the sauce is spooned over slices of hot game pâté.☐

Bordelaise: a Brown Sauce with Wine and Aromatics

1 Adding wine flavouring. Make a basic brown sauce (*page 46*). Put the reduced and cleansed sauce in a large pan. Prepare a reduction of red wine and aromatics (*page 10*), then put the pan containing the sauce over a medium heat and pour in an equal quantity of the red wine reduction (*above*).

2 Enriching the sauce. Bring the sauce to the boil, reduce the heat and draw the pan half off the heat. Let the sauce boil gently until it has reduced to just over a third of its original volume, skimming off any skin that forms on the cooler side of the pan. Add a spoonful of meat glaze (*above; page 44*) and stir it into the sauce with a little lemon juice.

3 Serving the sauce. If you like, the sauce can be finished with a garnish. To avoid clouding the sauce's clear colour, do not add any garnish that has been sautéed in fat. Here, poached and diced bone marrow (*page 11*) is added. Transfer the sauce to a warmed sauceboat and serve at once. In this case, the sauce is ladled over fillet steaks.☐

Velouté: a Base to Build On

Any meat or fish stock thickened only with a roux will produce a light, smooth sauce known as a velouté—literally, a velvety sauce. A velouté is usually enriched with cream or extra butter, and provides a base for innumerable finishes. Vegetable purées and flavoured butters will add colour and flavour, and garnishes—ranging from chopped herbs to small pieces of vegetables or seafood—can be used to give both texture and flavour to a basic velouté (*page 50*).

The sauce demonstrated here (*recipe, page 162*) is made with a fish fumet and provides a delicately flavoured accompaniment for a wide variety of fish. The roux is made first, in the same way as for a white sauce (*page 28*); it must not be allowed to brown lest it discolour the finished sauce. The fumet is whisked into the roux and the sauce is cooked for at least 45 minutes to eliminate any taste of flour.

To make a more full-bodied sauce, the cleansed and reduced liquid may be combined with egg yolks. A little warm velouté is first stirred into lightly beaten yolks and the mixture is then added to the rest of the velouté in the pan. The sauce is returned to a very low heat just until the liquid begins to thicken. Once egg yolks have been added, the liquid must not come near the boil: too high a heat would cause the yolks to thicken unevenly and turn the sauce grainy.

A pale velouté enriched with cream is quickly transformed into a vividly coloured sauce. A purée of sweet red peppers (*page 9*), spinach or tomato, for example, or a little saffron dissolved in hot water will add colour as well as extra flavour. Flavoured butters (*pages 12-13*) may be whisked in to give further enrichment. Garnishes (*pages 10-11*) should be chosen to complement the sauce's basic flavour. Prawns and mussels, for instance, make good partners for a fish velouté. Poached bone marrow goes well with a game velouté, and mushrooms or truffles with all veloutés—fish, meat and game.

A velouté can serve as an integral part of a dish as well as an accompaniment. On page 50 (*top*), strips of poached sole are served with a butter-enriched velouté; on page 51 (*bottom*), a sauce flavoured with mushrooms and onion provides a protective coating for a gratin of fish.

1 **Whisking in fish fumet.** In a pan set over medium heat, blend butter and flour to make a roux (*page 28*). After a minute or two, when the roux has begun to foam, ladle fish fumet (*page 42*) into the pan, whisking continuously (*above*). When all the fumet has been added, whisk until the mixture comes to the boil, then reduce the heat so that the liquid simmers.

2 **Cleansing the sauce.** Set the pan half off the heat and simmer the sauce for at least 45 minutes, repeatedly skimming off the skin of fatty impurities that forms on the surface of the sauce at the cooler side of the pan (*above*). When the sauce has reduced to half its original volume and only a thin skin forms, put the pan fully back on the heat.

3 **Enriching with cream.** Pour in double cream (*inset*) and stir it into the velouté with a wooden spoon (*above*). The finished sauce should have a light, creamy consistency that is just thick enough to coat the spoon. Remove the sauce from the heat. Before finishing the sauce with the flavouring or garnish of your choice, taste it and adjust the seasoning if necessary. □

A Satin-Smooth Coating for Fragments of Fish

1 Whisking in butter. Prepare a velouté with fish fumet and enrich it with cream (*page 49*). Remove the pan from the heat and set it on a trivet. Whisk small cubes of chilled butter, a handful at a time, into the sauce (*above*).

2 Adding fish fillets. Cut sole fillets into strips about 1 cm (½ inch) wide. Put the strips of fish in a buttered pan and cook them briefly in a little hot fish fumet (*page 42*). Drain the fillets in a sieve and tip them into the pan of sauce (*above*).

3 Serving the sauced fish. Gently stir the fillets into the sauce, taking care not to break the fish. If necessary, return the pan briefly to the heat to warm the sauce through before serving (*above*).☐

Enrichment and Colour from a Herb Butter

1 Adding herb butter. Prepare and chill herb butter (*page 12*), then break it into pieces. Make a fish velouté and add cream (*page 49*). Off the heat, whisk in the butter, a few pieces at a time (*above*). Here, about 30 g (1 oz) of butter is added for every 30 cl (½ pint) of sauce.

2 Serving the finished sauce. When all the herb butter has been incorporated and the sauce is evenly coloured, pour it into a warmed sauceboat (*above*). Serve the sauce immediately. In this instance, the sauce provides a colourful accompaniment for a fillet of brill poached in fish fumet (*inset*).☐

Golden Tint from Saffron

1 Colouring velouté with saffron. Prepare a garnish of prawns and mussels (*page 10*) and dissolve powdered saffron in a little hot water. Make a fish velouté and stir in cream (*page 49*). Remove the pan from the heat. Stir the saffron liquid into the sauce (*above*).

2 Ladling the sauce over the fish. Stir the garnish of prawns and mussels into the saffron-coloured velouté sauce. Transfer the sauce to a warmed sauceboat and ladle it over the fish you are serving—here, poached fillet of brill.☐

exture and Flavour from Duxelles

1 Combining with mushrooms. Prepare *duxelles* with onion, mushrooms, parsley and lemon juice (*page 9*). Prepare a fish velouté and stir in cream (*page 49*). Remove the pan from the heat. Stir the *duxelles* into the sauce, adding about 60 g (2 oz) to every 30 cl (½ pint) of sauce.

2 Coating fish. Sauté white breadcrumbs in butter. Spread half the sauce in the bottom of a shallow ovenproof dish. Place a trimmed fish—here, sole—on the sauce. Cut along the fish's backbone, partially separating the fillets from the bones, and insert butter beneath the fillets. Ladle the rest of the sauce over the fish; sprinkle the breadcrumbs on top.

3 Serving the gratin. Put the dish in a preheated 190°C (375°F or Mark 5) oven for about 20 minutes, until the fish is cooked and the surface of the gratin is golden and crisp. To serve, lift portions of fish off the bone and accompany them with a little sauce spooned out from under the fish (*above*).☐

Chaud-Froid: a Cool Coating of Jelly

Stock-based sauces are usually served hot. However, the gelatinous quality of a reduced stock causes it, on cooling, to set into a firm, light jelly that may be used as the base for a delicious cold coating sauce called *chaud-froid*—literally, "hot-cold".

Chaud-froid is made from cleansed, reduced velouté that is supplemented with concentrated stock, flavoured and then cooled. The flavouring should be chosen to enhance the food that the sauce is to cover. In this demonstration (*recipe, page 163*), half the velouté is flavoured with game brown sauce to make a *chaud-froid* for coating dark meats such as partridge. The other half is enriched with double cream to make a pale sauce for covering chicken breasts. For further variations of colour and flavour, you could add tomato or pepper purée (*page 9*) or dissolved saffron to a cream-enriched *chaud-froid*.

Any stock-based velouté can be used to make *chaud-froid*. To coat cooked hare or pheasant, you could choose a game stock velouté, enriched with game brown sauce. A velouté made from veal stock, with its unassertive flavour, is suited to all kinds of meats; it is an especially good choice if you want to flavour and colour the *chaud-froid* for contrasting effects.

The foods to be coated and any garnishes must be prepared in advance so that they are ready to hand when the sauce has cooled to a coating consistency. The sauce should be liquid enough to coat the meat evenly, yet thick enough to set firmly. The best way to achieve the right consistency is to cool the sauce rapidly, over ice, in a bowl made of metal that allows heat to be drawn quickly and evenly out of the liquid.

Garnishes should be applied to each piece immediately after you have dipped it; as the sauce sets, it will hold the garnish in place. Chopped truffles, pickled tongue, hard-boiled egg white, sprigs of blanched herbs and slices of olive are just a few of the garnishes you might use.

For a glittering presentation, the assembled dish can be given a final coating of aspic—jellied veal stock. A dash of fortified wine in the aspic—Madeira, port or sherry—will add piquancy to the flavour.

1 Making velouté. Prepare a roux and, over a low heat, whisk in veal stock (*above*) to make a velouté (*page 49*). Increase the heat, whisking continuously until the mixture boils, then reduce the heat so that the liquid simmers.

2 Adding coulis. Set the pan half off the heat and simmer the sauce until it is reduced by about a third—about 45 minutes—skimming off skin as it forms on the cooler side of the pan. Add a couple of tablespoons of *coulis* (*page 44*) and continue to cook the velouté, stirring, until the *coulis* is evenly incorporated.

6 Making white chaud-froid. Place the pan containing the reserved velouté over a low heat and bring it to a simmer. Add double cream (*above*)—here, 12.5 cl (4 fl oz) was added to 30 cl (½ pint) of velouté. Then cook the sauce, skimming occasionally, until it has reduced by about a third. Transfer the *chaud-froid* sauce to a metal bowl and cool it.

7 Coating chicken breasts. Have ready the meat—in this case, roasted chicken breasts. Dip each piece in the sauce (*above*), place it on a rack set over a tray and garnish it. In this case, the garnish is a mixture of finely chopped pickled tongue and hard-boiled egg white. Coat and garnish all the chicken breasts and then refrigerate them.

3 **Making brown chaud-froid.** Pour half the velouté into a small pan; stir it until cool to prevent a skin from forming, then set it aside. Pour the rest of the velouté into another pan and set it over a low heat. Add a few tablespoons of brown sauce (*above; page 46*), then simmer the sauce until it has reduced by about a third. Transfer the sauce to a metal bowl.

4 **Cooling the chaud-froid.** Set the metal bowl in a larger bowl filled with ice. Stir the sauce with a figure-of-eight motion until it has cooled and thickened enough to coat the spoon. Remove the bowl from the ice. If the sauce becomes too thick for coating, thin it over a larger bowl of warm water, then return it to the ice and stir until the correct consistency is achieved.

5 **Dipping.** Have ready pieces of meat—in this case, roasted partridges, halved and skinned. Place a piece in the sauce, turn it with a fork, then lift it out. Allow excess sauce to drip back into the bowl (*above*), then put the meat on a rack over a tray. Apply a garnish—here, finely chopped truffles. Repeat with the remaining pieces of meat, then chill them.

8 **Preparing aspic.** Take the meats from the refrigerator; trim them evenly. Melt veal stock (*page 42*) over heat; allow it to cool to nearly room temperature; stir in Madeira. Pour a few tablespoons of the stock into a metal bowl set in a bowl of ice. Stir the stock until it thickens and is on the point of setting (*above*); remove it from the bowl of ice.

9 **Glazing with aspic.** Transfer the meats to clean racks set over trays. Spoon the aspic over each piece of meat (*above*), preparing more aspic as necessary (*Step 8*). Return the meats to the refrigerator for the glaze to set. After about 10 minutes, apply another coat of aspic and let it set. Continue the process until the meats are completely glazed.

10 **Serving.** Arrange all the partridge halves and the chicken breasts on a platter—in this instance, they are laid on a bed of chicken mousse. Cover the entire surface of the dish with more aspic; refrigerate it to set the glaze. Serve the platter over crushed ice to keep the aspic from melting.□

Exotic Enhancements for Basic Sauces

Enrichments for stock-based sauces can go far beyond the classic finishes of egg yolks, butter and cream. The traditional finish for a brown game sauce to be served with rabbit or hare is some of the animal's blood (*right*). Mixed with the puréed raw liver, the blood gives the sauce a velvety texture and a dramatic, very dark colour.

An unusual thickener for a fish velouté is the puréed orange-pink roe—usually called the coral—of the sea urchin. Coral velouté (*below*) can be served with almost any simply cooked fish.

Both blood and coral will coagulate at high temperatures. The basic sauce must be partially cooled before either is added and the mixture then kept well below the boil. Blood also coagulates when exposed to the air and must be mixed with vinegar as soon as it is drawn.

To make the coral velouté, choose sea urchins that are moist and bright. Opening a sea urchin is a simple matter of snipping round the base with scissors; you then scoop out the coral with a spoon.

When furred game is hung, the blood collects in the chest cavity. Ask your butcher in advance to gut the animal and reserve the blood, or purchase the animal whole and gut it yourself, as here.

If skinning the animal yourself, suspend it by one of its hind legs so that the head rests on the work surface. Make a circular incision below the heel joint, then slit the skin down the inside of the leg to the tail. Grasp the leg near the paw and roll the skin back over the leg and thigh. Skin the other hind leg in the same way.

To skin the body, slit the skin at the base of the tail, then carefully along the belly until you reach the neck. Grasp the skin detached from the hind legs and peel back the body skin up to the shoulders. Skin the forelegs in the same way as the hind legs. Roll the skin over the animal's neck and head and cut it free at the eyes and mouth: the whole skin will fall free, leaving the animal ready for gutting.

Dark Colour from Hare's Blood

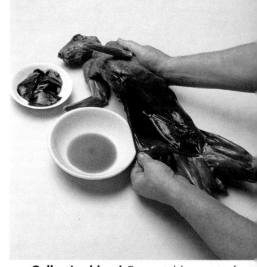

1 Collecting blood. Pour a tablespoon of vinegar—here, red wine vinegar—into a bowl. Slit the hare's belly, draw out the innards and discard everything but the liver, cutting it free from the gall bladder. To release the blood, hold the animal over the bowl and slit the diaphragm with the tip of the knife; pour out the blood into the bowl of vinegar (*above*).

Puréed Corals for a Taste of the Sea

1 Extracting corals. Prepare a fish velouté (*page 49*). While it is cooking, cup the rounded side of each sea urchin in your hand and use sharp-pointed scissors to cut out a circular piece from the dimpled underside. Shake the urchin to empty out the viscera; discard them. With a spoon, scoop out the five orange-pink corals inside the shell (*above*).

2 Puréeing the corals. Discard the urchin shells and transfer the corals to a sieve set over a bowl. Use a pestle to break down the corals' soft flesh, then press it through the sieve (*above*) to form a liquid purée.

3 Adding cream. With a whisk, stir the purée gently until it has an even texture. Then, to enrich it, whisk in double cream (*above*)—here, 12.5 cl (4 fl oz) of cream is added to about 15 cl (¼ pint) of purée obtained from three dozen urchins.

2 **Thickening the sauce.** Make a brown game sauce (*page 48*). To prepare the thickening, purée the liver by passing it through a metal sieve or grinding it in a food processor, then mix it with the blood. Remove the cooked sauce from the heat; allow it to cool slightly—stirring it to prevent a skin from forming—then stir in the blood and liver mixture (*above*).

3 **Finishing and serving the sauce.** Over a fireproof mat and a very low heat, reheat the sauce, stirring until it thickens slightly and turns dark chocolate brown—do not allow the sauce even to approach a simmer lest it curdle. Transfer the sauce to a warmed sauceboat and serve it at once. Here, the sauce is ladled over a serving of roast saddle of the hare from which the blood was drawn.☐

4 **Combining corals and velouté.** Allow the prepared velouté to cool slightly. To avoid curdling the purée, whisk it into the sauce in two stages: first whisk a ladleful of warm velouté into the purée (*above*), then whisk the mixture of velouté and coral purée into the pan containing the rest of the velouté.

5 **Finishing the sauce.** Over a fireproof mat and a low heat, reheat the sauce, stirring it until it thickens slightly—do not allow the sauce to approach a simmer or it will curdle. Remove the sauce from the heat and, for further enrichment, whisk in a few cubes of butter (*above*).

6 **Serving the sauce.** Transfer the sauce to a warmed sauceboat. Serve the sauce immediately—here, with a whole sea bass that is garnished with the carrot and onion slices from the court-bouillon in which it was poached.☐

3
Egg Sauces
Elegant Emulsions

The prime importance of the egg in sauce-making lies in the ability of the yolk to form emulsions with different liquids. Vigorous beating of egg yolk together with oil, butter or stock, for example, causes the liquid to become evenly suspended in the egg, so that the two elements are bound permanently together. The resulting rich, smooth sauces, both hot and cold, are among the most impressive in all cookery.

Mayonnaise—a mixture of egg yolks and oil, sharpened with a dash of vinegar or lemon juice—is perhaps the best-known uncooked egg emulsion (*page 58*). The essential trick in making mayonnaise is to have the ingredients at room temperature and to add the oil to the yolks very gradually—literally drop by drop at first—while beating vigorously. The result is a voluptuously thick emulsion that lends itself to emphatic flavourings: garlic, anchovies, tomatoes and herbs, for example.

Subjected to heat, egg yolks thicken as well as emulsify, giving cooked egg sauces their body and texture. But cooking with eggs always requires care. If the sauce gets too hot, the emulsion will break—the yolk will separate from the liquid. To prevent the sauce from curdling in this way, heat must always be kept very gentle. The best method is to use a bain-marie or water bath so that the heat remains indirect and therefore low.

Hollandaise, the archetypal hot egg sauce, is made by cooking egg yolks with butter and oil and flavouring the sauce with lemon juice (*page 60*). With additional flavourings, a basic hollandaise is easily transformed into other sauces (*pages 62-63*)—tarragon, for example, makes a béarnaise, tomato purée a *choron* and the juice of blood oranges a *maltaise*.

Other liquids that can be emulsified with egg yolks to make smooth sauces include stock and wine. On page 64, eggs are whisked over heat with fumet to make a savoury fish sabayon, and with wine and sugar to make a sweet one. The whisking incorporates air, making sabayons very light and fluffy. Custard, made with eggs and milk, is a creamier, more substantial sweet sauce (*page 66*).

One way to provide extra thickening for an egg sauce is to start with a roux of butter and flour. The swiftly prepared *sauce bâtarde* shown on page 68 is made by simply whisking water and egg yolks into the roux. The sauce's neutral taste makes it a suitable vehicle for all manner of flavourings—such as lemon juice, mustard, fresh herbs or tomato purée.

Sauce maltaise (page 62)—a variation on a basic hollandaise sauce—completes an hors-d'oeuvre serving of boiled asparagus spears. The sauce, made by combining butter with egg yolks and lemon juice over gentle heat, gets its dramatic colour from its flavouring: the freshly squeezed juice of a blood orange.

Mayonnaise: Simple Magic

Mayonnaise is the result of a remarkable transformation: two disparate ingredients, oil and egg yolks, combine as if by magic to form a glistening, golden emulsion with a thick, jelly-like consistency. Continued whisking disperses the oil into tiny droplets, and these remain suspended in the beaten yolk. Egg is such an efficient emulsifier that a single yolk can hold ½ litre (16 fl oz) of oil, producing a sauce thick enough to be cut cleanly with a knife. Here, proportions of one yolk to 17.5 cl (6 fl oz) produce a mayonnaise that holds its shape when spooned.

Mayonnaise (*right; recipe, page 167*) is easy to make, provided a few essential rules are observed. The ingredients—egg yolks, oil, and vinegar or lemon juice (or a combination of the two) to season—should all be at room temperature. Beat the yolks in advance and, most important of all, add the oil slowly, a drop at a time at first, then in a controlled trickle.

Too much oil added at once will cause the emulsion to separate; if this happens, you can restore it by beating a fresh yolk in another bowl and slowly whisking in the broken mayonnaise. If the sauce is too thick, add a little warm water, lemon juice or vinegar. Mayonnaise can also be made in a blender or food processor, but the result will be fluffier and less rich.

By adding different ingredients, you can vary the colour, flavour and texture of mayonnaise to complement seafood, cold meat and salad dishes. Almost any cooked vegetable, diced or puréed, can be incorporated. Green mayonnaise (*below*) is created by stirring in chopped herbs and spinach; for a tangy pink mayonnaise, use puréed sweet red peppers and tomato purée. A classic French recipe includes jellied veal stock (*page 42*) to thicken and flavour the sauce.

Gribiche (*opposite page, below; recipe, page 167*) is an unusual form of mayonnaise based on hard-boiled yolks pounded to a paste—here, with raw yolk to help emulsify the oil. Mustard, capers and gherkins add substance and pungency.

A Smooth Blend of Eggs and Oil

1 **Adding lemon juice.** Separate eggs and put the yolks in a mixing bowl. Season with salt and pepper. Whisk the yolks with a wire whisk until they are smooth in texture and pale in colour. Pour the juice of half a lemon into the bowl in a thin, slow stream (*above*), constantly whisking the ingredients to blend them.

A Herb-Flecked Mayonnaise

1 **Adding herbs and spinach.** Make some mayonnaise (*Steps 1 and 2, above*). Stem and parboil spinach, then drain it, squeeze it well and chop it. Prepare *fines herbes*; sprinkle them on the mayonnaise (*above*), then add the spinach.

2 **Mixing the ingredients.** Stir the chopped herbs and spinach into the mayonnaise until they are evenly incorporated (*above*). The finished sauce should be a pale green with darker flecks. If you wish, add other flavourings; in this case, the sieved coral of a poached lobster.

3 **Serving green mayonnaise.** Serve this coloured and flavoured sauce with any fish or shellfish dish—here, it garnishes a cold lobster arranged on a bed of lettuce leaves (*above*). Or, without the addition of the lobster coral, serve the green mayonnaise with dishes such as chicken, brains or vegetables.□

2 **Incorporating oil.** Begin to add olive oil drop by drop (*above, left*), whisking continuously; control the flow by inserting your thumb in the bottle's neck. When the mixture begins to emulsify, dribble the oil in a thin stream (*above, centre*), continuing to whisk steadily. As the sauce becomes paler and thickens, increase the flow of oil (*above, right*). To test the consistency, use the whisk to lift out some sauce and drop it back into the bowl; if the drop holds its shape, the sauce is ready. To thin it, add a few drops of lemon juice or water.

3 **Serving mayonnaise.** The sauce is best served at once with a salad or simple cold dish, such as chicken garnished with gherkins (*above*). To store mayonnaise, cover it and put it in the refrigerator or a cool place. It will keep for up to three days. Stir or whisk before using.□

Gribiche: Piquancy from Capers and Gherkins

1 **Mashing yolks.** Hard boil eggs. Place the yolks in a bowl and reserve the whites. Add one raw egg yolk and a teaspoonful of mustard to the yolks. With a pestle, mash the ingredients to a smooth paste. Add lemon juice and oil, turning with the pestle to incorporate the oil.

2 **Adding flavourings.** Cut half of the egg whites into *julienne*. Wash, drain and chop capers and gherkins. Prepare *fines herbes*. Add all these ingredients to the mayonnaise (*above*) and stir until they are thoroughly blended.

3 **Serving gribiche.** A *gribiche* sauce may be served with hot or cold fish or shellfish. In this instance, the sauce is spread on a platter and topped with warm poached scallops cut into halves.□

Hollandaise: Theme and Variations

Egg yolks whisked with butter over a low heat combine with the fat and thicken to form a rich emulsion. Flavoured with lemon juice, the result is hollandaise—a celebrated preparation in its own right, and the foundation for a range of egg-thickened sauces. Two ways of preparing a basic hollandaise and three variations (*recipes, page 165*) are demonstrated here and on the following pages.

A hollandaise can be made with either butter cubes (*right*) or melted butter (*box, opposite page*); in the latter case, the butter is first melted in a separate pan and clarified to separate the clear fat from the milky solids butter always contains.

Whichever method you use, there are two rules to observe in making the sauce. The butter must be whisked into the yolks a little at a time, and each portion must be incorporated before the next is added—otherwise the emulsion will separate. Even more important, the sauce must not overheat, or the eggs will begin to solidify and the sauce will be ruined. To make the yolks more fluid, mix them with a little water before heating. Prepare the sauce in a pan set in a bain-marie—a deep pan partly filled with water. Keep the water at just below simmering point.

Classic hollandaise is flavoured only with lemon juice. *Sauce maltaise*, made by adding blood orange juice, has a bitter-sweet taste and a pink to deep mauve colour, depending on the variety of orange used. A béarnaise is made like a hollandaise, except that the yolks are combined with a reduction of flavoured wine and vinegar before butter—or, as in this demonstration, oil—is whisked in. Tarragon gives the sauce its distinctive taste, and chervil and shallots usually lend support. For *sauce choron*, coarse tomato purée is stirred into the completed béarnaise.

Egg-thickened sauces are best served immediately. As soon as the desired consistency is reached, remove the pan from the bain-marie to prevent the sauce from thickening further. If necessary, you can hold the sauce for a short time before serving by standing the pan in a warm—but not hot—bain-marie.

1 **Heating egg yolks and water.** Cut chilled butter into small cubes. Squeeze the juice from a lemon, remove the pips and reserve the juice. Set a trivet in a large pan and pour in water until the trivet is just covered. Heat the water to just below simmering point. Combine egg yolks with a little water, salt and pepper in a saucepan and rest the pan on the trivet (*above, left*). Beat the yolks with a whisk (*above, right*) until the mixture begins to thicken slightly.

2 **Thickening the sauce.** Whisking continually, add the butter cubes, a handful at a time. Allow each batch of butter to be incorporated before adding more (*above, left*). Whisk until all of the butter is blended in and the sauce begins to thicken (*above, right*). Turn off the heat but continue to whisk the sauce.

A Method with Melted Butter

1 **Clarifying butter.** Melt butter gently in a heavy pan set over a low heat. Remove the pan from the heat, place it on a trivet and leave the butter to cool and settle. Spoon away the scum that rises to the surface (*above*). Carefully pour off the clarified liquid butter into another pan, leaving the milky residue behind.

2 **Adding the clarified butter.** Heat water in a bain-marie and put egg yolks, water and seasoning in a saucepan (*Step 1, opposite page*). Whisk the yolks until they thicken slightly. Add the clarified butter, a ladleful at a time, whisking the mixture continually as you pour (*above*). When the sauce begins to thicken, add lemon juice to flavour it.

3 **Completing the sauce.** Whisk over heat until the sauce's consistency is thick and creamy (*above*). If the sauce becomes too thick to pour, whisk in a little warm water or a few more drops of lemon juice. Taste for salt.

3 **Adding lemon juice.** Still whisking, pour the lemon juice into the sauce (*above*) and blend it thoroughly into the mixture. Remove the pan from the bain-marie. The sauce should have a firm, velvety consistency but still be pourable.

4 **Serving hollandaise.** Serve the sauce warm—with poached fish, vegetables or egg dishes, Here, it is ladled over spinach topped with poached eggs. The spinach was parboiled, squeezed and sautéed in butter, then moulded in small ramekins.□

Béarnaise: the Tang of Tarragon

1 Reducing the flavourings. Finely chop shallots, tarragon and chervil and place them in a pan. Add white wine and white wine vinegar. Bring the mixture to the boil, then reduce the contents slowly over low heat, stirring from time to time. Boil it until the liquid has been reduced to a couple of tablespoonfuls.

2 Straining the liquid. Strain the contents of the pan through a sieve; press the herbs and shallots to extract all the liquid, then discard them. Pour the liquid into a small, heavy saucepan (*above*). Add egg yolks; set the saucepan on a trivet in a bain-marie partly filled with water heated to just below simmering point. Whisk the yolks and liquid together.

3 Adding oil. When the egg mixture pales in colour and thickens slightly, add oil in a thin, steady stream (*above*). Whisking continually, gradually increase the flow of oil. Two V-shaped cuts along the oil bottle's cork will allow an even flow. The sauce will thicken and become lighter in colour as more oil is whisked into it.

Choron: a Rosy Tint from Tomatoes

1 Adding tomato. Make a coarse tomato purée (*page 30, above*). Prepare a béarnaise sauce (*Steps 1 to 5, above*); if you wish, omit the final addition of herbs. Stir the tomato purée into the sauce.

2 Serving the sauce. Transfer the sauce to a warmed sauceboat (*above*). In this case, the sauce is served with grilled kidneys (*inset*); it can also be served wth grilled meats, poultry, or robust-flavoured fish such as salmon, tuna or sturgeon.□

4 Adding water. The finished sauce should be thick but pourable and its colour a clear lemon yellow. If the sauce is too thick, thin it slightly by whisking in warm water (*above*) or a little lemon juice.

5 Adding herbs. When you are ready to serve the sauce, remove the pan from the bain-marie. Stir in some finely chopped tarragon and chervil (*above*). Transfer the finished béarnaise from the pan to a warmed sauceboat.

6 Serving the sauce. Béarnaise sauce is traditionally served with grilled poultry or meat. Here, it is spooned over a grilled rump steak (*above*). Alternatively, it can be served with poached or grilled fish or with vegetables.□

Maltaise: Brilliant Colour from Blood Oranges

1 Whisking. Squeeze the juice from one or two blood oranges, depending on their size, and set it aside. Mix egg yolks with lemon juice; put the mixture in a pan in a bain-marie. Whisk butter into the mixture over a low heat (*page 60*) until it is thick and smooth (*above*).

2 Adding orange juice. Pour the orange juice in a steady stream into the sauce, whisking all the time. As more juice is added, the sauce will take on a deep raspberry colour. Remove the pan from the heat, continuing to whisk.

3 Serving the sauce. Pour the finished sauce into a warmed sauceboat. This sauce most often accompanies boiled asparagus spears, served hot or tepid (*above*); alternative vegetables include broccoli, cauliflower or small leeks.□

Sweet and Savoury Sabayons

Sabayon is a frothy but thick sauce made by whisking egg yolks and a liquid together over heat. Depending on the liquid and flavourings used, the sauce can be sweet or savoury; in either case, the whisking beats air into the hot yolks so that the mixture foams and more than doubles its original volume. For a savoury sabayon (*right; recipe, page 166*), the liquid used is reduced fish fumet (*page 42*). For a sweet sabayon (*right, below; recipe, page 166*), wine is whisked into yolks that are first combined with sugar.

Savoury sabayon is closely related to hollandaise (*page 60*) in the way that it is made, and the same principle of gradual, gentle cooking applies. With the pan resting in a bain-marie over a low heat, combine the liquid and egg yolks, in roughly equal proportions. Keep the surrounding water at just below simmering point to provide sufficient heat for the yolks to thicken and bind the mixture, but not so much heat that the yolks solidify and cause the sauce to curdle. Towards the end of cooking, which takes about 10 minutes, whisk in butter cubes to enrich the sauce.

To make sweet sabayon, the method is a little different. Beat sugar into the egg yolks to form a pale, creamy mixture; then slowly whisk in wine over low heat until the sauce becomes frothy and light. Any sweet or dry white wine, including sparkling wine, is suitable for a sweet sabayon. Fortified wines—for example, Madeira or sherry—give the sauce a more pronounced flavour. You can vary the texture of the sauce by whisking whipped double cream or beaten egg whites into the finished sabayon.

Eggs and Fumet Whisked to a Froth

1 **Forming an emulsion.** Put some fish fumet (*page 42*) in a pan and reduce it over heat. Remove the pan from the heat and leave the fumet until cool, then add egg yolks. Place the pan in a bain-marie containing water at just below simmering point. Whisk the yolks into the fumet (*above, left*) until they are thoroughly blended. Continue whisking until the mixture thickens (*above, right*).

Wine and Sugar Lightly Whipped

1 **Mixing egg yolks and sugar.** Pour castor sugar into a large pan. Separate eggs and add the yolks to the sugar. Place the saucepan in a bain-marie containing water heated to just below simmering point. Begin to beat the yolks and sugar with a wire whisk (*above*).

2 **Adding wine.** Continue to whisk until the sugar has thoroughly dissolved in the yolks and the mixture becomes creamy and pale. Begin to pour in white wine, (*above*) whisking all the time.

2 **Enriching with butter.** Cut butter into small cubes. Take a handful of the cubes and drop them, a few at a time, into the egg and fish fumet mixture, whisking continuously. When the first batch of butter has been completely absorbed, add a second portion. Continue adding handfuls of butter until all the cubes have been incorporated.

3 **Serving the sauce.** The sabayon is ready to be served when it is thick and frothy, and coats the side of the pan. Transfer the completed sauce to a warmed sauceboat. Here, the sabayon accompanies a fish terrine; it may also accompany any poached white fish dish.□

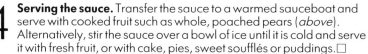

3 **Completing the sweet sabayon.** Continue to whisk the wine into the eggs and sugar; the mixture will slowly become whiter and frothier and will double in volume after about 5 minutes (*above, left*). Whisk for a further 5 to 10 minutes to finish the sauce: it should be thick, light and foamy (*above, right*).

4 **Serving the sauce.** Transfer the sauce to a warmed sauceboat and serve with cooked fruit such as whole, poached pears (*above*). Alternatively, stir the sauce over a bowl of ice until it is cold and serve it with fresh fruit, or with cake, pies, sweet soufflés or puddings.□

The Creamy Richness of a Classic Custard

A mild sweet sauce with a velvety texture, custard is the perfect partner for all kinds of puddings, and for many other hot or cold desserts. Like sweet sabayon (*page 64*), custard sauce is made by beating together egg yolks and sugar, then whisking in a liquid. However, for a custard, hot milk is substituted for wine, and the proportion of liquid is much greater. The result is a thin pouring sauce of uniform smoothness (*right; recipe, page 166*).

The richness and consistency of the custard depend on the proportion of eggs to milk. Here, six yolks to 60 cl (1 pint) of milk are used to make a custard that will evenly coat a spoon. For a thinner sauce, use a little more milk; for a thicker, richer custard, add an extra yolk.

As with other egg-thickened sauces, care must be taken not to curdle a custard by overheating it. Mixing the yolks with sugar helps to keep them fluid. Cooking begins by scalding the milk—heating it to just below boiling point—then whisking it into the yolks off the heat. The hot milk starts the yolks cooking gently and dilutes the mixture so cooking can safely be completed in a heavy pan over a low direct heat. Stir the sauce constantly, alternating figure-of-eight with circular motions, to distribute the heat evenly throughout.

Custard sauce lends itself to many different flavourings. To make the caramel custard shown here (*box, right*), liquid caramel (*page 38*) is stirred into the finished custard; alternatively, the caramel can be incorporated with the hot milk. For a vanilla custard, a vanilla pod is steeped in the scalded milk and removed before the liquid is whisked into the egg and sugar mixture. You could also flavour custard with rum or coffee.

Custard and its variations are equally good served hot, warm or cold. For cold custard, stir the sauce over ice (*Step 4, opposite page*) until it is chilled; or stir the sauce until cool, then cover and refrigerate until you wish to serve it.

1 Combining egg yolks with sugar. Separate eggs, place the yolks in a mixing bowl and add castor sugar. Using a wire whisk, break up the yolks (*above, left*), then whisk the ingredients together until the sugar is completely absorbed and the mixture is smooth (*above, centre*). As you whisk, the beaten yolks will become paler and increase in volume. After about 10 minutes, when the mixture is thick and almost white, test the consistency by lifting out a little on the whisk and dribbling it across the surface of the bowl: it should form a ribbon-like trail (*above, right*).

A Last-Minute Addition of Caramel

1 Incorporating flavouring. Boil a sugar syrup to the caramel stage and stir a little water into it to make a caramel sauce (*page 38*). Prepare a custard (*Steps 1 to 5, above*) and whisk in the caramel until it is thoroughly blended.

2 Serving the custard. When the caramel is evenly incorporated, pour the sauce into a warmed jug (*above*). Serve at once with a hot or cold dessert; or stir until cool, then cover and refrigerate.

2 **Adding scalded milk.** Scald milk, stirring as it heats to prevent a skin forming. Remove the pan from the heat and allow the milk to cool slightly; then pour the milk into the egg yolk and sugar mixture, whisking slowly but continuously. When the mixture is well blended, transfer it from the bowl to a heavy saucepan.

3 **Cooking the custard.** Place the heavy saucepan over a very low heat. Stir the custard continuously as it heats, making sure you cover the entire surface of the pan. The correct consistency has been achieved when the custard is smooth and coats the spoon evenly.

4 **Arresting the cooking.** Remove the pan from the heat and dip it at once in a bowl of ice to stop the sauce from thickening further. Stir the sauce gently so that it does not form a skin. If the sauce is not to be served immediately, keep it warm by covering the pan and placing it in a warm—but not hot— bain-marie.

5 **Straining the sauce.** Pour the custard through a sieve into a warmed bowl (*left*) and serve immediately with a dessert—in this case, moulded chocolate pudding (*below*). If you prefer to serve the custard cold, stir it over ice until it cools in order to prevent a skin forming, then cover it and put it in the refrigerator.□

Bâtarde: a Savoury Sauce Made in Minutes

A light, yolk-bound sauce can be easily and very quickly made by using a second thickening agent in addition to the eggs. The *sauce bâtarde* shown here (*recipe, page 166*) is begun with a roux of butter and flour and finished with beaten egg yolks. Unlike other roux-based sauces (*page 28*), *bâtarde* does not need any reduction because, once the sauce is bound by the flour, the egg yolks complete the thickening in just a few minutes.

Speed is the key to success when making *sauce bâtarde*: cooking it for more than a few minutes would bring out the taste of flour from the roux which could then only be eliminated by lengthy simmering. To avoid any delay in moving from one stage to the next, it is advisable to prepare all the ingredients in advance. Have ready egg yolks beaten with a little water, a jug of lightly salted warm water, freshly squeezed lemon juice, butter cut into cubes and the flavouring of your choice—here, it is finely chopped parsley.

As soon as the flour and butter begin to bubble, the water is whisked in over low heat. Off the heat, the yolks are mixed in; the pan is returned to a low heat and the sauce stirred gently for a few minutes while the eggs thicken it. Butter and flavourings are then added and the sauce is ready to serve.

Bâtarde is a suitable accompaniment for grilled fish, poultry, or steamed or boiled vegetables. For a richer effect, the yolks may be combined with a little cream instead of water. Flavourings for the finished sauce can include chopped herbs, capers or a spoonful of prepared mustard. In one variation traditionally served with grilled mackerel, a purée of cooked gooseberries is stirred into the plain *bâtarde*.

1 Preparing the ingredients. Squeeze the juice from a lemon; reserve it. Separate eggs, dropping the yolks into a bowl. Add cold water to the bowl and beat the mixture until it is smooth.

2 Adding water. Melt butter in a heavy pan set over a low heat. Add flour and stir the roux until it begins to foam. Then pour in lightly salted warm water, whisking the mixture rapidly (*above*).

5 Thickening the sauce. Return the pan to a low heat and continue whisking until the sauce becomes slightly thicker (*above*). Take care that the mixture does not approach the boil.

6 Finishing the sauce. Place the pan on a trivet. Add to the thickened sauce the reserved lemon juice, then add finely chopped parsley (*above*), whisking until it is evenly distributed in the sauce. Whisk in handfuls of butter cubes, blending in each handful before adding the next.

3 **Bringing to the boil.** Continue to whisk the mixture as it heats, so that all the ingredients are smoothly blended. As soon as the mixture reaches the boil, remove the pan from the heat.

4 **Whisking in egg yolks.** Stand the pan on a trivet and leave it for a minute or two to allow the mixture to cool slightly. Then whisk in the reserved mixture of egg yolks and water (*above*).

7 **Serving the sauce.** The sauce is ready when all the butter is incorporated and the mixture has a smooth and velvety consistency (*left*). Taste it for seasoning, transfer it to a warmed sauceboat and serve immediately; here, it is poured over boiled cauliflower (*above*).□

4
Integral Sauces
Making the Most of Cooking Liquids

Most methods of cooking a main dish—especially sautéing, roasting, poaching and braising—offer an opportunity to make an accompanying sauce from flavouring elements that would otherwise be lost. In sautéing, for example, meat juices coagulate in the bottom of the pan to form a savoury deposit that can be incorporated into a sauce by being dissolved with liquid. This process, known as deglazing, is not confined to sautéing. Braised and stewed meats, too, are often given a preliminary browning, and the residues that remain in the pan can be deglazed with the braising liquid. And during roasting, meat juices that form a glaze in the bottom of the roasting pan are the starting point for a gravy.

Since the deglazing liquid can be chosen to suit the finished dish, the process permits considerable variation. Plain water, for example, may be all that is required to turn the rich residues of a juicy steak or roast into a straightforward and excellent sauce; but red wine, beer, veal stock or suitable combinations of these and other liquids can be used instead. For more delicately flavoured meats, such as pork, veal or chicken, the harmonious blend of Madeira and cream described on page 72 is one of many options for enriching the finished dish. Sauces for sautés and roasts in particular lend themselves to further elaboration by the addition of herb and vegetable garnishes after the deglazing stage.

In braised dishes, the relatively small amount of cooking liquid used for cooking absorbs enough flavour from the main ingredients to stand as a sauce by itself; no further embellishment is needed for the highly reduced sauce that coats the leg of lamb on page 78. In some braises, however, and in all poached dishes, additional body and flavour is required to turn a dilute cooking medium into a finished sauce. Cream, alone or with egg yolks, will thicken and enrich sauces for fish and white meats, while the addition of one of the concentrated savoury essences described in Chapter 2 will give substance to sauces for red meats, game and offal.

Most of the dishes described in this chapter are composed of two complementary elements: a fluid sauce and a solid main ingredient that share common flavour but retain separate identities. However, when all of the solid ingredients are chopped very finely and cooked together with the liquid, the elements merge. The result is a thick, yet pourable blend appropriate for serving over rice, potatoes or pasta (*page 84*).

A glistening red wine sauce is spooned over slices of tender rump steak. The sauce was made by using red wine to deglaze the pan in which the steak was fried, reducing the liquid until it was concentrated in flavour and then enriching it with butter (*page 74*).

Savoury Residues from Sautéed Meats

As meat and poultry are roasted or sautéed, they release juices that form rich pan deposits; these can then be used as the savoury starting point for sauces. Preparing these sauces entails no more work than deglazing the pan deposits by dissolving them in a liquid. However, despite their culinary simplicity, deglazed sauces can be endlessly varied by changing the choice of liquid—plain or fortified wine, stock, beer, cider or plain water. In the demonstration on the right, Madeira and double cream form a voluptuous alliance in a sauce for thick slices of pork loin.

Whatever the liquid, the sauce is made in the same way. After the meat or poultry is fully cooked, it is removed from the pan. Any excess fat is then poured or spooned off, to leave the cooking deposits. Over high heat, liquid is added, and the bottom and sides of the pan are scraped vigorously until the caramelized deposits dissolve in the liquid to form the sauce.

A large joint of roasted meat will often exude such an abundant supply of flavourful deposits that water is all that is needed to create a sauce richly flavoured with the meat's own unaltered essences. Such is the case with the silverside of veal on page 76. White wine, instead of water, would bring an extra dimension of taste; veal stock would lend extra body.

Red wine contributes a robust flavour and an appropriate colour to sauces for dark meat, as with the pan-fried steak in the upper demonstration on page 74. On the same page, a reduction of red wine and aromatics, blended with a little meat glaze, yields a full-bodied sauce of concentrated flavour for sautéed calf's kidneys.

Fullness of flavour with a hint of sweetness is the hallmark of sauces made with fortified wines—such as Marsala, Madeira or port. Such sauces go especially well with the naturally sweet taste of pork (*right*) or the richness of game.

1 Preparing pork. Trim pork—in this case, an eye of loin—free of all membranes and fat. Cut the meat into 2.5 cm (1 inch) thick slices. To brown the meat and to give the sauce extra body, coat the slices lightly in flour on each side. In a wide pan, heat some butter; when it foams, add the slices of pork (*above*).

2 Turning the pork. When, after a few minutes, the pork slices have browned on the underside, turn them over with a fork (*above*). Continue to sauté them, and when the slices are evenly coloured on both sides, remove them from the pan and transfer them to a warm platter. Set the platter aside in a warm place.

5 Enriching with cream. To lend volume and richness to the sauce, pour in double cream (*above*). The quantity can be varied according to taste and how much sauce you require. Here, cream equal to about double the quantity of deglazing liquid is added to the pan.

6 Blending the sauce. Stir the cream and deglazing liquid together, scraping the bottom of the pan to bring the syrupy liquid to the surface (*above*). When the sauce is evenly blended, boil it for a few minutes to concentrate the flavours.

3 **Adding liquid.** Pour off and discard any excess fat from the pan, leaving behind the pan deposits. Return the pan to a high heat and pour in a generous splash of liquid—in this case, Madeira (*above*).

4 **Deglazing.** When the liquid comes to the boil, use a wooden spatula or spoon to scrape up the deposits from the bottom of the pan (*above, left*). Scrape and stir until all the deposits have dissolved in the liquid. Boil the liquid for a few minutes, drawing the spatula across the bottom of the pan to check the liquid's consistency. When the spatula leaves a clean trail (*above, right*) the liquid is thick enough and deglazing is completed.

7 **Straining the sauce.** To ensure that the sauce is entirely smooth and free of any undissolved solids, strain it through a sieve into another pan (*above*). Cook the sauce for another minute or two, until it thickens to a coating consistency.

8 **Serving the sauce.** As soon as the sauce has the consistency of thick cream (*inset*), it is ready to serve. Spoon it from the pan over each serving of pork (*above*). Here, glazed carrots lend a complementary sweetness to the pork, and provide an attractive touch of colour.□

Tender Beef Allied with Red Wine

1 Sautéing steak. Trim away excess fat from steak—here, a 5 cm (2 inch) thick piece of rump. Coat a pan with oil and set it over a high heat. When the oil sizzles, place the steak in the pan and sear one side for up to 1 minute. Reduce the heat to medium and cook the steak for 3 to 4 minutes. Increase the heat; turn the steak over (*above*) and sear the other side.

2 Pouring off excess fat. Reduce the heat and sauté the steak for a further 2 to 5 minutes, depending on how rare you want the meat to be. Remove the pan from the heat. Transfer the steak to a warm platter and set it aside. Let the pan juices cool slightly so that excess fat rises to the surface. Pour off and discard excess fat (*above*).

3 Deglazing the pan. Return the pan to the heat. Pour in a generous amount of full-bodied red wine (*above*). With a wooden, flat-edged spatula, scrape up the pan deposits until they have all been loosened and dissolved in the liquid. Reduce the liquid to a syrup, then remove the pan from the heat.

An Aromatic Finish for Calf's Kidneys

1 Sautéing kidneys. Cut the membrane and suet from calf's kidneys. Halve each kidney lengthwise and trim away the core fat. Slice the kidneys into 1 cm (½ inch) wide pieces. In a pan, heat butter until it foams. Add the kidneys (*above*); sauté them over a high heat for about 4 minutes, stirring and tossing frequently, until they lose their surface pinkness.

2 Deglazing. Tip the kidneys into a strainer set over a bowl. Return the pan to the heat. Add a little butter to the pan. Put in finely chopped shallots; when they are lightly coloured, add enough red wine reduction (*page 10*) to cover the bottom of the pan (*above*). Scrape the deposits from the bottom of the pan until they all dissolve in the liquid.

3 Adding meat glaze. Boil the liquid until it has reduced to a syrupy consistency, then add 2 to 3 tablespoons of meat glaze (*page 44*) for extra flavour and body. Stir until the glaze has melted and the liquids are all blended into a smooth sauce. Add a dash of lemon juice.

4 **Finishing the sauce.** Add a few cubes of butter (*above*), swirling the pan so that the butter is evenly absorbed into the sauce. Carve the steak, cutting it on the bias to make broad slices. Spoon the sauce over the slices and serve them immediately (*right*).□

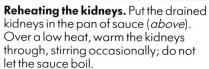

4 **Reheating the kidneys.** Put the drained kidneys in the pan of sauce (*above*). Over a low heat, warm the kidneys through, stirring occasionally; do not let the sauce boil.

5 **Finishing with butter.** When the kidneys are thoroughly reheated, remove the pan from the heat and stand it on a trivet. Add a few cubes of butter. Stir all the ingredients together (*above*) until the butter is completely absorbed.

6 **Serving the kidneys.** Transfer the kidneys and their sauce to a warm serving platter. If you like, sprinkle some finely chopped parsley over the dish as a garnish before serving (*above*).□

Recouping a Roast's Rich Juices

1 **Wrapping meat in caul.** Trim a joint of veal—in this case, silverside—free of all fat and membrane. Mix water with a little vinegar; soak caul in it for about 10 minutes. Rinse well, dry and lay the caul on a work surface. Place the meat on top. Wrap the caul round the joint so that the meat's surface is completely covered.

2 **Basting the veal.** Put the veal in a shallow roasting pan just large enough to contain it, then place the pan in a preheated 220°C (425°F or Mark 7) oven. After 10 minutes, reduce the heat to 180°C (350°F or Mark 4) and roast the meat, basting it frequently (*above*); allow 20 minutes per 500 g (1 lb). Test the meat by pinching it; if it feels firm, the meat is done.

3 **Deglazing with water.** Transfer the veal to a carving board or platter and place it in a warm place. Spoon off any excess fat from the pan. Set the pan over high heat and pour in water (*above*). As the water comes to the boil, scrape up the pan deposits and blend them into the liquid.

4 **Serving.** Stir the sauce as it boils and reduces, then transfer it to a sauceboat. Carve the veal and transfer the slices to serving plates; reserve any meat juices and add them to the sauce. Spoon a little of the sauce over the meat (*right*) and serve the rest separately. Here, the veal is accompanied by boiled new potatoes, tossed in butter and parsley.□

Sweetbreads Bathed in Wine and Stock

An integral sauce for many braised and poached foods is formed by simply straining, cleansing and reducing the liquid used to cook them. The main difference between braised and poached dishes is that more liquid is used in poaching—making the reduction of the sauce take proportionately longer—but in each case the principle is the same. During cooking, the liquid becomes imbued with flavours from the main ingredients—meat, poultry, fish or vegetables—and their accompanying aromatics and herbs.

The most important factor in the taste and consistency of the finished sauce is the nature of the liquid that you start with: wine, stock or fumet, and plain water all have advantages. Wine brings its complexity of flavour; a rich veal stock supports the flavours of meat, poultry or vegetables, just as fish fumet reinforces fish, and also lends the sauce considerable body; water leaves the flavour of the main ingredients unaltered. A combination of white wine and veal stock is used here to braise calf's sweetbreads (*right*) and a leg of lamb (*page 78, above*). In the lower demonstration on page 78, fortified wine, together with veal stock, provides a rich liquid that envelops artichokes.

The addition of *coulis* or meat glaze (*page 44*) to a sauce for meat or offal will lend even more body and also intensify the dish's succulence. A similar effect can be produced by including gelatinous calf's feet or pig's trotters in the pot at the start of cooking. These additions, though, take at least 3 hours to render their gelatine: use them only in dishes that have a lengthy cooking time.

For fish dishes, a fumet alone is the appropriate choice if you want to intensify natural flavour. In the upper demonstration on page 80, coils of filleted sole are poached in a white wine fumet with mushroom cooking liquid as well to give the sauce more complexity; the mushrooms, supplemented by mussels and a little of their cooking liquid, flavour and garnish the finished sauce. By contrast, a red wine fumet is the liquid used to cook firm-fleshed salmon (*page 80, below*); supplemented with a red wine velouté, it yields a robust sauce that is finished with pungent anchovy butter.

1 Preparing the sweetbreads. Soak calf's sweetbreads in several changes of cold water. Simmer them gently for 5 minutes in fresh water; drain and refresh them in cold water. Peel off surface membranes, cartilage and fat. Put the sweetbreads, between two towels, under a weighted board for 3 hours. Place them in a pan on a bed of *mirepoix* (*page 8*).

2 Braising. Pour in white wine and melted veal stock (*page 42*) to barely cover the calf's sweetbreads, then press buttered greaseproof paper on top (*above*) and cover the pan with a lid. Either simmer the sweetbreads over a low heat for 40 minutes, or bring them to the boil, then transfer them to a 150° to 170°C (300° to 325°F or Mark 2 to 3) oven.

3 Cleansing. Take out the sweetbreads. Strain the liquid through a sieve into a pan. Return the sweetbreads and the *mirepoix* to the braising pan; keep them warm. Simmer the liquid, half off the heat, skimming off the thick skin as it forms. The sauce is ready when only a thin skin, free of fat, forms. For extra body, stir in a spoonful of *coulis* (*above*).

4 Serving. When the *coulis* has melted and the sauce is smooth, pour it over the sweetbreads. Warm the assembled dish over a very low heat before you present it. Serve the sweetbreads straight from the pan, coating each portion with a few spoonfuls of sauce (*above*).□

Special Treatment for Glazed Lamb

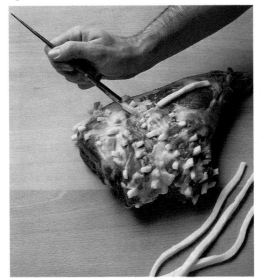

1 **Larding.** Remove fat from a leg of lamb. cut out the pelvic bone; reserve it. Cut chilled pork back fat into 1cm (½ inch) thick strips. Thread a larding needle with a strip and draw it through the surface of the meat, making stitches at 2.5 cm (1 inch) intervals (*above*); leave 2.5 cm of fat protruding . Repeat until the leg's upper surface and sides are larded.

2 **Assembling ingredients.** Tie the loose flesh with string. Split a couple of washed pig's trotters in half lengthwise; parboil them for 2 to 3 minutes; drain and rinse them. Prepare a bouquet garni (*page 7*). Put coarsely chopped onions and carrots and a few unpeeled garlic cloves in a braising pan; place the lamb on top.

3 **Adding veal stock.** Pack the pelvic bone the pig's trotters and the bouquet garni round the meat. Pour over two to three glasses of white wine, then hot veal stock (*page 42*) until the ingredients are barely covered (*above*). Cover the contents with buttered greaseproof paper and a lid; place the pan in a preheated 170°C (325°F or Mark 3) oven.

Braised Artichokes with Madeira and Cream

1 **Preparing artichokes.** Snap the stem, along with its fibres, off each artichoke. Bend and snap off the tough outer leaves until you reach the tender ones. Cut off two-thirds of the globe's top and, with a stainless steel knife, pare away the dark green exterior from the base. Scoop out the raw choke with a teaspoon (*above*). Rub the surfaces with lemon juice.

2 **Adding braising liquid.** To prevent the artichokes being spoiled by chemical reaction with metal, place them in an earthenware dish, packing them tightly in a single layer. Add liquid—in this case, veal stock and Madeira (*above*)—to reach about half way up the sides of the artichokes. Pour the liquid inside the globes as well as round them.

3 **Braising.** Over a fireproof mat, bring the liquid to the boil. Then cover and cook the artichokes in a preheated 170°C (325°F or Mark 3) oven for about 45 minutes, until they feel firm when pierced with a fork. Transfer them to a plate (*above*); pour the liquid into a pan, then return the artichokes to the dish. Bring the liquid to the boil, then cleanse and reduce it.

4 **Pressing out juices.** Cook the lamb until it is tender, about 3 hours. Transfer the lamb and trotters to a tray; discard the bone and the bouquet garni. Strain the braising liquid and vegetables through a sieve set over a pan. With a flat skimmer, press the juices out of the vegetables (*above*), then discard them. Cleanse and reduce the liquid.

5 **Glazing the lamb.** Put the lamb in a shallow ovenproof dish. Remove the bones from the trotters, then cut each half-trotter diagonally into three pieces; arrange them round the meat. Pour the cleansed sauce over the meat and cook it, uncovered, in a 200°C (400°F or Mark 6) oven for 30 to 45 minutes, basting it every 2 to 3 minutes (*above*).

6 **Serving.** Prepare an accompaniment for the lamb—in this case, a generously buttered, mixed purée of swede, onion, celeriac, potato and garlic is chosen, but you could substitute a potato purée or pasta. Carve the lamb and transfer the slices, along with pieces of trotter, to serving plates. Spoon the sauce over the slices of meat (*above*).☐

4 **Adding cream.** Pour the reduced liquid over the artichokes, then add double cream (*above*)—here, an amount about equal to the braising liquid. Cover the dish and return it to the oven for 20 to 30 minutes, basting regularly. Transfer the artichokes to a warm plate, draining them of all liquid, and keep them warm.

5 **Finishing the sauce.** Strain the cream-enriched braising liquid through a sieve set over a small pan (*above*). Over a high heat, boil the liquid briskly until it has reduced to the consistency you want.

6 **Serving.** If you like, prepare a garnish to go inside each artichoke. In this case, tiny onions were parboiled, then cooked gently in butter. Arrange the artichokes and the garnish on a warmed serving dish. Ladle the sauce over them (*above*) and serve them immediately.☐

Spirals of Fish with a Seafood Garnish

1 **Preparing sole.** Make a fish mousseline and colour it green with spinach (*recipe, page 167*); chill it until firm. Rinse and dry sole fillets and press them flat with a wide-bladed knife. Score each fillet in three or four places on the skinned side. Spread the mousseline thickly on the scored sides. Roll up the fillets (*above*); pack them in a heavy, buttered pan.

2 **Adding the liquid.** Ladle the poaching liquid—here, mushroom cooking liquid (*page 11*) and fish fumet (*page 42*)—around the fillets (*above*). Add enough for the fillets to be barely submerged.

3 **Poaching.** Cover the fillets with buttered greaseproof paper (*above*). Set the pan, covered, on a medium heat; bring the liquid to the boil. Remove from the heat and leave the fillets in the covered pan for about 10 minutes, or until the mousseline is firm to the touch. With a spatula or spoon, transfer the fillets to a serving platter and keep them warm.

Salmon Steaks in a Wine-Dark Sauce

1 **Enriching velouté.** Prepare a basic fish velouté (*page 49, Steps 1 and 2*), using a red wine fumet (*page 42*). Pour an equal quantity of red wine reduction (*page 10*) into the velouté, stirring as you pour (*above*). Boil the mixture briskly until it has reduced by about half.

2 **Poaching salmon.** Slice fresh salmon into 5 cm (2 inch) steaks and arrange them in a buttered pan. Cover them with tepid red wine fish fumet (*above*) and place buttered greaseproof paper on top; put on the lid. Bring the fumet to the boil, then turn off the heat and leave the salmon in the hot liquid for about 10 minutes to complete its cooking.

3 **Straining the poaching liquid.** Transfer the salmon steaks to a warm plate and keep them warm. Strain the poaching liquid through a sieve set over a small pan (*above*). Over a high heat, boil the liquid until it has reduced by about half.

4 **Reducing the liquid.** Set the pan over a high heat and boil the liquid briskly until it has reduced by about half. Add double cream to taste, then swirl the pan gently to mix the cream into the liquid (*above*).

5 **Adding a garnish.** Prepare a garnish for the sauce—here, cooked mushrooms and steamed, shelled mussels (*page 10*). Tip the garnish ingredients into the sauce (*above*). Stir the sauce gently over a low heat for a couple of minutes to warm the garnish, then transfer the sauce to a warmed sauceboat.

6 **Serving.** Slice the rolled sole fillets in half horizontally, to reveal the green spirals; arrange three halves on each serving plate for a portion. Ladle a little of the garnished sauce round each portion (*above*) and serve the rest separately.☐

4 **Combining the two liquids.** Pour the reduced poaching liquid into the pan containing the velouté (*above*). Stir the liquids to amalgamate them. Over a high heat, bring the liquid to the boil. Set the pan half off the heat, then cleanse and reduce the sauce.

5 **Finishing with anchovy butter.** Remove the pan from the heat and stand it on a trivet. A few pieces at a time, add chilled anchovy butter (*page 12*), whisking to blend it smoothly into the sauce. Here, about 40 g (1½ oz) of anchovy butter is used for 30 cl (½ pint) of sauce.

6 **Serving.** Pour the sauce immediately into a warmed sauceboat. Remove the skin from the salmon steaks and place them on individual serving plates. Ladle over them a generous helping of sauce.☐

Meat Stew: an Intricate Assembly of Flavours

When meat is browned in fat as a preliminary to further cooking, it yields savoury deposits in the same way as the sautéed and roasted meats shown on pages 72 to 76. But continuing to cook the meat in the pan after it is deglazed allows the meat's flavour to be drawn into the braising liquid. This liquid, cleansed and reduced, provides a rich, concentrated sauce to serve with the meat. A veal stew is shown here, but with the appropriate adjustments of cooking time the same technique could be applied with equal success to pieces of lean beef, lamb or rabbit, or to joints of chicken.

The sauce of a stew owes much to the character of the liquids employed—these can include red or white wine, beer, stock or plain water, depending on taste. Here, a dash of brandy and a generous amount of red wine are used to deglaze the pan in which pieces of knuckle of veal have been browned. The pair create an assertive flavour base for the sauce. Melted veal stock is then added. Rich in gelatine, the stock keeps the meat tender during its stewing, and gives body to the final sauce. The sauce's body will also be boosted, and its colour improved, if you sprinkle a little flour over the ingredients and let the flour brown before you deglaze the pan.

The stew is by no means finished when the meat is done. Lengthy cooking draws out fat and solids from the meat; these rise to the surface where they are trapped in a thick skin. This skin must be repeatedly skimmed off, just as for a stock (*page 42*). During this cleansing period, the sauce reduces and becomes thicker.

Garnishes for stews can include a variety of vegetables—peas, green beans, carrots, onions, turnips and mushrooms, for example. Garnish vegetables should be cooked in advance. Once they are added to the braised meat, the assembled dish should be gently reheated in its sauce before serving. Noodles, rice or potatoes all make suitable accompaniments, since they will soak up the rich sauce.

1 Sautéing onions. Heat butter in a wide, shallow pan until it foams, then gently sauté finely chopped onions. When they are soft, remove the onions with a slotted spoon (*above*), transfer them to a plate and set them aside.

2 Browning veal. Put the veal—in this case, thick pieces from the knuckle—in the pan. Over a medium heat, cook them on one side for about 15 minutes. Turn them over (*above*) and cook them for a further 15 minutes to brown the undersides.

6 Transferring the meat. Remove the pan from the heat and set it on a trivet. With a slotted spoon, transfer the veal to a plate (*above*). Press juices from the bouquet garni into the pan, then discard it.

7 Puréeing the onions. Pour the braising liquid and onions from the pan into a fine-meshed sieve set over a bowl. To add body to the sauce, press the onions through the sieve with a pestle (*above*). Transfer the liquid to a small pan. Return the meat to the braising pan and keep it covered in a warm place.

3 **Adding flour.** Return the softened onion to the pan. To thicken the sauce and deepen the colour, sprinkle a couple of tablespoons of flour over the ingredients (*above*). With a wooden spatula, lift the pieces of meat slightly and stir in the flour, then turn the meat over.

4 **Deglazing.** Pour in 1 to 2 tablespoons of brandy; then, over a high heat, add red wine (*above*)—here, about 30 cl (½ pint). With the wooden spatula, deglaze the pan by scraping up the residues from underneath the meat.

5 **Braising.** Pour in hot veal stock (*page 42*) until the meat is barely covered (*above*). Prepare a bouquet garni (*page 7*) and tuck it under the meat. Put a lid on the pan and simmer the meat gently, on a low heat, for about 1½ hours.

8 **Cleansing the sauce.** Bring the sauce to a boil, then set the pan half off the heat. With a ladle or metal spoon, pull to one side the thick skin of impurities that forms on the cooler side of the pan (*above*) and discard this skin. Continue to skim every time a thick skin forms until—after 20 to 30 minutes—only a thin skin appears and it contains no fat.

9 **Reassembling the stew.** Add a garnish to the meat in the braising pan—in this case, mushrooms (*page 11*), chopped and parboiled carrots, and tiny onions that were plunged briefly into boiling water to loosen their skins, then cooled, peeled and parboiled for 10 minutes. Pour the sauce into the pan (*above*).

10 **Serving the stew.** Cover the pan and simmer the stew gently for 15 to 20 minutes so that all its elements heat through and the flavours intermingle. The stew is served here directly from the pan, over noodles (*above*). □

Ragù: Pasta's Perfect Partner

When meat is minced and then braised, the resulting stew is so fine in texture that it constitutes a sauce in itself. Here, beef is braised with aromatic vegetables in stock and tomato purée until it is meltingly tender (*recipe, page 131*). Any raw lean meat, poultry or furred game, or leftover roasted or grilled meat can be treated in the same way. The coating consistency of such sauces makes them perfect partners for boiled potatoes, rice and pasta.

The meat should be lean and well-flavoured, but there is no need to choose an expensive cut, since the combination of fine chopping and slow cooking will tenderize it. To minimize any loss of juices, you can chop the meat by hand, using two heavy knives of equal size and weight. Alternatively, pass the meat through a meat grinder or simply cut it into small pieces.

The minced beef in this demonstration is supplemented by finely chopped prosciutto. Other possible flavourings include chopped chicken livers, mushrooms or celery. The cooked sauce may be enriched with a few spoonfuls of cream.

1 Browning meat. Finely chop onions and carrots. Heat butter or oil in a heavy pan over a low heat. Sauté the vegetables, stirring, until they are soft. Increase the heat and add minced lean raw beef (*above*). Brown the beef, stirring so that the heat sears it on all sides.

2 Adding flavourings. When the meat is well browned, reduce the heat and stir in any flavouring ingredients you wish to add, such as diced cooked ham, leftover meat or, as here, prosciutto. Season the mixture—in this case, salt, pepper, lemon rind and a grating of nutmeg are used.

3 Adding liquid. Add a little tomato purée (*page 30*) or puréed canned tomatoes. Pour in hot, melted veal stock (*page 42*), scraping the pan to dissolve any meaty deposits. Cook the mixture over a low heat, with the lid set slightly ajar, so that you can control the simmer.

4 Finishing the sauce. Cook the sauce for about 1½ hours, until the meat is tender and the sauce has reduced to the desired consistency; if necessary, add a little more liquid during cooking. The sauce should have sufficient body for the meat and liquid not to separate. To enrich the sauce, stir in double cream (*above*).

5 Serving the sauce. Boil rice, polenta or pasta—here, spaghetti—and drain it. Transfer the spaghetti to a warm serving dish, spreading it out evenly with a fork. Ladle the sauce over the pasta (*above*) and serve the dish immediately. □

Anthology of Recipes

In choosing the 222 recipes that make up the Anthology, the Editors and consultants have drawn upon the cooking literature of 22 countries. A large number of the recipes are French, and these include sauces from the classic tradition as well as recipes from masters of the *nouvelle cuisine*. Recipes from other countries represent both simple mixtures such as the Thai chili sauce *nam prik* or the Mexican fresh vegetable *salsa cruda*, and elaborate concoctions such as a Polish fish dish with gingerbread sauce, or *shahi raan*, a spiced lamb dish from India.

The Anthology spans three centuries and includes the work of 109 authors. While many famous culinary authorities of the past and present are represented, so too are little-known authors of rare and out-of-print books held in private collections. Some of these recipes have never been published in English. What they have in common is authenticity, and an emphasis on the meticulous preparation of fresh, natural ingredients.

Since many early cookery writers did not specify amounts of ingredients, these have been judiciously added and, where appropriate, introductory notes printed in italics have been supplied by the Editors. Modern terms have been substituted for archaic language, but to preserve the character of the original and to create a true anthology, the authors' texts have been changed as little as possible. Some cooking instructions have been expanded, but in cases where the directions seem somewhat abrupt, the reader should refer to the appropriate demonstration in the front of the book to find the technique in question explained. Unfamiliar cooking terms and ingredients are explained in the combined General Index and Glossary at the end of the book.

The Anthology is organized according to the chapters in the front of the book, with the addition of a category for dessert sauces. The section of integral sauces includes both dishes where the sauce is produced as part of the cooking process, and recipes which give instructions for a main dish and its separate sauce. Recipes for standard preparations—basic and classic sauces, stocks, flavoured butters—appear at the end. The serving suggestions included in some recipes are, of course, optional.

All recipe ingredients are listed in order of use, with the title ingredients first. Metric and imperial measures for each ingredient are listed in separate columns. The two sets of figures are not always exact equivalents, but are consistent for each recipe. Working from either set of figures will produce equally good results, but the two sets should not be mixed for the same recipe.

Simple Sauces

Gascony Garlic Butter

Beurre de Gascogne

To make 225 g (7½ oz)

12	garlic cloves	12
200 g	butter	7 oz
	salt and pepper	
	grated nutmeg	
	cayenne pepper	

Boil the garlic cloves in plenty of water over a high heat until they are soft, about 20 minutes. Drain. Pound the garlic and butter together. Season with salt, pepper, grated nutmeg and cayenne pepper. Reserve and use as required.

ARISTIDE QUILLET
LA CUISINE MODERNE

Blue Cheese Sauce for Steaks

To make about 20 cl (7 fl oz)

125 g	blue cheese, softened	4 oz
1	garlic clove, crushed and macerated in 1 to 2 tbsp brandy for 15 minutes	1
4 tbsp	olive oil	4 tbsp

Pound the garlic and brandy to a paste and blend in the cheese and the oil. Grill a thick steak, slice it, spread it with this mixture and slip it under the grill to melt the cheese.

HELEN BROWN
HELEN BROWN'S WEST COAST COOK BOOK

Sea Urchin Butter

Beurre d'Oursins

The technique of opening sea urchins is shown on page 54.

Use this butter to coat cooked fish fillets or lobster meat. It will melt as it comes into contact with the heat of the fish.

To make 75 g (2½ oz)

3 or 4	sea urchins	3 or 4
50 g	butter, softened	2 oz

Open the sea urchins and remove the coral from each one. Purée the corals by pushing them through a nylon sieve. Then work the purée into the softened butter.

JEAN AND PAUL MINCHELLI
CRUSTACÉS, POISSONS ET COQUILLAGES

Valentinoise Sauce

Sauce Valentinoise

The technique of making this sauce is shown on page 20.

This sauce is served as an accompaniment to all meats, white or red, grilled over glowing charcoal.

To make 15 cl (¼ pint)

6	shallots, finely chopped, placed in a cloth, washed in running water and squeezed dry	6
4 tbsp	chopped parsley	4 tbsp
1	ripe tomato, skinned, seeded and finely chopped	1
60 g	butter, chilled	2 oz
	salt and pepper	
1	lemon, juice strained	1
1 tbsp	jellied meat roasting juices	1 tbsp

Put the shallots and the parsley in a long, fairly deep dish and keep warm by the stove. Add the tomato and butter. Season with salt and pepper, pour the lemon juice over all and add the jellied meat juices.

Make sure that the serving dish in which the sauce is mixed does not get too hot, as the sauce must not liquefy. With a fork, mix all the ingredients together well. Take the grilled meat straight from the hot grill and place it on top of the sauce.

PAUL BOUILLARD
LA GOURMANDISE À BON MARCHÉ

Ravigote Butter

Beurre de Ravigote

To make 250 g (8 oz)

4	sprigs parsley	4
4	sprigs chervil	4
4	sprigs tarragon	4
6	chives	6
1	shallot	1
1	small garlic clove	1
250 g	butter, softened	8 oz
	salt and pepper	

Clean and trim the herbs and blanch them in boiling water for 2 minutes with the shallot and garlic. Drain and squeeze to remove all the water. Pound them together in a mortar, press through a sieve and then mix this paste carefully with the butter. Add salt and pepper to taste. Store the butter in the refrigerator until it is required.

ARISTIDE QUILLET
LA CUISINE MODERNE

Ibizan Parsley Sauce

Salsa de Juvert

This sauce is especially good with poached or grilled fish. If you serve it with poached fish, thin the sauce with a few tablespoons of the liquid in which the fish was cooked.

To make ¼ litre (8 fl oz)

60 g	parsley	2 oz
2	garlic cloves	2
	salt	
	cayenne pepper	
1	lemon, juice strained	1
10 cl	oil	3½ fl oz

Pound the garlic and parsley in a mortar with a pinch of salt and cayenne pepper to taste. Add the lemon juice and oil, and beat the mixture well.

JUAN CASTELLO GUASCH
¡BON PROFIT!

The Perfect Mint Sauce

To make about 8 cl (3 fl oz)

40	fresh mint leaves	40
About 1 tsp	castor sugar	About 1 tsp
About 1 tbsp	boiling water	About 1 tbsp
About 1 tbsp	lemon juice or wine vinegar	About 1 tbsp

Pound down the mint leaves with a pestle and mortar. Cover with castor sugar to take up all the juice. Add just enough boiling water as will dissolve the sugar. Sharpen the sauce with lemon juice or wine vinegar to taste.

BEE NILSON (EDITOR)
THE W. I. DIAMOND JUBILEE COOKBOOK

Fresh Mexican Sauce

Salsa Mexicana Cruda

Although this can be made up to 3 hours ahead, it is best made at almost the last minute. You will find this sauce on Mexican tables at any time of day, for it goes well with breakfast eggs, with roast or grilled meat at lunchtime, or *tacos* in the evening, and there are people who put a spoonful of it into their *frijoles de olla* (stewed beans). It is marvellously crunchy and refreshing served just with tortillas. The Sinaloa version calls for some spring onions and lime juice in place of the onions and water, and the Yucatan version, *x-ni-pec*, substitutes Seville orange juice for the water.

To make about 35 cl (12 fl oz)

One 175 g	tomato	One 6 oz
½	medium onion	½
6	sprigs fresh coriander	6
3	chili peppers, preferably *serranos*	3
About ½ tsp	salt	About ½ tsp
8 cl	cold water	3 fl oz

Chop the tomato, onion, coriander and chili peppers finely. Do not skin the tomato or seed the chili peppers. Mix them together in a bowl and add the salt and water.

DIANA KENNEDY
CUISINES OF MEXICO

Italian Green Sauce

Salsa Verde

To make 35 cl (12 fl oz)

100 g	Italian mixed pickled vegetables, well rinsed	3½ oz
2	salt anchovies, soaked, filleted, rinsed and dried	2
1	hard-boiled egg	1
50 g	cooked tuna fish	2 oz
1	sweet green pepper, seeded	1
90 g	parsley	3 oz
30 g	basil	1 oz
1	lemon, juice strained	1
15 cl	olive oil	¼ pint
1 tsp	mustard (optional)	1 tsp

Put all the solid ingredients through a meat grinder, or chop them finely in a food processor. Add the lemon juice, oil and, if you wish, the mustard, and leave the sauce to rest for several hours before it is served.

GINO BRUNETTI
CUCINA MANTOVANA DI PRINCIPI E DI POPOLO

Vietnamese Chili Sauce

Nuoc Cham

Nuoc mam (Vietnamese fish sauce) can be bought from food shops specializing in Oriental groceries.

This exciting sauce is almost always served at Vietnamese meals, just as Westerners serve salt and pepper. Its base is *nuoc mam* (bottled fish sauce). To appreciate best the results of its superb blending qualities at the table, use it sparingly at first, gradually adding more until the result is just right for your palate. If you find it a trifle strong at first, dilute it with an additional $\frac{1}{2}$ tablespoon of water.

To make 5 tablespoons

$\frac{1}{2}$	fresh red chili pepper or 2 dried chili peppers, split down the centre, seeds and membrane removed, cut into pieces	$\frac{1}{2}$
1	garlic clove	1
2 tsp	granulated sugar	2 tsp
$\frac{1}{8}$	lime	$\frac{1}{8}$
2 tbsp	*nuoc mam*	2 tbsp
$2\frac{1}{2}$ tbsp	water	$2\frac{1}{2}$ tbsp

Put the garlic, chili pepper pieces and sugar into a mortar. Pound them to a paste. Squeeze the lime juice into the paste, then, with a small knife, remove the pulp from the lime section and add it as well. Mash this mixture, then stir in the fish sauce and the water.

BACH NGÔ AND GLORIA ZIMMERMAN
THE CLASSIC CUISINE OF VIETNAM

Provençal Anchovy Sauce

Anchoïade

This sauce can accompany raw vegetables, cold meats and poached fish. You can also spread it on slices of toasted bread and reheat the bread very gently before serving.

To make about 20 cl (7 fl oz)

10	salt anchovies, soaked, filleted, rinsed and drained	10
3	garlic cloves	3
15 cl	olive oil	$\frac{1}{4}$ pint
	pepper	

In a mortar, pound the anchovy fillets with the garlic cloves. When they have been reduced to a paste, pour in the olive oil in a thin trickle, beating all the time, as though you were making mayonnaise. Season with pepper. Serve chilled.

LUCETTE REY-BILLETON
LES BONNES RECETTES DU SOLEIL

Thai Hot Sauce

Nam Prik

Dried shrimps can be bought from Oriental food shops. If nam pla (Thai fish sauce) is unobtainable, Chinese oyster sauce can be substituted.

This basic Thai hot sauce is on the table at every meal. There are as many versions of *nam prik* as there are cooks to prepare it. *Makeua puong*, the tiny pea aubergine, is often chopped and added, as are some other miniature aubergine varieties. If not available, *makeua puong* may be omitted, but the sauce characteristically contains small fragments of chili peppers and other ingredients.

To make about 20 cl (7 fl oz)

30 g	whole dried shrimps, chopped	1 oz
6	garlic cloves, chopped	6
4	dried red chili peppers (including seeds), chopped	4
1 tsp	granulated sugar	1 tsp
3 tbsp	*nam pla*	3 tbsp
3 tbsp	lime juice	3 tbsp
2	red or green *serrano* chili peppers, seeded and finely chopped	2
3	*makeua puong*, chopped (optional)	3

In a mortar or food processor, pound or grind the shrimps, garlic, dried chili peppers and sugar until the mixture is fragmented and well blended. Gradually add the fish sauce and lime juice, spoonful by spoonful, until you have a consistent mixture. Pour into a serving bowl and stir in the chopped fresh chili peppers and pea aubergines (if available).

This sauce keeps well for several weeks, refrigerated, and even tastes better after a day or so of storage.

JENNIFER BRENNAN
THAI COOKING

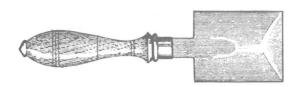

Mexican Avocado Sauce

Guacamole

If serrano chili peppers are unavailable, any hot green chili peppers can be used instead.

Use this as a sauce or a salad. It also makes an excellent dip with fried tortilla triangles. The inclusion of the avocado stone in the dish is supposed to keep the *guacamole* from turning a dark colour. If you are not using the *guacamole* immediately, cover it with aluminium foil or plastic film to exclude the air and refrigerate it (possibly a more reliable formula than the retention of the avocado stone).

To make about 60 cl (1 pint)

2	large, very ripe avocados, peeled and stoned	2
One 175 g	tomato, skinned, seeded and chopped	One 6 oz
½	small onion, finely chopped	½
2 or more	*serrano* chili peppers, chopped	2 or more
3 or 4	sprigs fresh coriander, finely chopped	3 or 4
	salt and pepper	
	sugar	

Mash the avocados. Mix them well with all the other ingredients and season with salt, pepper and a pinch of sugar. Pile the *guacamole* into a serving dish and place an avocado stone in the centre of the mixture.

ELISABETH LAMBERT ORTIZ
THE COMPLETE BOOK OF MEXICAN COOKING

Avocado Sauce for Fish and Shellfish

Avocado makes a good sauce for salmon and salmon trout in particular, though it also goes well with crab and lobster, or tomato and egg salad. If the sauce is to be served with cold fish, mix in two chopped spring onions after the sauce has been seasoned. If the sauce is for hot fish, omit the spring onions and warm the sauce in a basin over a pan of simmering water until the sauce is hot, but nowhere near boiling point.

To make ½ litre (16 fl oz)

2	ripe avocados, peeled and stoned	2
1	small lemon, juice strained	1
1	large garlic clove, crushed	1
30 cl	soured cream	½ pint
	salt and pepper	

Mash the avocados with the lemon juice and garlic. Mix in the cream gradually. Taste and season with salt and pepper.

JANE GRIGSON
JANE GRIGSON'S VEGETABLE BOOK

Whipped Cream Dressing for Salads

Punajuurikermakastike

To make beetroot juice, grate a small beetroot finely. Put it into a muslin bag and squeeze it well. Alternatively, use a food processor fitted with a juice extractor.

This sauce is fluffy and light pink. Serve it in a small bowl or arranged in a mound on a bed of beetroot or red cabbage salad. It also goes well with a herring and beetroot salad.

To make ½ litre (16 fl oz)

¼ litre	double cream, whipped	8 fl oz
2 tbsp	lemon juice	2 tbsp
2 tsp	beetroot juice	2 tsp
	salt	
	sugar	

Combine the cream with the lemon juice, beetroot juice and a pinch each of salt and sugar. Blend the sauce thoroughly.

BEATRICE A. OJAKANGAS
THE FINNISH COOKBOOK

Cold Horseradish Sauce with Soured Cream

Umak od Hrena

Serve this sauce with boiled beef or fish or ham.

To make ¼ litre (8 fl oz)

60 g	horseradish, grated	2 oz
4 tbsp	soured cream	4 tbsp
	salt	
1 tsp	sugar	1 tsp
2 tbsp	vinegar or lemon juice	2 tbsp
1	hard-boiled egg yolk	1

Pour the soured cream over the horseradish. Add salt to taste, the sugar and the vinegar or lemon juice. Press the egg yolk through a sieve into the sauce and mix well.

INGE KRAMARZ
THE BALKAN COOKBOOK

Mustard Cream Sauce

Sauce Moutarde à la Crème

This sauce can accompany many hors-d'oeuvre dishes.

To make 20 cl (7 fl oz)

3 tbsp	French mustard	3 tbsp
15 cl	double cream or *crème fraîche*	¼ pint
	salt and pepper	
1	lemon, juice strained	1

In a bowl, mix the mustard with salt and pepper and the lemon juice. Gradually whisk in the cream, in the same way as you would whisk oil into a mayonnaise.

EUGENIE BRAZIER
LES SECRETS DE LA MÈRE BRAZIER

Tomato and Yogurt Sauce

Tomaten-Joghurt-Sauce

To make 35 cl (12 fl oz)

2	tomatoes, skinned, seeded and finely chopped	2
30 cl	yogurt	½ pint
4 tbsp	chopped parsley	4 tbsp
1 tbsp	white wine vinegar	1 tbsp
	salt and freshly ground pepper	

Stir the yogurt until it is smooth. Mix in the tomatoes and parsley. Season with the vinegar and salt and pepper.

BERND NEUNER-DUTTENHOFER
DIE NEUE DEUTSCHE KÜCHE

Yogurt Raita

To balance spicy Indian grills there is nothing better than a refreshing yogurt sauce. For a spicy raita add one or more of the following, to taste, a pinch at a time: about 1 teaspoon of paprika; a good pinch of cayenne pepper; about 1.5 cm (½ inch) of fresh ginger root, squeezed in a garlic press to extract the juice; a good pinch of *garam masala*; a good pinch of cumin; a good pinch of ground coriander; a few fresh coriander leaves, chopped. Other ingredients which are ordinarily added to yogurt for a raita include: grated carrots with chopped al-

monds; sliced bananas with sultanas; diced boiled new potatoes; roasted aubergine pulp.

You can turn it into a salad by adding raw vegetables such as half a cucumber, peeled and grated or finely chopped, a tomato, finely chopped, an onion, finely chopped or grated, or four chopped spring onions and one green chili pepper, finely chopped or minced (optional).

To make about 55 cl (18 fl oz)

½ litre	yogurt	16 fl oz
½	lemon, juice strained	½
2	garlic cloves, crushed	2
2 tbsp	chopped fresh mint leaves	2 tbsp
1	green chili pepper, finely chopped	1

Beat all the ingredients together in a bowl. Chill the mixture thoroughly before serving.

CLAUDIA RODEN
PICNIC

Pounded Almond Sauce

Romesco

The technique of making this sauce is shown on page 24. Cayenne pepper can be substituted for the paprika.

This is very good with whelks and with all kinds of fish and shellfish, grilled or poached.

To make about 30 cl (½ pint)

60 g	almonds, blanched	2 oz
1	slice white bread, crusts removed, cut into cubes	1
About 17.5 cl	olive oil	About 6 fl oz
4 to 6	garlic cloves	4 to 6
4	small tomatoes, skinned, seeded and coarsely chopped	4
	salt and pepper	
1 tsp	paprika	1 tsp
4 tbsp	sherry	4 tbsp

Fry the cubes of bread in a little of the oil until they are golden. Take them out of the pan and fry the almonds and garlic cloves, adding a little more oil if necessary. When the almonds and garlic cloves are golden, remove them from the pan and fry the tomatoes for a few minutes.

Place all the fried ingredients in a mortar and pound them with salt and pepper, the paprika and sherry. Stir in enough of the remaining oil, a little at a time, to make a thick sauce.

JAUME CIURANA AND LLORENÇ TORRADO
ELS OLIS DE CATALUNYA

Greek Garlic Sauce

Skorthaliá

This is the famous *skorthaliá* as it is made in Greek villages, usually served over fried cod or fried aubergine slices. It is always served chilled, even over hot foods. In addition to being used over fried foods, it is good as a dip with an assortment of crisp raw vegetables. With boiled globe artichokes, serve 3 tablespoons alongside each artichoke as a dip. The mixture may be a bit thick if you use a blender; if it is, turn the machine off every couple of seconds and mix with a rubber spatula, then turn the blender on again.

To make ½ litre (16 fl oz)

4	garlic cloves, crushed	4
4 tbsp	water	4 tbsp
½ tsp	salt	½ tsp
2	potatoes, peeled, boiled and mashed	2
75 g	almonds, blanched and finely ground	2½ oz
4 tbsp	wine vinegar	4 tbsp
¼ litre	olive oil	8 fl oz

Place all the ingredients in a mixer bowl or blender container. Mix or blend at high speed. When the sauce is white and creamy, pour it into a bowl, cover and chill for at least 2 hours.

ANNE THEOHAROUS
COOKING THE GREEK WAY

Catalan Garlic Sauce

Picada

This sauce is used to flavour soups or fish or meat stews. It is usually added to the main dish as it cooks, about half way through the cooking time.

To make ¼ litre (8 fl oz)

6	garlic cloves	6
4	sprigs parsley	4
30 g	almonds, pine-nuts, hazelnuts or walnuts, toasted	1 oz
1	plain sweet biscuit or slice of white bread fried in olive oil	1
10 cl	lukewarm water or stock (*page 158*)	3½ fl oz

Pound the garlic cloves in a mortar until they form a paste. Add the parsley and continue to pound. When the parsley is combined with the garlic, pound in the nuts, then the biscuit or fried bread. Gradually work in the water or stock. When the sauce is smooth, add it to the dish it is to flavour.

FERRAN AGULLÓ
LLIBRE DE LA CUINA CATALANA

Yogurt Almond Sauce

Skorthaliá me Yaourti

This mild variation of *skorthaliá* should be served cold or at room temperature. Greeks almost always serve it with fried vegetables. It also makes an unusual dip served chilled with lots of crisp raw vegetables.

To make ½ litre (16 fl oz)

½ litre	yogurt	16 fl oz
8	almonds, blanched and finely ground	8
1	small garlic clove, crushed	1
¼ tsp	almond extract	¼ tsp
2 tbsp	olive oil	2 tbsp
1½ tbsp	white wine vinegar	1½ tbsp
¼ tsp	salt	¼ tsp
15 g	parsley, finely chopped	½ oz

Combine the garlic, almonds, almond extract, olive oil and vinegar in a bowl. Drain off any excess water from the yogurt. Add the yogurt, salt and parsley to the bowl and whisk the sauce until it is smooth.

ANNE THEOHAROUS
COOKING THE GREEK WAY

Garlic and Almond Sauce

Ajo Blanco

This sauce, from Malaga in southern Spain, is sometimes used as a soup base, garnished with seeded grapes and bread crusts. Use the sauce to accompany fish or vegetables.

To make 60 cl (1 pint)

2	garlic cloves	2
75 g	almonds, blanched	2½ oz
	salt	
150 g	fresh white breadcrumbs	5 oz
10 cl	oil	3½ fl oz
3 tbsp	vinegar	3 tbsp

Put the garlic and almonds in a mortar, add a little salt and pound until a fine paste is formed. Moisten the breadcrumbs with a little water and add them to the paste. Continue to pound, adding a little more water if necessary, until everything is well blended. Add the oil, a little at a time, in a fine stream, and continue to pound and work the mixture until it resembles mayonnaise. Then add the vinegar, a tablespoon at a time, and work it in thoroughly. Adjust the seasoning.

COCINA REGIONAL ESPAÑOLA

Pesto Sauce

The technique of making pesto is demonstrated on page 22. A mixture of pecorino and Parmesan cheese can be used instead of Parmesan alone. If the sauce is to be used to dress pasta, thin it with a little of the pasta's cooking water before tossing the sauce and pasta together.

To make about ¼ litre (8 fl oz)

3	large garlic cloves	3
	salt	
2 tbsp	pine-nuts	2 tbsp
60 g	basil leaves, washed, stems removed	2 oz
2 or 3	sprigs summer savory, stems removed (optional)	2 or 3
100 g	freshly grated Parmesan cheese	3½ oz
About 15 cl	olive oil	About ¼ pint

In a mortar or heavy bowl, pound the garlic to a smooth purée with a little salt. Add the pine-nuts and continue pounding to an even paste. Add the herbs and mash them to a purée. Mix in alternately spoonfuls of cheese and olive oil until a sauce of good body results. *Pesto* is usually required to be the consistency of mayonnaise.

JUDITH OLNEY
SUMMER FOOD

A Delicate Green Sauce

Salsa Verde Delicata

This sauce is served with cauliflower and capon.

To make 45 cl (¾ pint)

100 g	pine-nuts	3½ oz
50 g	pistachio nuts	2 oz
	salt	
10 cl	strong white vinegar	3½ fl oz
15 cl	oil	¼ pint

Soak the nuts in tepid water for 2 hours, until softened. Drain them, then pound them together in a mortar until reduced to a homogeneous mixture. Add a pinch of salt and dilute with the vinegar. Stir in the oil.

G. B. RATTO
LA CUCINIERA GENOVESE

Tarator with Pine-Nuts

This is the favourite accompaniment to fish in the Lebanon.

To make about 90 cl (1½ pints)

350 g	pine-nuts	12 oz
2	slices white bread, crusts removed, soaked in water and squeezed dry	2
2	garlic cloves	2
	salt and white pepper	
1 to 2	lemons, juice strained, made up to ¼ litre (8 fl oz) with water	1 to 2

Pound the pine-nuts, bread, garlic, salt and pepper to taste, and the lemon juice and water to a paste in a mortar, or blend the ingredients to a very smooth cream in a blender.

CLAUDIA RODEN
PICNIC

Genoese Piquant Sauce

Salsa Piccante

Use this to season a small capon, boiled scorzonera, beans cooked in herbs, cauliflower, fish and other dishes.

To make 75 cl (1¼ pints)

250 g	tomatoes, skinned, seeded and chopped	8 oz
2 tbsp	chopped parsley	2 tbsp
60 g	pine-nuts	2 oz
1 tbsp	capers	1 tbsp
1	garlic clove	1
2	salt anchovies, soaked, filleted, rinsed and drained	2
125 g	fresh white breadcrumbs	4 oz
20 cl	vinegar	7 fl oz
20 cl	oil	7 fl oz
	salt	

Put the tomatoes, parsley, pine-nuts, capers, garlic and anchovies in a mortar. Soak the breadcrumbs in 15 cl (¼ pint) of the vinegar and add them to the tomato mixture. Pound everything together, then press it through a sieve. Dilute the sieved mixture with the oil and the rest of the vinegar, and season with a little salt.

G. B. RATTO
LA CUCINIERA GENOVESE

Piquant Garlic and Hazelnut Sauce

Salvitjada

This sauce, usually garnished with grilled and peeled spring onions, accompanies grilled chops or sausages.

To make 35 cl (12 fl oz)

4	garlic cloves	4
12	hazelnuts, toasted and skinned	12
6	fresh mint leaves	6
	salt and pepper	
2	dried *romesco* peppers, soaked in hot water, or 1 tbsp cayenne pepper	2
3	slices white bread, moistened in 8 cl (3 fl oz) vinegar	3
¼ litre	olive oil	8 fl oz

Put the garlic, mint and a little salt in a mortar and pound well. Add the hazelnuts and pound again. When the mixture has formed a smooth paste, add the flesh of the *romesco* peppers or the cayenne pepper and the bread. Continue pounding to form a very fine paste. Finally, add the oil, drop by drop, until the sauce is thick but runny. Add salt and pepper if necessary.

NESTOR LUJAN AND JUAN PERUCHO
EL LIBRO DE LA COCINA ESPANOLA

Walnut Sauce

Salsa di Noci

To peel the walnuts, blanch them briefly in boiling water to loosen the skin, then remove it with your fingers.

Use this sauce to season gnocchi and pasta.

To make 45 cl (¾ pint)

100 g	walnuts, peeled	3½ oz
60 g	pine-nuts, toasted	2 oz
15 cl	oil	¼ pint
4 tbsp	finely chopped parsley	4 tbsp
1	garlic clove, finely chopped	1
15 cl	hot water	¼ pint

Crush the walnuts and the pine-nuts together in a mortar. Heat half the oil and fry the parsley and garlic lightly in it. Put in the pounded nuts and fry them lightly. When they are light brown in colour, dilute the mixture with the remaining oil and the hot water.

G. B. RATTO
LA CUCINIERA GENOVESE

Garlic Sauce

La Sauce d'Ail

Chopped chervil, hyssop or marjoram may be added to the sauce; avoid chives and tarragon.

To make 10 cl (3½ fl oz)

6	garlic cloves, any green centre shoots removed	6
12	walnuts	12
1 tsp	Armagnac	1 tsp
	salt and pepper	
About 10 cl	olive oil	About 3½ fl oz
	chopped herbs (optional)	

In a mortar, pound together the garlic cloves, walnuts and Armagnac to form a smooth paste. Season with salt and pepper, and gradually add the oil, pounding and turning with the pestle. The amount of oil should be equal to the combined weight of the garlic and walnuts. Finally, if you wish, add chopped herbs of your choice.

ANDRÉ DAGUIN
LE NOUVEAU CUISINIER GASCON

Turkish Nut Sauce

Khiyàr Tèrèturu

Present this sauce with cucumber, cauliflower or another such salad, with a dribbling of olive oil poured over it.

To make about 60 cl (1 pint)

250 g	walnuts or blanched almonds	8 oz
1 to 2	slices white bread, crusts removed, soaked in water and squeezed dry	1 to 2
1 to 2	garlic cloves, crushed	1 to 2
About 4 tbsp	wine vinegar or the juice of 1 to 2 lemons	About 4 tbsp
	salt and pepper	
About 10 cl	water	About 3½ fl oz

Grind the nuts in a blender; add the bread, garlic, wine vinegar or lemon juice and salt and pepper to taste. Blend all the ingredients, adding enough water to bring the mixture to the consistency of a light cream.

CLAUDIA RODEN
PICNIC

German Apple Sauce

Apfelsauce

Should the sauce be too thick, dilute it with white wine. This is an excellent sauce for game and poultry.

To make about ¾ litre (1¼ pints)

4	large apples, peeled, cored and cut into pieces	4
30 g	butter	1 oz
2 tbsp	dark rye breadcrumbs	2 tbsp
12.5 cl	white wine	4 fl oz
30 g	sultanas, chopped	1 oz
	ground cinnamon	
½	lemon, rind grated	½
About 1 tbsp	sugar	About 1 tbsp

Sauté the apple pieces in the butter until soft. Remove them from the pan and fry the breadcrumbs in the butter that remains. Mix the apples and breadcrumbs, add the wine, sultanas and a pinch of cinnamon, and bring to the boil with the lemon rind and sugar to taste.

HANS GUSTL KERNMAYR
SO KOCHTE MEINE MUTTER

Apple Sauce

This goes well with goose, roast pork and other pork dishes.

To make about 30 cl (½ pint)

3	cooking apples, peeled, cored and sliced	3
6	almonds, blanched and sautéed	6
1	onion, chopped	1
1	orange, rind grated	1
1	slice white bread, toasted and dipped in white wine vinegar	1
	pepper	
½ tsp	ground mixed spices	½ tsp
3 tbsp	white wine	3 tbsp
3 tbsp	white wine vinegar	3 tbsp

Place the apple slices in a saucepan with the almonds, onion, grated orange rind and bread. Season with pepper and mixed spices, moisten with the wine and vinegar and boil until the apple slices are soft, about 15 minutes. Pass the sauce through a sieve and serve hot.

PAUL DINNAGE
THE BOOK OF FRUIT AND FRUIT COOKERY

Apple Sauce with Madeira

Sauce Dino

The technique for making apple purée is shown on page 36.

This is a sauce for cold game, and was created in honour of the Duke of Dino by his chef, Bichot, in 1877.

To make ½ litre (16 fl oz)

20 cl	thick apple purée	7 fl oz
30 cl	Madeira	½ pint
2	oranges, rind grated, juice strained	2
1	lemon, juice strained	1

Heat the Madeira with the orange rind until the liquid has reduced by half. Add the apple purée and stir over heat to reduce the sauce to the thickness you desire. Let it cool. Finally, stir in the juice of the oranges and the lemon.

JOSEPH FAVRE
DICTIONNAIRE UNIVERSEL DE CUISINE PRATIQUE

Morello Cherry Sauce

Saure Kirschensauce

This sauce is traditionally served with wild boar; it can be served with other kinds of game. If dried and fresh morello cherries are not available, use either 100 g (3½ oz) each of redcurrants and black cherries, or 200 g (7 oz) of redcurrants.

To make 1 litre (1¾ pints)

100 g	dried morello cherries, soaked overnight	3½ oz
100 g	fresh morello cherries, poached in water for 15 minutes, then drained and stoned	3½ oz
½ litre	red wine	16 fl oz
2.5 cm	stick cinnamon	1 inch
1	lemon, rind thinly pared	1
2 tbsp	fresh white breadcrumbs, fried in butter for 5 minutes	2 tbsp
	sugar	

Place the soaked morello cherries in a saucepan with half of their soaking liquid, the wine, cinnamon and lemon rind. Boil until the cherries are soft. Press the cherries through a sieve, combine the purée with the cooking liquid and breadcrumbs, and bring to the boil to thicken the sauce slightly. Season with a little sugar and add the poached fresh morello cherries. If the sauce is too thick, dilute it with a little of the poaching liquid. Serve hot.

WALTER BICKEL AND RENÉ KRAMER
WILD UND GEFLUGEL

Green Gooseberry Sauce

To make spinach juice, pound cleaned spinach leaves in a mortar until they form a paste. Place the paste on a square of muslin and fold the cloth round to enclose the spinach. Hold the cloth over a dish and twist the ends so that the juice is squeezed out of the spinach.

This is the standard sauce to serve with grilled mackerel. It is best when served very hot.

To make about 17.5 cl (6 fl oz)

250 g	green gooseberries	8 oz
4 tbsp	spinach juice or 4 sorrel leaves, finely chopped	4 tbsp
15 g	butter	½ oz
	grated nutmeg	
	sugar	
	salt and pepper	

Boil the gooseberries in water until soft, about 20 minutes. Drain off the water and pass them through a sieve. Put the purée into a non-reactive saucepan and add the spinach juice or sorrel. Add the butter and a pinch of nutmeg. Season with sugar and salt and pepper to taste, then heat through.

PAUL DINNAGE
THE BOOK OF FRUIT AND FRUIT COOKERY

Gooseberry Mint Sauce

Serve this gooseberry and mint sauce with dishes of lamb.

To make about 20 cl (7 fl oz)

175 to 250 g	gooseberries, topped and tailed	6 to 8 oz
1 tbsp	finely chopped mint leaves	1 tbsp
2 tbsp	water	2 tbsp
15 g	butter	½ oz
	salt and pepper	
	sugar	

Put the gooseberries in a pan with the water and butter, salt and pepper to taste and a pinch of sugar. Bring to the boil, cover and simmer gently until the fruit is cooked and tender—about 20 minutes. Either rub the fruit through a sieve or pass it through a blender to form a purée. Just before serving, reheat the purée and stir in the finely chopped mint leaves.

JOAN CATLIN AND JOY LAW (EDITORS)
ROYAL COLLEGE OF ART COOK BOOK

Cold Cranberry Sauce, Bosnian-Style

Umak od Brusnica

Serve this cranberry sauce with cold meat or with poultry.

To make about ½ litre (16 fl oz)

500 g	cranberries	1 lb
12.5 cl	water	4 fl oz
2 tbsp	capers, chopped	2 tbsp
2 tsp	mustard	2 tsp

Cook the cranberries in the water until very tender (20 to 25 minutes). Pass them through a fine sieve or crush them thoroughly in a blender. Cool.

Add the capers to the cranberry purée. Dilute the mustard with a small quantity of the cranberry purée, then combine it with the cranberry mixture.

INGE KRAMARZ
THE BALKAN COOKBOOK

Prune Sauce

Zwetschgensauce

This sauce traditionally accompanies pork or dumplings.

To make ½ litre (16 fl oz)

250 g	prunes, soaked overnight and drained	8 oz
	water	
15 g	butter	½ oz
1 tbsp	flour	1 tbsp
½	lemon, rind grated, juice strained	½
1 tbsp	rum	1 tbsp
	ground cinnamon	
30 g	sugar (optional)	1 oz
	salt	

Boil the prunes in enough water to cover them for 10 minutes or until they are soft. Drain them and reserve the liquid. Stone the prunes and chop them finely.

Melt the butter in a pan and stir in the flour. Let it cook for a minute, without browning. Pour on 30 cl (½ pint) of the liquid in which the prunes were cooked and add the lemon rind, rum and a pinch of cinnamon. Add a little sugar, if necessary, then the chopped, stoned prunes. Bring to the boil and season with the lemon juice and salt.

HANS GUSTL KERNMAYR
SO KOCHTE MEINE MUTTER

Green or Sorrel Sauce

To prevent the sorrel from discolouring, it should be cooked in a non-reactive pan.

Serve this sauce with lamb, veal, sweetbreads, etc. Cayenne pepper, nutmeg and lemon juice are sometimes added.

To make about 15 cl (¼ pint)

250 g	sorrel, washed	8 oz
60 g	butter	2 oz
	salt, pepper and icing sugar	

Put the sorrel into a stew-pan that will just hold it, with the butter. Cover the pan closely and set it over a low heat for 15 minutes. Then pass the sorrel through a fine-meshed sieve with the back of a wooden spoon. Season it with salt, pepper and a small pinch of icing sugar. Return the sorrel purée to the heat, make it hot and serve it.

DR. KITCHINER
THE COOK'S ORACLE

Potato Sauce

Salsa de Patatas

This sauce is typical of the Sierra Morena region of Andalusia, and goes very well with fish dishes.

To make about 45 cl (¾ pint)

250 g	potatoes, peeled and sliced	8 oz
4 tbsp	olive oil	4 tbsp
2	sweet red peppers, seeded and chopped	2
300 g	tomatoes, skinned, seeded and chopped	10 oz
	salt	
4	cumin seeds	4
1	bay leaf	1
15 cl	water	5 fl oz

Heat the oil in a pan, add the potato slices and fry them for 5 minutes. Add the sweet peppers and tomatoes. Cook for about 15 minutes, until the potatoes are soft. Add salt to taste and the cumin seeds, bay leaf and water. Allow the mixture to boil for 5 minutes, then rub it through a fine-meshed sieve. Return the sauce to the heat for a further 2 minutes, skimming off any froth that appears.

ANA MARIA CALERA
COCINA ANDALUZA

Tomato Sauce

Salsa di Pomodoro

Out of season, you can use canned tomatoes for this sauce. It should be served hot.

To make ½ litre (16 fl oz)

1 kg	ripe tomatoes, skinned and chopped	2 to 2½ lb
30 g	butter	1 oz
1	stick celery, diced	1
½	carrot, diced	½
½	onion, sliced	½
1 tbsp	olive oil	1 tbsp
½ tsp	salt	½ tsp

Melt the butter and cook the celery, carrot and onion in it for 5 minutes or until they are softened. Add the tomatoes, oil and salt, and simmer for 30 minutes or until the sauce is thick and all excess liquid has been absorbed. Sieve the sauce.

GINO BRUNETTI
CUCINA MANTOVANA DI PRINCIPI E DI POPOLO

Mexican Tomato Sauce

Salsa de Jitomate

Any hot green chili peppers may be used for this sauce if serrano *chili peppers are not available.*

To make about 30 cl (½ pint)

2	large tomatoes, skinned, seeded and chopped	2
2 tbsp	olive oil	2 tbsp
1	onion, finely chopped	1
1	garlic clove, finely chopped	1
½ tsp	sugar	½ tsp
2 or more	*serrano* chili peppers, chopped	2 or more
	salt and freshly ground pepper	
1 tbsp	chopped fresh coriander	1 tbsp

Heat the oil and fry the onion and garlic until limp. Add all the other ingredients, except the coriander, and cook gently for 15 minutes. Season to taste with salt and pepper. Add the coriander and cook the sauce for a minute or two longer. This sauce can be served either hot or cold.

ELISABETH LAMBERT ORTIZ
THE COMPLETE BOOK OF MEXICAN COOKING

Samfaina Sauce

Salsa Samfaina

Serve this sauce hot to accompany either meat or fish dishes.

To make about 20 cl (7 fl oz)

1	onion, cut into large pieces	1
4 tbsp	oil or 60 g (2 oz) lard (or half quantities of each)	4 tbsp
1	sweet red or green pepper, seeded, cut into strips	1
1	aubergine or courgette, cut into strips	1
2 or 3	ripe tomatoes, skinned and chopped	2 or 3
	salt	

Heat the oil or lard in a large frying pan and fry the onion until transparent. Add the sweet green or red pepper. After 7 to 8 minutes cooking, add the aubergine or courgette. Cool for a further 3 minutes and then add the tomatoes. Season with salt and let the sauce cook for 5 minutes more over a low heat.

MARÍA DOLORES CAMPS CARDONA
COCINA CATALANA

Andalusia Sauce

Salsa Andaluza

To make about 30 cl (½ pint)

250 g	pumpkin, peeled, seeded and diced	8 oz
1	garlic clove	1
2	black peppercorns	2
1	large tomato, skinned and seeded	1
3 tbsp	white wine vinegar	3 tbsp
	salt	

Boil the pumpkin in a little water for 10 to 15 minutes, until tender, then drain it and set it aside. Pound the garlic and peppercorns together in a mortar. Add the tomato and the pumpkin. Pound the ingredients well, then add the vinegar and a little salt. Pour into a dish and serve.

ANA MARIA CALERA
COCINA ANDALUZA

Catalan Vegetable Sauce

Samfaina

Pumpkin may be used instead of aubergine in this recipe.

To make about 60 cl (1 pint)

250 g	Spanish onions, sliced	8 oz
2 tbsp	olive oil or 30 g (1 oz) lard	2 tbsp
2 or 3	sweet green or half-red peppers, peeled, seeded and cut into 2.5 cm (1 inch) squares	2 or 3
1	aubergine, cubed, salted and drained for 30 minutes	1
300 g	tomatoes, skinned, seeded and diced	10 oz

Fry the onion in the oil or lard until it is soft but not browned. Add the sweet peppers. Cook for 8 minutes, then add the aubergine. After 5 more minutes cooking, add the tomatoes. Cook for 15 minutes until all the vegetables are soft and any excess liquid has been absorbed.

FERRAN AGULLÓ
LLIBRE DE LA CUINA CATALANA

Catalan Sauce

Sauce à la Catalane

The author suggests serving this sauce with pork or with dishes of game such as wild boar, hare or venison.

To make ¾ litre (1¼ pints)

1	onion, sliced	1
10	garlic cloves	10
8 cl	oil	3 fl oz
½ litre	tomato purée (*page 164*)	16 fl oz
2	oranges, rind grated, juice strained	2
1	lemon, rind grated, juice strained	1
	cayenne pepper	
2 tbsp	chopped parsley	2 tbsp
2 tbsp	chopped fresh mint leaves	2 tbsp
	mustard	
10 cl	Madeira	3½ fl oz

Let the onion and garlic colour in the oil over a medium heat, then stir in the tomato purée, orange rind and juice, lemon rind and juice, a pinch of cayenne pepper, the parsley and mint, a little mustard and the Madeira. Heat the sauce through before serving.

JOSEPH FAVRE
DICTIONNAIRE UNIVERSEL DE CUISINE PRATIQUE

Lyonnaise Sauce

Sauce Lyonnaise

To make 60 cl (1 pint)

3	onions, chopped	3
30 g	butter	1 oz
20 cl	white wine vinegar	7 fl oz
20 cl	white wine	7 fl oz
½ litre	tomato purée (*page 164*)	16 fl oz

Place the onions and the butter in a thick-bottomed saucepan. Cook gently for about 30 minutes, or until the onions are golden and quite soft. Add the vinegar and wine and allow the sauce to reduce by two-thirds.

Add the tomato purée. Cook very gently for 5 to 6 more minutes, removing the skin as it forms. You can sieve the sauce or leave it unsieved, as you wish.

EUGENIE BRAZIER
LES SECRETS DE LA MÈRE BRAZIER

Onion Sauce

Some cooks mix the pulp of apples or turnips with the onions, others add mustard to them.

To make about 15 cl (¼ pint)

2	large onions, unpeeled	2
60 g	butter, melted	2 oz

Put the onions into a bowl of salted cold water and let them lie for 1 hour. Then wash them, put them into a saucepan with plenty of salted water and boil them until they are tender, 30 to 40 minutes. Now peel them, pass them through a sieve and mix the melted butter with them.

DR. KITCHINER
THE COOK'S ORACLE

Lemon-Wine Steak Sauce

To make about 35 cl (12 fl oz)

4 tbsp	lemon juice	4 tbsp
½ litre	red wine	16 fl oz
30 g	onion, finely chopped	1 oz
1	garlic clove, lightly crushed	1
30 g	butter	1 oz
2 tbsp	olive oil	2 tbsp
	salt and pepper	
1 tbsp	finely chopped parsley	1 tbsp

Cook the chopped onion and the crushed garlic clove in the red wine until the liquid is reduced by one half. Remove the garlic, stir in the butter and olive oil, the lemon juice, salt and pepper and the chopped parsley.

HELEN BROWN
HELEN BROWN'S WEST COAST COOK BOOK

Cumberland Sauce

This sauce may have been named after Ernest, Duke of Cumberland, the brother of King George IV, or one of his descendants. It is traditionally served with roast venison or cold meats such as ham, pressed salt beef, tongue or pork brawn. The technique of making this sauce is shown on page 20.

To make 20 cl (7 fl oz)

2	shallots, finely chopped	2
1	lemon, rind thinly pared and cut into short *julienne*, juice strained	1
1	orange, rind thinly pared and cut into short *julienne*, juice strained	1
About 2 tbsp	redcurrant jelly	About 2 tbsp
15 cl	port	¼ pint
1 tbsp	wine vinegar	1 tbsp
	ground ginger	
	salt	
	cayenne pepper	

Blanch the chopped shallots in boiling water for 2 minutes, then drain. Blanch the strips of lemon and orange rind similarly, for 1 minute, and drain them. Melt the redcurrant jelly in a bain-marie over a medium heat. Add the shallots, lemon and orange rind *julienne*, port, vinegar, a pinch of ground ginger and the orange and lemon juice. Season to taste with a little salt and a pinch of cayenne pepper.

ALFRED SUZANNE
A BOOK OF SALADS

A Travelling Sauce

This recipe dates from the early 18th century. Verjuice is the juice of sour green grapes, though in Britain the juice from sour apples or crab apples was sometimes used. Lemon juice may be substituted for verjuice.

This general sauce is always ready to be used with all kinds of flesh, fowl or fish that require rich sauces. It is a good companion for travellers, who more frequently find good meat than good cooks. Those who are admirers of the taste of garlic may add it to this sauce, or diminish or leave out any particular ingredient that they do not approve of. The sauce may also be made of water only, or of verjuice, or of wine, or of orange or lemon juice; but if it is made of water, it will keep only a month; if it be made of verjuice, it will last three months; if we make it of vinegar it will last a year; or of wine it will last as long. You must keep it in a dry place. Use a little of this sauce at a time, stirring it well when you use it.

To make about 3 litres (5¼ pints)

2.3 litres	claret	4 pints
15 cl	wine vinegar	¼ pint
15 cl	verjuice	¼ pint
125 g	salt	4 oz
30 g	black peppercorns	1 oz
½ tsp	finely grated nutmeg	½ tsp
½ tsp	ground cloves	½ tsp
¼ tsp	powdered ginger	¼ tsp
2 or 3	pieces dried orange rind	2 or 3
15 g	mustard seeds, bruised with a pestle	½ oz
6	shallots, pounded lightly	6
5 or 6	bay leaves	5 or 6
1	small sprig basil or marjoram	1
1	sprig thyme	1
10 cm	stick cinnamon	4 inches

Place the claret, vinegar and verjuice together in a clean stone jar that can be tightly closed. Add to this the salt, peppercorns, nutmeg, cloves, ginger, orange rind, mustard seeds, shallots, bay leaves, herbs and cinnamon. Close the jar tightly and let the mixture infuse for 24 hours in the oven at its lowest possible setting.

When this is done, strain your composition through a linen cloth until you have pressed out as much liquor as possible, and put it in a dry stone bottle or jar. Close the jar tightly as soon as the liquid is cold.

RICHARD BRADLEY
THE COUNTRY HOUSEWIFE AND LADY'S DIRECTOR

A Standing Sauce

This sauce should keep for up to four months. Use it in small quantities to add zest to gravies and sauces.

To make 1 litre (1¾ pints)

1 litre	claret or dry white wine	1¾ pints
2	lemons, rind thinly pared, juice strained	2
5	salt anchovies, soaked, filleted, rinsed and dried	5
1 tsp	allspice berries	1 tsp
30 g	fresh ginger root, sliced	1 oz
2	blades mace	2
1 tsp	cloves	1 tsp
15 g	horseradish, sliced	½ oz
1	bouquet garni of parsley, thyme and marjoram	1
6	shallots, sliced	6
2 tbsp	capers, with juices	2 tbsp

Take the claret or white wine and put it in a glazed jar, with the lemon juice. Put the anchovies, allspice, ginger, mace, cloves, a little of the lemon rind, the horseradish, herbs, shallots and capers in a linen bag and put the bag into the wine; stop the jar closely, set it in a large pan of hot water and keep it in a warm place for 1 hour.

A spoonful or two of this liquor is good in any sauce.

SUSANNAH CARTER
THE FRUGAL COLONIAL HOUSEWIFE

Garlic and Anchovy Sauce from Provence

Bagna Caudà

This sauce provides a pleasant accompaniment to cooked vegetables such as cardoons and turnips, or raw vegetables such as celery and fennel.

To make about 20 cl (7 fl oz)

3	garlic cloves	3
6	salt anchovies, soaked, filleted, rinsed and drained	6
	olive oil	
75 g	butter, cut into small cubes	2½ oz

Heat the oil in a saucepan and fry the garlic in it, without letting it brown. Add the anchovy fillets and cook them until they dissolve. Stir the ingredients together to make a paste. Take the saucepan off the heat and stir in the cubes of butter with a wooden spoon. Serve the sauce hot.

LUCETTE REY-BILLETON
LES BONNES RECETTES DU SOLEIL

Garlic and Anchovy Sauce

Bagna Caôda

Sixty g (2 oz) of butter may be used instead of the cream, or a wine glass of Barbera, a local red wine of the Piedmont region, or any full-flavoured Italian wine.

To make ½ litre (16 fl oz)

3	garlic cloves, finely chopped	3
200 g	salt anchovies, soaked, filleted, rinsed, dried and pounded to a paste	7 oz
50 g	butter	2 oz
10 cl	oil	3½ fl oz
17.5 cl	double cream	6 fl oz
2	white truffles, very finely sliced (optional)	2

Place the garlic, anchovies, butter and oil in a saucepan. Cook over a very low heat—it should not boil—for about 10 minutes or until well blended. Towards the end of the cooking time, stir in the cream and add the truffles, if available.

FELICE CÙNSOLO
LA CUCINA DEL PIEMONTE

Rocambole, Garlic and Anchovy Sauce

Sauce Perlée

Rocambole (also known as sand leek and Spanish garlic) is a member of the onion family and has a mild garlic flavour. If it is unavailable, use an extra garlic clove. The author states that this sauce is particularly good for meats without much flavour; for other meats, he recommends diluting the sauce with 15 cl (¼ pint) of concentrated broth (recipe, page 159).

To make 55 cl (18 fl oz)

15 g	rocambole	½ oz
2	garlic cloves	2
3	salt anchovies, soaked, filleted, rinsed, dried and pounded	3
15 cl	white wine vinegar	¼ pint
15 cl	Champagne	¼ pint
8 cl	oil	3 fl oz
1	lemon or orange, juice strained	1
	salt and coarsely ground black pepper	

Place the rocambole, garlic, anchovies, vinegar, Champagne, oil and lemon or orange juice in a pan and bring to the boil. Set aside for the liquid to cool and the flavours to infuse. When it is cold, pass through a sieve. Serve the sauce cold or hot with whatever you wish, adding salt and pepper to taste.

LOUIS AUGUSTE DE BOURBON
LE CUISINIER GASCON

A Sauce for Boiled Fish

Salsa per Condire il Pesce Lessato

To make ½ litre (16 fl oz)

250 g	salt anchovies, soaked, filleted, rinsed and drained	8 oz
20 cl	oil	7 fl oz
2 tbsp	capers or tomato purée (*page 164*) (optional)	2 tbsp

Put the anchovies into a saucepan with the oil and stir them with a spoon, over a low heat, until the anchovies dissolve. Take care that the oil does not boil. Add the capers or the tomato purée if you wish.

G. B. RATTO
LA CUCINIERA GENOVESE

Crab Sauce or Dip

Poo Lon

To make coconut milk, infuse the grated flesh of one coconut in 60 cl (1 pint) of boiling water for 1 hour. Strain the milk through a muslin-lined sieve and squeeze the coconut flesh remaining in the muslin until no more liquid will come out.

Lon are boiled sauces; they are commonly served with fresh vegetables and small dried and fried fish of the herring family, called *pla too*. This combination of vegetables, fish and sauce eaten with rice provides the basic meal of the Thai, eaten throughout Thailand.

To make 60 cl (1 pint)

175 g	cooked crab meat, flaked	6 oz
40 cl	coconut milk	¾ pint
½ tsp	salt	½ tsp
3	shallots, finely chopped	3
1 tsp	granulated sugar	1 tsp
15 g	dried tamarind, soaked in 1 tbsp hot water and sieved	½ oz
2	green *serrano* chili peppers, thinly sliced into rounds	2
1 tbsp	chopped fresh coriander leaves	1 tbsp

In a medium-sized saucepan, mix the crab meat, coconut milk and salt. Bring to the boil, stirring. Reduce the heat and simmer for 5 minutes, stirring occasionally. Add the shallots, sugar, tamarind liquid and chili peppers and continue to cook, stirring, for another 5 minutes until a thick, homogeneous sauce is formed. Transfer the sauce to a serving bowl and sprinkle it with the coriander.

JENNIFER BRENNAN
THAI COOKING

Bread Sauce

To make 45 cl (¾ pint)

100 g	soft white breadcrumbs	3½ oz
1	onion stuck with 4 cloves	1
¼ litre	milk	8 fl oz
	powdered mace	
6	peppercorns	6
15 g	butter	½ oz
2 tbsp	double cream	2 tbsp
	salt and pepper	

Put the onion into a saucepan with the milk, a pinch of powdered mace and the peppercorns. Bring to the boil, then remove from the heat and leave to stand for 30 minutes. Strain the milk into another pan and add the breadcrumbs. Heat until boiling, stirring gently. Stir in the butter and cream, and season to taste with salt and pepper.

MARY NORWAK
THE FARMHOUSE KITCHEN

Bread Sauce for Poultry

The author suggests that, instead of milk, this sauce can be made with a stock prepared from the giblets, neck and legs of the poultry that the sauce is to accompany.

To make ¼ litre (8 fl oz)

30 g	fresh white breadcrumbs	1 oz
About 17.5 cl	milk	About 6 fl oz
1	onion	1
12	peppercorns or allspice berries, tied in muslin, or ½ tsp powdered mace	12
2 tbsp	cream, melted butter or broth (*page 159*)	2 tbsp

Put the bread into a saucepan and pour on as much milk as it will soak up and a little more. Put the pan on a gentle heat and add the onion and the pepper, allspice or mace. Bring the mixture to the boil, then stir it well and let it simmer until it is quite stiff. Remove the pan from the heat and stir in the cream, melted butter or broth. Take out the onion and the peppercorns or allspice berries, and the sauce is ready.

DR. KITCHINER
THE COOK'S ORACLE

Norman White Sauce

Sauce Blanche Normande

To make ¼ litre (8 fl oz)

1 tsp	cornflour or flour	1 tsp
1 to 2 tbsp	water	1 to 2 tbsp
30 g	butter	1 oz
¼ litre	double cream	8 fl oz
1 tsp	white wine vinegar (optional)	1 tsp

Mix together the cornflour or flour and the water; add the butter and cream and place the mixture over a low heat. Stir until the sauce boils up. Serve.

You may acidulate this sauce with a little vinegar, but do not add it until the sauce has been removed from the heat.

ÉMILE DUMONT
LA BONNE CUISINE FRANÇAISE

Meat-Based Béchamel Sauce

Sauce Béchamel

To make about ½ litre (16 fl oz)

125 g	butter	4 oz
250 g	raw veal scraps and trimmings, diced	8 oz
125 g	cooked ham, diced	4 oz
2	carrots, sliced	2
2	onions, finely sliced	2
2	cloves, crushed	2
1	bay leaf, crumbled	1
2	shallots, finely sliced	2
1 tbsp	chopped parsley	1 tbsp
1 tbsp	chopped spring onion	1 tbsp
½ tsp	coarsely ground white pepper	½ tsp
¼ tsp	grated nutmeg	¼ tsp
¼ tsp	salt	¼ tsp
1 tbsp	flour	1 tbsp
60 cl	milk	1 pint

Melt the butter in a heavy-based pan, and add all the meat, vegetables and seasonings. Cook over a medium heat, stirring frequently, until the meat has stiffened. Do not let the meat brown. Stir in the flour, then gradually add the milk. Simmer gently, stirring constantly, until the sauce is very thick and well reduced, about 40 minutes. Strain the sauce through a fine-meshed sieve.

B. ALBERT
LE CUISINIER PARISIEN

Warm Chive Sauce

Warme Schnittlauchsauce

To make about 30 cl (½ pint)

3 tbsp	finely chopped chives	3 tbsp
15 g	butter	½ oz
1	small onion, very finely chopped	1
1 tbsp	flour	1 tbsp
¼ litre	milk	8 fl oz
	salt and pepper	
	grated nutmeg	
2 tbsp	soured cream	2 tbsp

Melt the butter and fry the onion in it for about 1 minute, without letting it brown. Stir in the flour, then pour on the milk and season with salt and pepper and a pinch of nutmeg. Bring to the boil, then let the sauce simmer for 5 minutes. Finally, add the chives and the soured cream.

HANS GUSTL KERNMAYR
SO KOCHTE MEINE MUTTER

Horseradish and Almond Sauce

Mandelkren

The technique of making a white sauce is shown on page 28.

To make 35 cl (12 fl oz)

3 tbsp	finely grated horseradish	3 tbsp
60 g	ground almonds	2 oz
45 g	butter	1½ oz
45 g	flour	1½ oz
30 cl	milk, or half milk and half stock (*page 158*)	½ pint
	salt	
1 tbsp	sugar	1 tbsp
4 tbsp	double cream	4 tbsp
1 tbsp	lemon juice	1 tbsp

Prepare a white sauce with the butter, flour and milk (or milk and stock), seasoned with salt and the sugar. Cook slowly for about 20 minutes or until all taste of raw flour has disappeared. Stir in the ground almonds, the cream and the lemon juice, taking care not to curdle the sauce.

Add the grated horseradish; do not boil the sauce after putting this in. Check the seasoning. Serve hot.

ROSL PHILPOT
VIENNESE COOKERY

Marseilles Sauce

Sauce Marseillaise

To make 15 cl (¼ pint)

1 tbsp	olive oil	1 tbsp
2	garlic cloves, crushed	2
1 tbsp	flour	1 tbsp
¼ litre	white wine	8 fl oz
1	sprig parsley	1
⅛ tsp	powdered saffron	⅛ tsp
	salt and pepper	

Place the olive oil in a saucepan with one of the garlic cloves. Heat, stirring, without allowing the garlic to brown. When it is very hot, sprinkle in the flour. Cook and stir until the mixture is just beginning to brown.

Gradually stir in the wine; then add the parsley, powdered saffron, the remaining garlic clove and salt and pepper. Bring to the boil, then lower the heat and move the pan to one side. Simmer for 20 minutes, removing the skin as it forms on the surface of the sauce.

At the end of the cooking time, skim off all traces of grease from the surface of the sauce, pour it through a fine-meshed sieve into a sauceboat and serve hot.

F. BARTHÉLÉMY
LES MENUS EXPLIQUÉS DE CUISINE PRATIQUE

Buttermilk Sauce

Karnemelksaus

Serve this sauce warm with a salad of lettuce, potato and hard-boiled eggs, or chicory and potato, or brown kidney beans and lettuce. Each diner should mix the salad and sauce together on his own plate.

To make ½ litre (16 fl oz)

½ litre	buttermilk	16 fl oz
75 g	smoked fatty bacon, cut into cubes	2½ oz
45 g	flour	1½ oz
	salt	

Fry the bacon slowly to extract the fat, stirring now and then. Mix the flour with an equal quantity of buttermilk until smooth, and then stir in the remaining buttermilk. Bring to the boil in a small pan, stirring all the time, and cook until the sauce thickens, about 4 minutes. Season with salt. Stir in the bacon cubes and fat.

RIA HOLLEMAN
UIT GROOTMOEDERS KEUKEN

White Sauce for Boiled Fowls

To serve, put some of the sauce in a tureen and the remainder in the dish with the boiled fowl.

To make 75 cl (1¼ pints)

1	large blade mace	1
2	cloves	2
15	peppercorns	15
30 cl	water	½ pint
4	salt anchovies, soaked, filleted, rinsed, dried and finely chopped	4
125 g	butter, kneaded with 1 tbsp flour	4 oz
30 cl	double cream	½ pint

Boil the mace, cloves and peppercorns in the water until the water is flavoured with the spices, about 10 minutes. Strain the liquid into a saucepan and add the chopped anchovies, the kneaded butter and flour, and the cream. Boil the sauce, stirring well, for 2 minutes.

MRS. RUNDELL
MODERN DOMESTIC COOKERY

Mussel Sauce

Sauce aux Moules

The technique of preparing mussels is shown on page 10.

To make 35 cl (12 fl oz)

36	small, well-rounded mussels, scrubbed	36
2	onions, thinly sliced	2
3	sprigs parsley	3
	coarsely ground black pepper	
20 cl	dry white wine	7 fl oz
1	shallot, finely chopped	1
60 g	butter	2 oz
1 tbsp	flour	1 tbsp

Put the mussels in a saucepan with the onions, parsley, pepper and half the white wine. Cover and cook for 3 to 5 minutes over a high heat, shaking the pan from time to time, just until the mussels open. Decant the cooking liquid and set it aside so that any sediment settles at the bottom, then strain it through a very fine-meshed sieve into a saucepan. Keep it warm over a very low heat. Do not allow it to boil. Remove the mussels from their shells and place them in the cooking liquid to keep them warm.

Fry the shallot gently in 30 g (1 oz) of the butter without browning it. Sprinkle on the flour and mix it in to make a white roux. Pour in the remaining wine, stirring continuously, and add 20 cl (7 fl oz) of the cooking liquid and a little pepper. Allow the sauce to reduce until it is thick enough to coat the spoon. Add the mussels to the sauce and heat them without letting the sauce boil. Finally, remove the pan from the heat and whisk in the remaining butter in small pieces.

ARISTIDE QUILLET
LA CUISINE MODERNE

Spanish Mussel Sauce

Salsa Marinera

Use this sauce to accompany fish and egg dishes.

To make ¼ litre (8 fl oz)

12	mussels, scrubbed	12
20 cl	water	7 fl oz
2 tbsp	white wine	2 tbsp
1	onion, finely chopped	1
2	garlic cloves, finely chopped	2
1 tbsp	olive oil	1 tbsp
250 g	tomatoes, skinned, seeded and chopped	8 oz
2 tbsp	flour	2 tbsp
	salt and pepper	
2	sprigs parsley, finely chopped	2
12	almonds, blanched and toasted	12
⅛ tsp	powdered saffron	⅛ tsp

Boil the mussels in the water and wine until they open. Shell the mussels and split them down the middle. Strain and reserve the cooking liquor.

Fry the onion and garlic in the oil until they start to brown. Add the tomatoes and, when they have softened, stir in the flour and the reserved mussel cooking liquor. Season with salt and pepper, add the parsley and simmer gently until the sauce thickens, about 5 minutes.

Pound the almonds and saffron together in a mortar. Add the almond mixture to the sauce and cook for a few minutes. Finally, add the mussels.

MAGDALENA ALPERI
TRATADO COMPLETO DE COMIDAS Y BEBIDAS

Crayfish Sauce

La Sauce Nantua

Sauce nantua accompanies all kinds of fish simply poached in white wine or a court-bouillon.

To make about 90 cl (1½ pints)

About 80	small live crayfish	About 80
1.75 litres	court-bouillon (*page 159*)	3 pints
300 g	butter	10 oz
3 tbsp	flour	3 tbsp
½ litre	double cream	16 fl oz
	salt	
	cayenne pepper	

Bring the court-bouillon to the boil, throw in the crayfish and let them cook for 8 minutes on a high heat. Drain and shell them. Reserve the tails and keep them hot.

Put the shells into a mortar with the butter and pound them together. When they are well amalgamated, put this mixture into a saucepan and cover it with cold water. Bring to the boil and simmer for 15 minutes. Take the pan from the heat, to allow the crayfish butter to rise and spread out over the surface. Gather the butter with a ladle and pour it through a fine sieve into a bowl filled with cold water with a few ice cubes floating in it. The cold will quickly make the crayfish butter solidify and form a disc-shaped block. Lift out this block, turn it over on the kitchen table and use a knife to scrape off any scum which sticks to it.

Put half the crayfish butter into a sauté pan, let it melt, add the crayfish tails and heat them without bubbling. Sprinkle the flour in, mix carefully, pour in the cream and bring to the boil, stirring all the time. Cook until the sauce thickens, about 10 minutes. Season with salt and a pinch of cayenne pepper and incorporate the remaining crayfish butter, stirring constantly. Do not let the sauce boil again. The crayfish sauce is now ready to serve.

PAUL BOUILLARD
LA GOURMANDISE À BON MARCHÉ

A Good Fish Sauce

This is the best sauce to serve with skate, maids (small rays) and thornback rays.

To make 30 cl (½ pint)

2	salt anchovies, soaked, filleted, rinsed and dried	2
¼ litre	water	8 fl oz
1	clove	1
1	blade mace	1
2	strips lemon rind	2
1 tsp	black peppercorns	1 tsp
1 tbsp	dry red wine	1 tbsp
15 g	butter	½ oz
15 g	flour	½ oz

Boil all the ingredients except the butter and flour together until your anchovies have dissolved, about 10 minutes. Then strain the liquid. Roll the butter in the flour, add the mixture to the strained sauce and heat gently for a few minutes until the sauce has thickened.

SUSANNAH CARTER
THE FRUGAL COLONIAL HOUSEWIFE

Bound Butter Sauce

Sauce au Beurre Lié

To make 35 cl (12 fl oz)

175 g	butter	6 oz
25 g	flour, sifted	1 oz
¼ litre	water	8 fl oz
3 to 4 tbsp	lemon juice	3 to 4 tbsp
	salt and pepper	

Place in a saucepan 25 g (1 oz) of the butter and the flour. Mix with a wooden spoon to obtain a smooth paste, then gradually stir in the water and 2 tablespoons of the lemon juice. Season to taste with salt and pepper.

Place the saucepan over a medium heat and stir constantly. When the mixture comes to the boil, remove it from the heat and stir vigorously while adding the remaining butter, bit by bit. The sauce will become creamy. Finish by beating in 1 to 2 more tablespoons of lemon juice, to taste.

F. BARTHÉLÉMY
LES MENUS EXPLIQUÉS DE CUISINE PRATIQUE

My Special Butter Sauce

Mon Beurre Blanc

To make 30 cl (½ pint)

250 g	butter, chilled and cut into 10 slices	8 oz
4	shallots, very finely chopped	4
20 cl	dry white wine	7 fl oz
3 tbsp	distilled vinegar	3 tbsp
½ tsp	salt	½ tsp
6	black peppercorns, crushed	6
1 tbsp	*crème fraîche* or double cream	1 tbsp

Place the chopped shallots in a thick-bottomed saucepan. Add the white wine, vinegar, salt and peppercorns and place the pan over a medium heat. Bring the liquid to the boil, then lower the heat and leave the liquid to reduce by boiling very gently, until only a tablespoonful remains at the bottom of the pan. This will take about 10 minutes.

Add the *crème fraîche* or double cream and stir it in. Let the mixture boil for 1 minute, then take the pan from the heat and allow it to cool until you can place your hand on the pan without burning yourself.

Place the pan back on a very low heat and add two of the pieces of butter. Mix them in with a hand whisk until they have been completely incorporated into the mixture. Whisking continuously, incorporate another piece of butter into the sauce, and, when it has been completely amalgamated, whisk in another. Continue until all the butter has been whisked in and you have a fine, smooth sauce. Adjust the seasoning if necessary and strain the sauce through a very fine-meshed sieve into a sauceboat. Serve immediately.

MICHEL OLIVER
MES RECETTES À LA TÉLÉ

Egg Sauce

This egg sauce is an agreeable accompaniment to roasted poultry or salted fish.

To make 35 cl (12 fl oz)

3	eggs	3
30 cl	*sauce bâtarde* (*page 166*)	½ pint

Put the eggs into boiling water and boil for about 12 minutes, when they will be hard. Put them into cold water until you want them. This will make the yolks firmer and prevent their surface turning black, and you can cut them neatly.

Use only two of the whites; cut the whites into very small dice and all the yolks into bits about 5 mm (¼ inch) square. Put them into a sauceboat, pour on them the melted *sauce bâtarde* and stir them together.

DR. KITCHINER
THE COOK'S ORACLE

Stock-Based Sauces

Horseradish Sauce with Apples

Umak od Hren sa Jabukom

Serve this horseradish sauce with cooked beef or ham.

To make 17.5 cl (6 fl oz)

3 to 4 tbsp	grated horseradish	3 to 4 tbsp
3	apples, peeled, cored and grated	3
12.5 cl	cold broth (*page 159*)	4 fl oz
1	lemon, juice strained	1

Mix the apples and the horseradish, pour in the broth and add the lemon juice so that the mixture remains white.

INGE KRAMARZ
THE BALKAN COOKBOOK

Russian Walnut Sauce

Sousye "Satsyebyeli"

This sauce is for trout. It is served separately from the fish, which should be poached in water to which wine vinegar has been added. A garnish of radishes, spring onions and chopped parsley also accompanies the trout.

To make about 45 cl (¾ pint)

250 g	walnuts, finely chopped	8 oz
15 g	garlic, pounded	½ oz
	salt	
	cayenne pepper	
2 tbsp	chopped mint	2 tbsp
8 tbsp	white wine vinegar	8 tbsp
About 15 cl	cold fish fumet (*page 159*)	About ¼ pint

Mix together the walnuts and garlic and a pinch each of salt and cayenne pepper. Pass the mixture through a meat grinder. Add the mint and wine vinegar and sufficient cold fish fumet to form a sauce.

PAUL DINNAGE
THE BOOK OF FRUIT AND FRUIT COOKERY

Essence of Sage and Onions

Serve with goose, duck and breadcrumbed pork escalopes.

To make 8 cl (3 fl oz)

12	sage leaves, chopped	12
2	large onions, chopped	2
30 g	butter	1 oz
	pepper and salt	
15 cl	veal stock (*page 158*)	$\frac{1}{4}$ pint

Fry the onions and sage in a small saucepan on a low heat with the butter and a little pepper and salt. As soon as the onion begins to get lightly coloured, add the veal stock. Boil the sauce until it is reduced by half, about 15 minutes, then sieve it into a small saucepan for use.

CHARLES ELMÉ FRANCATELLI
THE MODERN COOK

Genevoise Sauce

Sauce Genevoise

Serve this sauce with freshwater fish or with salmon.

To make $\frac{1}{2}$ litre (16 fl oz)

1 bottle	Bordeaux wine or other richly coloured, full-bodied red wine	1 bottle
1	onion, chopped	1
	chopped parsley	
4	shallots, chopped	4
2	garlic cloves, crushed	2
1	bay leaf	1
2	sprigs thyme	2
100 g	mushrooms or mushroom stems and peelings	$3\frac{1}{2}$ oz
$\frac{1}{4}$ litre	coulis (*page 158*)	8 fl oz
$\frac{1}{2}$ litre	fish fumet (*page 159*)	16 fl oz
30 g	anchovy butter (*page 163*), made with 2 soaked and filleted salt anchovies	1 oz
125 g	butter, cut into small pieces	4 oz

Pour the wine into a pan, add the onion, parsley, shallots, garlic, bay leaf, thyme and mushrooms. Place the pan over a medium heat and reduce the mixture slowly to a quarter of its original volume. Pour in the *coulis* and dilute it with fish fumet. Turn up the heat and boil rapidly, stirring and scraping with a wooden spatula, until the sauce is reduced by half. Strain the sauce, then whisk in the anchovy butter and the butter pieces to make the sauce thick and smooth.

VIARD AND FOURET
LE CUISINIER ROYAL

A Sauce for Eels

Salsa per l'Anguilla

The author suggests that the sauce should be poured into a serving dish and the portions of cooked eel that it is to accompany should be arranged on top.

To make 55 cl (18 fl oz)

2	onions, finely chopped	2
4	shallots, finely chopped	4
1	garlic clove, finely chopped	1
45 g	butter	$1\frac{1}{2}$ oz
3 tbsp	finely chopped parsley	3 tbsp
1 tbsp	finely chopped capers	1 tbsp
4	salt anchovies, soaked, filleted, rinsed and dried, then floured and chopped	4
45 cl	fish fumet (*page 159*) or water	$\frac{3}{4}$ pint
$\frac{1}{2}$	lemon, juice strained	$\frac{1}{2}$

Place the onions, shallots and garlic in a small saucepan with the butter and fry gently for 5 minutes. Add the parsley, capers and anchovies and mix everything together. Dilute with the fish fumet or water. Simmer for 10 minutes, stirring continuously with a wooden spoon. Add the lemon juice.

IL CUCINIERE ALL'USO MODERNE

Sauce for Roasted Meat

To make about 35 cl (12 fl oz)

1	salt anchovy, soaked, filleted, rinsed and dried	1
17.5 cl	red wine	6 fl oz
8 cl	strong broth (*page 159*) or brown sauce (*page 160*)	3 fl oz
$\frac{1}{4}$ tsp	grated nutmeg	$\frac{1}{4}$ tsp
1	shallot, shredded	1
1	Seville orange, juice strained	1
	meat roasting juices	

Take the anchovy and put to it the red wine, broth or brown sauce, nutmeg, shallot and orange juice. Stew these together for about 10 minutes, then pour the sauce into the juices that run from your roasted meat.

SUSANNAH CARTER
THE FRUGAL COLONIAL HOUSEWIFE

Languedoc Green Sauce or Bacchic Sauce

La Sauce Verte Languedocienne ou Sauce Bachique

This is an excellent sauce for serving with crustaceans, molluscs, fish and grilled meat.

To make about 45 cl (¾ pint)

½ litre	white wine	16 fl oz
¼ litre	broth (*page 159*)	8 fl oz
1 tbsp	olive oil	1 tbsp
2	garlic cloves, finely chopped	2
1	shallot, finely chopped	1
2 or 3	spring onions, finely chopped	2 or 3
30 g	watercress, finely chopped	1 oz
3	sprigs tarragon, finely chopped	3
2	sprigs parsley, finely chopped	2
1	sprig chervil, finely chopped	1
1	sprig rosemary or wild thyme, finely chopped	1
	salt and pepper	

In a small saucepan, boil together the white wine, the broth and the olive oil. When the liquid has been reduced to a little less than half its original volume, reduce the heat and add the remaining ingredients. Heat the sauce just until it boils, then pour it into a very hot sauceboat.

AUSTIN DE CROZE
LES PLATS RÉGIONAUX DE FRANCE

Tarragon Sauce

Sauce Purée d'Estragon

This sauce goes particularly well with white meats such as veal and chicken and with eggs.

To make 20 cl (7 fl oz)

50 g	freshly picked tarragon leaves, stems removed	2 oz
160 g	spinach, leaves washed, stems removed	5½ oz
20 cl	chicken stock (*page 158*)	7 fl oz
30	white peppercorns, crushed	30
30 g	butter	1 oz
	salt	

Throw the spinach into a saucepan of boiling salted water and cook, uncovered, for about 4 minutes; then plunge immediately into cold water. Drain.

Put the tarragon leaves in a sieve and dip them into boiling salted water for 1 minute. Refresh the leaves under cold water and drain them.

Bring the stock to the boil in a small saucepan. Add the crushed peppercorns and then the tarragon and boil rapidly, uncovered, until the liquid has almost completely evaporated, about 15 minutes. Add the spinach and heat through.

Turn the whole lot into a fine-meshed sieve placed over a small saucepan and work it through with a wooden spatula; scrape the bottom of the sieve with the back of a knife.

Heat the butter in a frying pan until it is the colour of hazelnuts and incorporate it with the purée, whisking it in thoroughly. Keep the tarragon sauce warm until it is required, but do not let it boil.

JEAN AND PIERRE TROISGROS
THE NOUVELLE CUISINE

German Sorrel Sauce

Sauerampfersauce

To make ¼ litre (8 fl oz)

50 g	sorrel, cut into fine strips	2 oz
10 cl	fish fumet (*page 159*)	3½ fl oz
10 cl	dry white wine	3½ fl oz
2	shallots, chopped	2
12.5 cl	double cream	4 fl oz
30 g	butter, cut into tiny pieces	1 oz
	salt and pepper	
	lemon juice	

Reduce the fish fumet with the white wine and shallots until only about 1 tablespoon of syrupy liquid remains in the bottom of the pan. Pour in the cream and bring to the boil. Remove from the heat and drop in the sorrel. Add the butter and mix it in by moving the pan to and fro. Do not stir or the leaves will tear. Season with salt, pepper and lemon juice.

BERND NEUNER-DUTTENHOFER
DIE NEUE DEUTSCHE KÜCHE

French Sorrel Sauce

La Sauce à l'Oseille

Serve this sauce as a garnish for grilled fish or as an accompaniment to a *pot-au-feu*.

To make 30 cl (½ pint)

500 g	sorrel, stems removed, leaves washed	1 lb
40 g	butter	1½ oz
10 cl	beef broth (*page 159*)	3½ fl oz
15 g	sugar	½ oz
	salt and pepper	
2	egg yolks	2

Cook the sorrel in the butter in a non-reactive pan over a low heat until it has melted to a purée. Stir in the beef broth. Strain through a sieve into another saucepan and put back on the heat. Add the sugar and season with salt and pepper. Leave the sauce to reduce until it has the consistency of a light purée, about 20 minutes. Take the pan from the heat. Stir in the egg yolks and mix them in well.

ÉDOUARD DE POMIANE
LE CODE DE LA BONNE CHÈRE

Shallot Sauce

Sauce aux Échalotes

To make ¼ litre (8 fl oz)

6 to 8	shallots, finely chopped	6 to 8
10 cl	red wine vinegar	3½ fl oz
½	garlic clove	½
	salt and coarsely ground pepper	
	grated nutmeg	
1	bay leaf	1
1 tbsp	*glace de viande* (*page 158*) or meat roasting juices	1 tbsp
¼ litre	stock (*page 158*)	8 fl oz
1 tbsp	olive oil	1 tbsp

Place the shallots in a small saucepan with the vinegar, garlic, seasonings and *glace de viande* or roasting juices. Bring to the boil and cook until reduced by two-thirds.

Add the stock and cook for a few minutes more. Just before serving, stir in the oil.

B. ALBERT
LE CUISINIER PARISIEN

Frothy Shallot Sauce

Sauce aux Échalotes

Serve this sauce with grilled fillet of beef or poached fish.

To make 17.5 cl (6 fl oz)

2	shallots, very finely chopped	2
2 tbsp	white wine vinegar	2 tbsp
125 g	butter, 100 g (3½ oz) cut into small pieces	4 oz
1	sprig parsley, chopped	1
	salt and pepper	
2 tbsp	dry white wine	2 tbsp
2 to 3 tbsp	broth (*page 159*) or fish fumet (*page 159*)	2 to 3 tbsp

Put the shallots and vinegar in a small enamelled saucepan and reduce over low heat for 10 minutes until only about 1 teaspoon of liquid remains. Watch carefully to ensure that the liquid does not dry up completely. Add 25 g (½ oz) of butter and the chopped parsley, season with salt and pepper and stir in the wine and broth or fumet. Simmer for 7 to 8 minutes. Before serving, whisk in the remaining butter, a few pieces at a time. The sauce should be thick and frothy.

PIERRE NOLOT
À LA RECHERCHE DES CUISINES OUBLIÉES

Devil Sauce

Sauce à la Diable

To make sweet red pepper butter, prepare a sweet red pepper purée as shown on page 9 and beat 1 tablespoon of the purée into 60 g (2 oz) of creamed butter. Press the flavoured butter through a drum sieve before use.

To make 35 cl (12 fl oz)

6	large shallots, very finely chopped	6
15 cl	white wine vinegar	¼ pint
1	garlic clove, crushed	1
1	bay leaf	1
15 cl	*glace de viande* (*page 158*)	¼ pint
15 cl	stock (*page 158*)	¼ pint
60 g	sweet red pepper butter	2 oz
1 tbsp	olive oil	1 tbsp

Wash the chopped shallots, then press them gently in a towel to dry them; put them in a pan, pour in the vinegar and add the garlic, bay leaf and *glace de viande*. Reduce the mixture until it has a thick, syrupy consistency, then dilute it with the stock. Finally, whisk in the red pepper butter and the oil.

VIARD AND FOURET
LE CUISINIER ROYAL

Génoise Sauce

Sauce Génoise

If you want to make a Génoise sauce to serve with fish or with plainly cooked vegetables, the authors suggest the following variation on the recipe given below. Omit the sugar, substitute an equal amount of sauce bâtarde *(recipe, page 166) for the* coulis *or tomato purée, then thicken the sauce by whisking in 30 g (1 oz) of anchovy butter (recipe, page 163).*

Serve this sauce with dishes of grilled or roast chicken.

	To make ¼ litre (8 fl oz)	
4	gherkins, finely chopped	4
2 tbsp	capers	2 tbsp
30 g	sultanas	1 oz
30 g	currants	1 oz
	cayenne pepper	
	grated nutmeg	
	pepper	
2 tbsp	chopped parsley	2 tbsp
2	shallots, chopped	2
1 tbsp	*glace de viande (page 158)*	1 tbsp
10 cl	vinegar	3½ fl oz
1 tbsp	sugar	1 tbsp
2 tbsp	*coulis (page 158)* or tomato purée *(page 158)*	2 tbsp
About 10 cl	veal stock *(page 158)*	About 3½ fl oz

Put the gherkins, capers, sultanas, currants, a pinch each of cayenne pepper, grated nutmeg and pepper, and the parsley and shallots into a pan; add the *glace de viande.* Pour over the vinegar and add the sugar. Reduce the mixture to a thick, syrupy consistency and moisten it with the *coulis* or tomato purée, then with a little light veal stock.

VIARD AND FOURET
LE CUISINIER ROYAL

Wild Duck Sauce

This sauce is intended to accompany roast wild duck, though the author suggests that it also provides a good accompaniment to any kind of grilled meat.

	To make 12.5 cl (4 fl oz)	
½	lemon, juice strained	½
2 tsp	mustard	2 tsp
1 tsp	salt	1 tsp
	cayenne pepper	
	black pepper	
2 tbsp	port	2 tbsp
5 to 6 tbsp	duck gravy or stock *(page 158)*	5 to 6 tbsp

Mix together the lemon juice, mustard and salt; add a good deal of cayenne pepper and black pepper with the port and duck gravy or good stock; mix the whole till quite smooth, let it be heated and sent to the table hot.

LADY MURIEL BECKWITH
SAUCES, SWEET AND SAVOURY

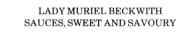

Sharp Sauce

La Sauce Pointue

This sauce goes well with hot meat pâtés and also with cold terrines, as long as it is served separately.

	To make 30 cl (½ pint)	
10 g	butter	⅓ oz
3	shallots, chopped	3
1 tbsp	Dijon mustard	1 tbsp
1 tsp	white wine vinegar	1 tsp
12	capers	12
45 cl	veal stock *(page 158)*	¾ pint
2 tbsp	double cream	2 tbsp

In a thick-bottomed copper pan, melt the butter and add the shallots and mustard. Cook for 3 to 4 minutes, watching carefully, then deglaze the pan with the vinegar and add the capers. Stir in the stock, and simmer for 40 to 45 minutes.

Just before serving, pour the cream into the middle of the simmering pan and allow it to disappear without stirring. The sauce will be smooth, shiny and thick.

ANDRÉ DAGUIN
LE NOUVEAU CUISINIER GASCON

Golden Sauce

Sauce Dorée

The technique of deglazing a roasting dish with wine to make a wine-flavoured gravy is shown on page 72.

To make 30 cl (½ pint)

½ litre	wine-flavoured meat gravy, or stock (*page 158*)	16 fl oz
10 cl	white wine	3½ fl oz
1	lemon, juice strained	1
5 or 6	hard-boiled egg yolks	5 or 6

Boil the gravy or stock together with the white wine until it is reduced by half. Add the lemon juice. Off the heat, press the egg yolks through a fine sieve so that they fall in fine threads into the sauce. Serve without reheating.

B. ALBERT
LE CUISINIER PARISIEN

White Sauce for Fish or Meat

Sauce au Blanc, en Gras et en Maigre

To make ½ litre (16 fl oz)

1 litre	broth (*page 159*) or fish fumet (*page 159*)	1¾ pints
60 g	fresh breadcrumbs	2 oz
60 g	parsley	2 oz
2	spring onions	2
2	garlic cloves	2
1	shallot	1
1	sprig thyme	1
1	bay leaf	1
1	sprig basil	1
2	cloves	2
¼ tsp	grated nutmeg	¼ tsp
4	mushrooms	4
20 cl	white wine	7 fl oz
	salt and pepper	
3	egg yolks	3
10 cl	double cream	3½ fl oz

Place in a saucepan all the ingredients except the egg yolks and cream. Simmer for 45 minutes or until the liquid has reduced by half, then strain the sauce.

When you are ready to use the sauce, beat together the egg yolks and double cream and add them to the sauce. Stir the sauce over a low heat until it has slightly thickened, being careful not to let it curdle. You can serve this sauce with whatever meat or fish dish you like.

MENON
LA CUISINIÈRE BOURGEOISE

Newburg Sauce

Sauce New-Burg

To cut up a raw lobster, hold it, underside down, on a work surface, keeping your hands clear of the claws. With the tip of a heavy knife, pierce the shell firmly in the centre of the cross-shaped mark behind the head to kill the lobster. Exerting a firm pressure on the knife, cut along the body and tail to divide the lobster into two. Pull out and discard the white gravel sac near the head and the thread-like intestinal canal. The tomalley is the grey-green substance beneath the intestinal canal. The coral is blackish coloured. These substances can be removed carefully with a spoon. Twist off the lobster's claws and crack them. Split each half of the lobster crosswise between the tail and body sections and cut the tail into pieces between segments of the shell.

Serve this sauce with fish such as salmon, trout or sole.

To make 35 cl (12 fl oz)

One 800 g	raw lobster, cut into pieces, coral and tomalley reserved	One 1½ lb
70 g	butter	2½ oz
4 tbsp	oil	4 tbsp
	salt	
	cayenne pepper	
10 cl	brandy	3½ fl oz
20 cl	Madeira	7 fl oz
20 cl	double cream	7 fl oz
20 cl	fish fumet (*page 159*)	7 fl oz

Pound the lobster coral and tomalley with 30 g (1 oz) of the butter, then put it aside until needed.

Sauté the lobster tail, claws and body in the remaining butter and the oil. Season with salt and cayenne pepper. When the carcass is quite red, pour off all the fat. Add the brandy to the pan and set it alight. When the flames die down, add the Madeira. Cook until the liquid is reduced by two-thirds. Add the cream and the fish fumet and continue to cook gently for 25 minutes.

Take out all the pieces of lobster, shell them and dice the

meat. Sieve the sauce and add the coral and tomalley butter. Bring the sauce to the boil, correct the seasoning and, if you wish, return the diced meat to the sauce.

EUGENIE BRAZIER
LES SECRETS DE LA MÈRE BRAZIER

Bilbaina Sauce

Salsa a la Bilbaína

To make 35 cl (12 fl oz)

1	large onion, finely chopped	1
1	garlic clove, finely chopped	1
4 tbsp	olive oil	4 tbsp
300 g	ripe tomatoes, skinned and mashed	10 oz
12	almonds, toasted and peeled	12
4	parsley sprigs	4
¼ litre	fish fumet (*page 159*)	8 fl oz
	salt	

Fry the onion and the garlic in the oil. When they begin to brown, add the tomatoes. Meanwhile, pound the almonds in a mortar with the parsley, until well mixed. Add them to the frying pan. Pour in the fumet, season with salt and leave the sauce to reduce for 10 minutes over a low heat. Pass the sauce through a sieve and serve very hot.

ANA MARIA CALERA
365 RECETAS DE COCINA VASCA

Romanian Bread Sauce

Semmelsoß

To make about ½ litre (16 fl oz)

2	bread rolls, crumbled	2
2	garlic cloves, crushed	2
8 cl	oil	3 fl oz
¼ litre	stock (*page 158*)	8 fl oz
	salt and pepper	

Soak the rolls in water, then squeeze them well. Fry the garlic lightly in the oil. Add the rolls. Pour in the stock, season with salt and pepper, and boil for 5 minutes, until thick. Sieve the sauce and reheat before serving.

MARIA HORVATH
BALKAN-KÜCHE

Fried Bread Sauce

This sauce can be served with all kinds of small game birds.

To make ¼ litre (8 fl oz)

4 tbsp	fresh white breadcrumbs, fried in butter until golden-brown	4 tbsp
60 g	lean ham, minced	2 oz
1	shallot, chopped	1
¼ tsp	grated nutmeg	¼ tsp
1 tsp	peppercorns, crushed	1 tsp
30 cl	brown sauce (*page 160*)	½ pint
	chopped parsley	
4 tbsp	reduced chicken stock (*page 158*)	4 tbsp
½	lemon, juice strained	½

Simmer the ham, shallot, nutmeg and peppercorns in the brown sauce until the liquid is reduced by half. Press through a sieve into a small saucepan containing the breadcrumbs, some parsley, the reduced chicken stock and the lemon juice. Bring to the boil, stirring, and serve.

CHARLES ELMÉ FRANCATELLI
THE MODERN COOK

White Bread Sauce

Sos de Piine Albă

Serve this bread sauce with either cold or warm fish.

To make ½ litre (16 fl oz)

4	thick slices white bread, crusts removed, crumb cubed	4
12.5 cl	hot water	4 fl oz
2	garlic cloves, crushed	2
1 tbsp	oil	1 tbsp
¼ litre	broth (*page 159*)	8 fl oz
	salt and pepper	

Soak the bread in the hot water, then squeeze it out. Fry the garlic in the oil for about 3 minutes. Add the soaked bread. Pour in the broth and bring to the boil, stirring all the time to make a smooth mixture. Season to taste and serve.

INGE KRAMARZ
THE BALKAN COOKBOOK

Poor Man's Hot Sauce

Sauce au Pauvre Homme Chaude

To make about 20 cl (7 fl oz)

2 tbsp	olive oil	2 tbsp
6	shallots, chopped	6
	bouquet garni	
	salt and pepper	
1	garlic clove	1
1 tbsp	fresh white breadcrumbs	1 tbsp
30 cl	broth *(page 159)*	½ pint
1 tbsp	chopped parsley	1 tbsp

Heat the oil in a saucepan and brown the shallots in the oil. Add the bouquet garni, salt and pepper, the garlic clove and breadcrumbs. Stir in the broth and leave the sauce to reduce for 20 minutes over a very low heat. Just before serving the sauce, stir in the chopped parsley.

ALOÏDE BONTOU
TRAITÉ DE CUISINE BOURGEOISE BORDELAISE

Chili Pepper and Garlic Sauce

Rouille

This sauce should be served from the mortar, to accompany fish soup. It can also be served with whelks.

To make 35 cl (12 fl oz)

2	chili peppers or ½ tsp cayenne pepper	2
2	garlic cloves	2
125 g	fresh white breadcrumbs	4 oz
15 cl	fish fumet *(page 159)* or liquid from the soup being served with this sauce	¼ pint
¼ tsp	powdered saffron	¼ tsp
15 cl	olive oil	¼ pint

Put the chili peppers and garlic into a wood or marble mortar, and crush them together. Soak the breadcrumbs in the fish fumet or soup, then add them to the garlic and pepper mixture and continue to pound until the mixture has a thick, creamy consistency. Add a pinch of saffron, then pour in the olive oil, a little at a time, in a thin stream, stirring all the time. If the sauce is too thick, dilute with a little more fish fumet or soup.

JEAN AND PAUL MINCHELLI
CRUSTACÉS, POISSONS ET COQUILLAGES

Curry Sauce

This sauce is used for curried vegetables and fish. Three apples, peeled, cored, sliced and added to the onions in the pan are an improvement.

To make 45 cl (¾ pint)

60 g	butter	2 oz
6	onions, sliced	6
1 tbsp	curry powder	1 tbsp
60 cl	stock *(page 158)* or brown sauce *(page 160)*	1 pint
1 tbsp	flour or arrowroot (optional)	1 tbsp

Melt the butter in a pan, add the onions and let them stew without browning for 5 minutes. Add the curry powder and mix them all together. Then moisten them with the stock or brown sauce and cook the mixture, stirring, for 20 minutes. Rub the sauce through a sieve. If it needs further thickening, stir a little of the sauce into the flour or arrowroot to make a thin paste. Return this to the rest of the sauce in a pan and cook it, stirring, for a further 2 minutes, or until it has the desired consistency.

MRS. C. F. LEYEL AND OLGA HARTLEY
THE GENTLE ART OF COOKERY

Lemon White Sauce for Boiled Fowls

To make 90 cl (1½ pints)

1	small lemon, rind thinly pared, juice strained	1
60 cl	double cream	1 pint
1	sprig lemon thyme	1
10	white peppercorns	10
125 g	butter, kneaded with 1 tbsp flour	4 oz
10 cl	chicken stock *(page 158)*, heated until almost boiling	3½ fl oz
	salt	

Place the lemon rind, cream, lemon thyme and peppercorns in a saucepan. Simmer very gently until the sauce has a good taste of lemon, about 10 minutes. Strain it and thicken it by whisking in the kneaded butter and flour. Bring to the boil and pour in the lemon juice, stirring well. Pour the hot stock into the sauce; do not boil them together. Add salt to taste.

MRS. RUNDELL
MODERN DOMESTIC COOKERY

Shallot Sauce for Scrag of Mutton Boiled

For those who love shallots, this is the prettiest sauce that can be served with a scrag of mutton.

To make about 12.5 cl (4 fl oz)

2 or 3	shallots, finely sliced	2 or 3
2 tbsp	lamb stock (*page 158*)	2 tbsp
2 tbsp	white wine vinegar	2 tbsp
	salt	
30 g	butter	1 oz
30 g	flour	1 oz

Pour the lamb stock and vinegar into a saucepan and add the shallots and a little salt. Roll the butter in the flour and add it to the shallot mixture. Stir everything together over a gentle heat and bring to the boil.

SUSANNAH CARTER
THE FRUGAL COLONIAL HOUSEWIFE

A Very Good Sauce for Boiled Chickens

To make 60 cl (1 pint)

1 set	chicken giblets	1 set
125 g	scrag of veal or lamb	4 oz
2	blades mace	2
1 tsp	white peppercorns	1 tsp
1	salt anchovy, soaked, filleted, rinsed and dried	1
1	stick celery, chopped	1
1	bouquet garni	1
1	small piece thinly pared lemon rind	1
1.25 litres	water	2 pints
125 g	butter, kneaded with 1 tbsp flour	4 oz
30 g	mushrooms, finely chopped	1 oz
2	egg yolks	2
17.5 cl	cream	6 fl oz

Place the chicken giblets and the scrag of veal or lamb in a saucepan with the mace, peppercorns, anchovy, celery, bouquet garni and lemon rind and boil them in the water until the liquid has reduced to 30 cl (½ pint). Strain, then thicken the liquid by whisking in the kneaded butter and flour. Boil this for 5 minutes and then add the mushrooms. Beat together the egg yolks and the cream and stir them into the sauce, off the heat. Keep stirring the sauce over a gentle heat until it is almost boiling, then pour it into a sauce tureen.

MRS. RUNDELL
MODERN DOMESTIC COOKERY

Almond Sauce with Horseradish

Sos de Migdale cu Hrean

Serve this almond sauce with boiled and roast meat.

To make ½ litre (16 fl oz)

90 g	almonds, blanched and finely chopped	3 oz
1 tbsp	grated horseradish	1 tbsp
1 tsp	flour	1 tsp
¼ litre	soured cream	8 fl oz
10 cl	stock (*page 158*)	3½ fl oz
1 tsp	sugar	1 tsp

Mix the flour and soured cream together well. Thin with the stock, adding it slowly to avoid lumps. Add the almonds and sugar and let the sauce simmer for 5 minutes. Just before serving the sauce, add the horseradish.

ANISOARA STAN
THE ROMANIAN COOK BOOK

Soured Cream and Tomato Sauce

Sos Pomidorowy ze Smietana

Serve this sauce with boiled beef, chops and meat patties.

To make about ½ litre (16 fl oz)

¼ litre	soured cream	8 fl oz
5 to 6	tomatoes, sliced	5 to 6
15 g	butter	½ oz
12.5 cl	broth (*page 159*)	4 fl oz
	salt and pepper	
1½ tsp	flour	1½ tsp
	sugar	

Melt the butter in a frying pan and sauté the tomatoes until mushy, about 15 minutes. Press them through a sieve, dilute them with the broth and season to taste.

Mix together the soured cream and flour, stirring until smooth. Add this to the tomato mixture. Sweeten very sparingly with sugar to give a sweet-and-sour taste. Simmer the sauce for 5 minutes, or until it is smooth and thick.

MARJA OCHOROWICZ-MONATOWA
POLISH COOKING

Oyster Sauce

Sauce aux Huîtres

To open an oyster, wrap it in a folded cloth and hold it on a firm surface with the flatter shell uppermost and the hinged end towards you. Insert the tip of an oyster knife into the small gap in the hinge. Twist the blade to snap the shells apart. Slide the knife blade along the inside of the upper shell to sever the muscle that holds the shells together. Discard the upper shell and lift the rounded lower shell off the cloth, making sure the liquid in it does not spill. Grip the lower shell firmly with your fingers. Cutting towards yourself, run the knife blade under the oyster to sever the muscle attaching it to the lower shell.

To make 45 cl (¾ pint)

24 to 36	small plump oysters	24 to 36
20 cl	dry white wine	7 fl oz
1	shallot, finely chopped	1
60 g	butter	2 oz
1 tbsp	flour	1 tbsp
	pepper	
	grated nutmeg	
2	egg yolks	2
1	lemon, juice strained	1

Open the oysters and drain their juices into a pan. Mix half of the white wine into the juices and place the pan over the heat. When the liquid comes to the boil, put the oysters in the pan and boil them for 1 to 2 minutes. Drain and trim them.

Fry the shallot in 30 g (1 oz) of the butter without browning. Sprinkle in the flour and mix it with the butter to make a white roux. Stir in the rest of the wine and add ¼ litre (8 fl oz) of the oyster cooking liquid, a little pepper and a dash of grated nutmeg. Leave the sauce to cook gently until it is thick enough to coat the spoon.

Beat together the egg yolks and lemon juice and stir in a few spoonfuls of the sauce. Then pour this mixture into the pan and stir the sauce on a low heat until it is thick. Finally, whisk in the remaining butter off the heat. Add the oysters to the sauce and serve.

ARISTIDE QUILLET
LA CUISINE MODERNE

Basic Sauce for Poached Fish

Kalakastike

Strain the liquid in which the fish was poached and use it as the fumet for this sauce.

To make ½ litre (16 fl oz)

45 g	butter	1½ oz
4 tbsp	flour	4 tbsp
½ litre	fish fumet (*page 159*)	16 fl oz
	salt	
2 tsp	chopped fresh or dried dill	2 tsp
1 tbsp	chopped parsley	1 tbsp
1 tbsp	chopped chives	1 tbsp
2	hard-boiled eggs, chopped (optional)	2

Melt the butter in a saucepan and stir in the flour. Slowly stir in the fish fumet and bring it to the boil. Cook until the sauce is thick, about 4 minutes. Season with salt and add the dill, parsley, chives and eggs (if used). Serve hot.

BEATRICE A. OJAKANGAS
THE FINNISH COOKBOOK

A Sauce for Cod

Sauce à la Morue

To make 60 cl (1 pint)

250 g	mushrooms, sliced	8 oz
1	bouquet garni	1
2	garlic cloves	2
60 g	butter	2 oz
1 tbsp	flour	1 tbsp
½ litre	cream	16 fl oz
1	sprig parsley, blanched and finely chopped	1
15 cl	reduced fish fumet (*page 159*)	¼ pint

Place the mushrooms, bouquet garni and garlic in a pan with the butter and fry gently. When they are cooked, sprinkle in the flour and mix in the cream. Cook, stirring continuously, until the sauce is thick, about 10 minutes. Strain the sauce through a muslin-lined sieve and add the parsley. Stir in the reduced fish fumet and serve.

LOUIS AUGUSTE DE BOURBON
LE CUISINIER GASCON

Almond Sauce for Turkey

To make 20 cl (7 fl oz)

60 g	almonds, blanched and finely chopped	2 oz
15 g	butter	½ oz
1 tbsp	flour	1 tbsp
15 cl	stock (*page 158*) or broth from cooking the turkey giblets	¼ pint
	salt	
	ground mace	
	sugar	
1 tbsp	double cream	1 tbsp

Melt the butter in a small saucepan and put the almonds into this, stirring them until they colour brown. Then sift in the flour and add the stock or broth. Flavour it with a pinch of salt, a pinch of mace and a pinch of sugar. Bring the sauce to the boil, then keep it hot in a bain-marie. Do not strain this sauce. Before serving, stir the cream into it.

MRS. C. F. LEYEL AND OLGA HARTLEY
THE GENTLE ART OF COOKERY

Poulette Sauce

Sauce Poulette

To make about 30 cl (½ pint)

75 g	butter	2½ oz
1 tbsp	flour	1 tbsp
½ litre	broth (*page 159*)	16 fl oz
	salt and pepper	
	grated nutmeg	
	bouquet garni	
	mushroom peelings or mushroom cooking liquid (optional)	
2	egg yolks	2
½	lemon, juice strained	½
1 tsp	chopped parsley	1 tsp

In a saucepan, make a pale roux with 15 g (½ oz) of the butter and the flour. Whisk in the broth and season the mixture with salt and pepper and a pinch of grated nutmeg. Add the

bouquet garni and, if you have any mushroom peelings or mushroom cooking liquid, add it too. Leave the sauce to reduce over a very gentle heat for 30 to 40 minutes, then pass it through a fine-meshed sieve.

Whisk together the egg yolks and the lemon juice, then stir in 1 to 2 tablespoons of the sauce. Pour this mixture into the sauce, return it to a low heat and whisk it as it thickens. Do not allow the sauce to boil. Remove the pan from the heat and whisk in the remaining butter, cut into small pieces. Stir in the parsley and serve.

ALOÏDE BONTOU
TRAITÉ DE CUISINE BOURGEOISE BORDELAISE

White Sauce from Ibiza

Salsa Blanca

This white sauce can be served with either meat or fish.

To make 20 cl (7 fl oz)

30 g	lard	1 oz
1	onion, finely chopped	1
1	carrot, finely chopped	1
1	turnip, finely chopped	1
2 or 3	sprigs chervil	2 or 3
	salt and pepper	
1 tbsp	chopped celery leaves	1 tbsp
1	bay leaf	1
1 tbsp	potato flour	1 tbsp
15 cl	veal stock (*page 158*)	¼ pint
8 cl	milk	3 fl oz
1	egg yolk, lightly beaten	1
1	lemon, juice strained	1

Heat the lard in a saucepan. Add the onion, carrot, turnip, chervil, salt and pepper, celery leaves and the bay leaf, and fry them gently. When they begin to brown, add the potato flour. Stir it in, then immediately pour in the stock and the milk. Continue to stir until the sauce begins to thicken, about 2 minutes. Then pour it through a sieve and return it to the heat to thicken a little more.

Mix together the egg yolk and lemon juice. Stir in a few tablespoons of the sauce, then pour this mixture into the remaining sauce in the saucepan. Stir everything together briefly over the heat, then serve.

GABRIEL SASTRE RAYO AND ANTONIA ORDINAS MARI (EDITORS)
LLIBRE DE CUINA DE CA'N CAMES SEQUES

Anchovy Sauce

Sardellen-Sauce

To make 35 cl (12 fl oz)

3	salt anchovies, soaked and rinsed, each cut into 3 pieces	3
60 g	butter	2 oz
1 tsp	flour	1 tsp
30 cl	stock (*page 158*)	½ pint
2	egg yolks, beaten	2

Put the anchovies in a small saucepan and fry them gently in the butter for 2 minutes. Stir in the flour and then pour on the stock. Let this boil, stirring, until it is slightly thick, about 4 minutes. Just before serving, pour some of the boiling sauce on to the egg yolks. Stirring constantly, add the egg yolk mixture to the saucepan. Quickly remove the sauce from the heat and pour it through a fine sieve into the sauceboat in which it is to be served.

FRAU RATH SCHLOSSER
URGROSSMUTTERS KOCHBUCH

Calf's Brain Sauce

Sos Mozgowy

This is excellent when reheated. Serve with veal cutlets.

To make about 1 litre (1¾ pints)

1	calf's brain	1
	salt	
1	onion	1
1	bay leaf	1
6	peppercorns	6
	thyme	
1	stick celery	1
1	lemon, rind grated, juice strained	1
15 g	butter	½ oz
1 tbsp	flour	1 tbsp
12.5 cl	broth (*page 159*)	4 fl oz
½ litre	soured cream	16 fl oz
2	egg yolks, beaten	2

Place the calf's brain in a saucepan of boiling, salted water, together with the onion, bay leaf, peppercorns, a pinch of thyme, the celery and the juice and rind of half the lemon. Bring the water back to the boil and simmer for 10 minutes.

Drain the brain and, when it is cool enough to handle, remove the membranes and cut the brain up finely.

Melt the butter in a saucepan, blend in the flour and then pour in the broth, stirring until it is smooth. Add the soured cream and the remaining lemon juice and let the sauce bubble up. Off the heat, stir 8 cl (3 fl oz) of the sauce into the egg yolks, then add this mixture slowly to the rest of the sauce. Reheat the mixture gently for a minute or two until it thickens. Finally add the brain and heat through.

MARJA OCHOROWICZ-MONATOWA
POLISH COOKING

Sorrel Sauce

Zuringsaus

To prevent the sorrel from discolouring, it should be cooked in a non-reactive pan.

Serve with fish. There is an even simpler and more old-fashioned way to make this sauce: boil some finely chopped sorrel with a little water and salt and then stir in some butter and crumbled brown bread or rusks until you have obtained a beautifully smooth sauce.

To make ¾ litre (1¼ pints)

250 g	sorrel, finely sliced or chopped	8 oz
2 tbsp	finely sliced leek	2 tbsp
50 g	butter	2 oz
½ litre	stock (*page 158*)	16 fl oz
30 g	flour	1 oz
	pepper	
2 tbsp	double cream or 30 g (1 oz) butter (optional)	2 tbsp

Fry the leek in 15 g (½ oz) of the butter, add the sorrel and let them cook together for 5 minutes. Add the stock and cook for another 15 minutes. Press through a sieve and reserve.

Melt the remaining butter over a low heat, stir in the flour and let it cook without browning for a few minutes. Then whisk in the sorrel purée and let the sauce cook gently for 5 minutes. Season with pepper. Add a dash of cream or a little extra butter, if desired, just before serving.

RIA HOLLEMAN
UIT GROOTMOEDERS KEUKEN

Celery Sauce

Sauce Céleri

To make ½ litre (16 fl oz)

125 g	celery, cut into small sticks	4 oz
1	onion, stuck with a clove	1
1	small bouquet garni	1
½ litre	broth (*page 159*)	16 fl oz
20 g	butter	⅔ oz
15 g	flour	½ oz
4 tbsp	double cream	4 tbsp
	salt and pepper	

Place the celery, onion and bouquet garni in a saucepan and cover them with the broth. Cover the pan and cook until the celery is soft enough to be crushed easily. Pour the contents of the pan through a sieve.

In another pan, melt the butter and stir in the flour. Stir in the broth used for braising the celery and cook, stirring, until the sauce comes to the boil.

While the sauce simmers, discard the bouquet garni and press the celery through the sieve. Stir the puréed celery into the sauce. Add the cream, season to taste with salt and pepper, and continue to cook, stirring, for a few minutes more, until the sauce is lightly creamy.

F. BARTHÉLÉMY
LES MENUS EXPLIQUÉS DE CUISINE PRATIQUE

Picardy Onion Sauce

La Sauce ou Soubise Picarde

This sauce is an excellent accompaniment to a joint of roast pork or pork chops or fried pork sausages. Large Spanish onions are very good for this sauce.

To make about ½ litre (16 fl oz)

400 g	onions, thinly sliced	14 oz
50 g	butter	2 oz
40 g	flour	1½ oz
	water	
About 1 tbsp	vinegar	About 1 tbsp
	salt and pepper	
	pork roasting juices or stock (*page 158*) (optional)	

In a heavy saucepan, make a pale roux with the butter and the flour. Take care that it does not colour at all. Add a very little water, the onions, the vinegar and salt and pepper. Cover the pan and leave the onions to cook, over a very gentle heat, for about 1 hour, stirring occasionally to prevent them colouring. Then add roasting juices from a joint of pork, if you have any; if not, depending on how much moisture the onions themselves have given out during cooking, you can, if you like, moisten the sauce with a little stock.

The sauce is ready when the onions have disintegrated into a purée. Stir well, but do not sieve the sauce. It should have the consistency of thick cream.

AUSTIN DE CROZE
LES PLATS RÉGIONAUX DE FRANCE

Mixed Sauce

Sauce Mêlée

To make ½ litre (16 fl oz)

2 tbsp	chopped parsley	2 tbsp
2 tbsp	chopped spring onions	2 tbsp
60 g	mushrooms, chopped	2 oz
½	garlic clove, chopped	½
30 g	butter	1 oz
1 tsp	flour	1 tsp
1 litre	broth (*page 159*)	1¾ pints
2	gherkins, chopped	2
3	egg yolks	3
	salt and pepper	

Place the parsley, onion, mushrooms and garlic in a saucepan with the butter. Cook for about 5 minutes, without letting them colour; stir in the flour. Gradually add all but about 3 tablespoons of the broth. Simmer the sauce for about 45 minutes or until it is reduced by half.

Add the gherkins to the sauce. Beat the egg yolks lightly with the remaining broth. Off the heat, stir this mixture into the sauce. Stir over a very low heat for another minute or two, or until the egg yolks have slightly thickened the sauce. Season to taste and serve with whatever you wish.

MENON
LA CUISINIÈRE BOURGEOISE

Red Wine Sauce with Raisins

Rode Wijnsaus met Rozijnen

This sauce goes well with slices of ox tongue or minced beef rolled up in tripe. Add the meat to the sauce before it is simmered, and cook the whole dish gently together.

To make 60 cl (1 pint)

20 cl	red wine	7 fl oz
75 g	raisins, washed	2½ oz
40 g	butter	1½ oz
35 g	flour	1¼ oz
40 cl	stock (*page 158*) or leftover gravy	14 fl oz
1	strip lemon rind	1
1	blade mace	1
2	cloves	2
	sugar (optional)	
	vinegar or lemon juice (optional)	

Melt the butter and add the flour; cook, stirring, until it turns dark yellow. Whisk in the stock or gravy gradually and then the wine. Add the raisins, lemon rind, mace and cloves. Leave the sauce to simmer for about 10 minutes or until the raisins have puffed up. Remove the spices and lemon rind from the sauce and season, if necessary, with a little sugar and with vinegar or a few drops of lemon juice.

RIA HOLLEMAN
UIT GROOTMOEDERS KEUKEN

Piquant Sauce

Sauce Piquante

To make about 20 cl (7 fl oz)

6	shallots, chopped	6
15 g	butter	½ oz
1 tbsp	flour	1 tbsp
30 cl	broth (*page 159*)	½ pint
	salt and pepper	
2 tbsp	vinegar, reduced to 1 tbsp	2 tbsp
1 tbsp each	chopped gherkins and capers	1 tbsp each
1 tsp	chopped parsley	1 tsp

Fry the chopped shallots in the butter for 5 minutes, then stir in the flour and let it brown lightly. Whisk in the broth, season with salt, pepper and the vinegar, and leave the sauce to reduce over a gentle heat for 20 minutes. Just before serving, stir in the gherkins, capers and parsley.

ALOÏDE BONTOU
TRAITÉ DE CUISINE BOURGEOISE BORDELAISE

Italian Sweet-and-Sour Sauce

Salsa Agrodolce

Sultanas, pine-nuts and a squeeze of lemon juice can be substituted for the capers.

To make 20 cl (7 fl oz)

50 g	butter	2 oz
1 tbsp	flour	1 tbsp
20 cl	chicken stock (*page 158*)	7 fl oz
2 tbsp	castor sugar	2 tbsp
2 tbsp	white wine vinegar, boiling	2 tbsp
1 tbsp	capers	1 tbsp

Melt the butter in a saucepan and add the flour, stirring until it dissolves. Dilute with the stock.

Heat the sugar in a small saucepan. When it turns brown, add the boiling vinegar and dissolve the sugar in the liquid. Pour the sugar and vinegar mixture into the pan containing the sauce. Simmer the sauce for 30 minutes. Just before serving, add the capers.

GIUSEPPE OBEROSLER
IL TESORETTO DELLA CUCINA ITALIANA

German Oyster Sauce

Austernsauce

To make ¾ litre (1¼ pints)

8	oysters, shelled, juices reserved	8
30 cl	dry white wine	½ pint
½ litre	fish velouté (*page 162*)	16 fl oz
1	egg yolk	1
1 tbsp	double cream	1 tbsp
60 g	butter, cut into pieces	2 oz
	lemon juice	
	cayenne pepper	

Simmer the oysters briefly in the white wine until they are firm, about 5 minutes. Pour the oysters' juices into the pan, then slowly stir in the fish velouté. Bring to the boil, then remove the pan from the heat. Whisk together the egg yolk and cream. Stir in about 8 cl (3 fl oz) of the sauce, then stir this mixture into the pan of sauce and heat it very gently, stirring all the time, until the sauce thickens, about 2 minutes. Off the heat, whisk in the butter, a little at a time, and season the sauce with lemon juice and cayenne pepper to taste.

THEODORE BÖTTIGER
SCHALEN UND KRUSTENTIERE

Seville Orange Sauce

Sauce Bigarrade

When preparing the orange rind, make sure that none of the bitter white pith is pared off with the rind. The julienne should be about half the width of a matchstick.

To make 60 cl (1 pint)

2	Seville oranges, rind thinly pared and cut into very fine *julienne*, juice strained	2
1	lemon, juice strained	1
1 litre	velouté sauce (*page 162*), reduced to 60 cl (1 pint)	1¾ pints

Parboil the strips of orange rind in plenty of boiling water for 3 minutes, then drain them and dry them with a cloth. Stir the orange and lemon juices into the velouté, strain the sauce through a sieve, then stir in the strips of orange rind.

URBAN DUBOIS AND ÉMILE BERNARD
LA CUISINE CLASSIQUE

Aromatic Sauce

Morels are a type of wild mushroom. If fresh morels are unavailable, use dried ones, soaked in hot water for 30 minutes before using.

To make ¼ litre (8 fl oz)

2	sprigs each of winter savory, sweet basil and lemon thyme	2
6	sage leaves	6
2	bay leaves	2
2	shallots, chopped	2
	grated nutmeg	
	pepper	
15 cl	beef broth (*page 159*)	¼ pint
8 cl	white sauce (*page 160*)	3 fl oz
4	egg yolks, beaten	4
24	morels, sliced and stewed in butter until soft	24
30 g	butter	1 oz
½	lemon, juice strained	½
1 tbsp	mixed chopped tarragon and chervil, blanched	1 tbsp

Place the herbs, shallots, a little nutmeg and pepper and the beef broth in a saucepan and boil rapidly for 10 minutes. Sieve this mixture into another saucepan, add the white sauce and reduce this by a quarter.

Off the heat, add the egg yolks, and pour this sauce into a double-boiler containing the morels. Simmer over a low heat until thick. Just before serving the sauce, add the butter, lemon juice and the tarragon and chervil.

CHARLES ELMÉ FRANCATELLI
THE MODERN COOK

Sauce for Boiled Fowl or Turkey

To make 1.5 litres (2½ pints)

3	cucumbers, sliced	3
3	lettuces, boiled for 2 to 3 minutes in salted water then drained, leaves shredded	3
1 litre	brown sauce (*page 160*)	1¾ pints
1	small onion, finely sliced	1
3 tbsp	double cream	3 tbsp
30 g	butter	1 oz
½	lemon, juice strained	½
	salt	

Put the cucumber and lettuce in a saucepan with the brown sauce and stew them together with the onion, until they become quite tender, about 10 minutes. Just before serving, stir in the cream, butter and lemon juice; add salt to taste.

IGNOTUS
CULINA FAMULATRIX MEDICINAE

Charcutière Sauce

Sauce Charcutière

To make ¼ litre (8 fl oz)

10 cl	wine vinegar	3½ fl oz
1 tbsp	finely chopped shallots	1 tbsp
¼ litre	brown sauce (*page 160*)	8 fl oz
60 g	very small gherkins, finely sliced	2 oz
1 tbsp	mustard	1 tbsp

Place the vinegar and the chopped shallots in a small pan over a gentle heat and simmer them together until the liquid has reduced by half. Add the brown sauce and continue to cook gently for 10 minutes. Stir in the sliced gherkins, then the mustard. The sauce should not be allowed to boil after the mustard has been added.

ÉDOUARD NIGNON
ÉLOGES DE LA CUISINE FRANÇAISE

Chopped Sauce

Sauce Hachée

To make 10 cl (3½ fl oz)

1 tsp	chopped shallots, blanched	1 tsp
1 tsp	finely chopped mushrooms	1 tsp
1 tsp	finely chopped parsley	1 tsp
4 tbsp	*sauce espagnole (page 160)*	4 tbsp
4 tbsp	broth (*page 159*)	4 tbsp
3 tbsp	red wine or sherry vinegar	3 tbsp
	pepper	
1 tbsp	chopped capers	1 tbsp
1 tbsp	chopped gherkins	1 tbsp
30 g	anchovy butter (*page 163*)	1 oz

Place the shallots, mushrooms and parsley in a saucepan and pour on the *sauce espagnole*, broth and red wine or vinegar. Add a pinch of pepper. Bring to the boil, skim, and simmer for several minutes. Sieve the sauce and, just before serving, add the capers, gherkins and anchovy butter. The sauce should not boil after these additions.

ALEXANDRE DUMAS
LE GRAND DICTIONNAIRE DE CUISINE

Moscow Sauce for Venison

Sauce Moscovite pour Venaison

Malaga wine is a sweet fortified wine from Spain. If it is unavailable, substitute port or Madeira.

To make ¾ litre (1¼ pints)

10 cl	reduced game stock (*page 158*)	3½ fl oz
10 cl	Malaga wine	3½ fl oz
½ litre	*poivrade ordinaire (page 161)*	16 fl oz
1 tbsp	juniper berries, crushed and infused in 8 cl (3 fl oz) of boiling water for five minutes	1 tbsp
40 g	almonds, blanched, toasted and slivered	1½ oz
40 g	raisins, soaked in warm water for 30 minutes and drained	1½ oz

Add the stock and the wine to the *poivrade ordinaire*. Strain the juniper berry infusion through a cloth and add the liquid to the sauce with the almonds and raisins. Heat the sauce without allowing it to boil.

EUGENIE BRAZIER
LES SECRETS DE LA MÈRE BRAZIER

Egg Sauces

A Salad Sauce

This mixture must not be poured upon the lettuce or vegetables used in the salad, but be left at the bottom, to be stirred up when wanted. This method preserves the crispness of the lettuce. Observe that the liquid ingredients must be proportioned to the quantity of vegetables used.

To make 15 cl (¼ pint)

2	hard-boiled egg yolks	2
1 tbsp	grated Parmesan cheese	1 tbsp
½ tsp	mustard	½ tsp
1 tbsp	tarragon vinegar	1 tbsp
1½ tbsp	mushroom ketchup	1½ tbsp
4 tbsp	oil	4 tbsp
1 tbsp	cider vinegar	1 tbsp

Take the egg yolks, Parmesan cheese, mustard, tarragon vinegar and mushroom ketchup and mix together. When they are well incorporated, add the salad oil and cider vinegar. Beat to incorporate the oil with the other ingredients.

IGNOTUS
CULINA FAMULATRIX MEDICINAE

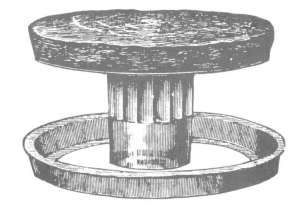

Mustard Sauce

Sauce Moutarde

Serve this sauce with grilled mackerel or herrings.

To make ¼ litre (8 fl oz)

2 tbsp	French mustard	2 tbsp
1 sprig each	parsley, tarragon, chives, chervil and salad burnet	1 sprig each
2	hard-boiled egg yolks	2
4 to 5 tbsp	olive oil	4 to 5 tbsp
2 tbsp	white wine vinegar	2 tbsp

Blanch the herbs in boiling water. Drain, freshen in cold water, then place them in a mortar and pound them with the egg yolks. Place this mixture in a sauceboat, then slowly add the olive oil, mustard and vinegar, stirring the mixture all the time with a wooden spatula.

LA CUISINE LYONNAISE

King Edward the Seventh's Sauce

This sauce was originally invented for His Royal Highness in the year 1861, long before he ascended the throne. It is to be eaten with boiled fish or meats. It also makes a good dressing for fish, game and poultry salads.

To make about ½ litre (16 fl oz)

4	hard-boiled egg yolks	4
4	salt anchovies, soaked, filleted, rinsed and dried	4
30 g	mixed tarragon, chervil, salad burnet and chives, parboiled, then pressed in a cloth	1 oz
1 tbsp	capers	1 tbsp
1 tbsp	French mustard	1 tbsp
3	egg yolks	3
30 cl	olive oil	½ pint
5 tbsp	tarragon vinegar	5 tbsp

Place the hard-boiled egg yolks, anchovies, herbs, capers, mustard and raw egg yolks in a mortar and bruise them together with a pestle. Then proceed to work in the olive oil and the vinegar, by degrees. When this is done, rub the sauce through a very fine sieve.

ELIZABETH CRAIG
COURT FAVOURITES

Chive Sauce from Vienna

Schnittlauchsosse

To make 30 cl (½ pint)

1 tbsp	chopped chives	1 tbsp
2	slices white bread, weighing about 90 to 125 g (3 to 4 oz), crusts removed	2
	milk	
2	hard-boiled egg yolks	2
½	lemon, juice strained	½
1 tsp	sugar	1 tsp
	salt and pepper	
	mustard	
3 tbsp	olive oil	3 tbsp

Soak the bread in a little milk. Squeeze it dry. Sieve the bread together with the egg yolks. Add the lemon juice, sugar, salt, pepper and a little mustard to taste. Stir in the olive oil, first drop by drop, then pouring more steadily. Taste for seasoning, and at the last moment add the chopped chives.

ROSL PHILPOT
VIENNESE COOKERY

Piedmont Green Sauce

Bagnet Verd

To make ¼ litre (8 fl oz)

30 g	parsley	1 oz
1	garlic clove	1
2	hard-boiled egg yolks	2
½	onion, chopped	½
30 g	fresh white breadcrumbs, soaked in 4 tbsp white wine vinegar	1 oz
8 cl	olive oil	3 fl oz
1 tbsp	vinegar	1 tbsp
	salt and pepper	
	sugar	

Crush the parsley, garlic, egg yolks, onion and breadcrumbs in a mortar. Pass the mixture through a sieve and work in the oil and vinegar and a little salt, pepper and sugar, stirring until the sauce becomes smooth.

FELICE CÙNSOLO
LA CUCINA DEL PIEMONTE

Green Sauce for Ox-Meat

Grüne Sauce zum Ochsenfleisch

The herbs for this recipe should include parsley, borage, salad burnet and tarragon.

To make 15 cl (¼ pint)

3	hard-boiled egg yolks	3
	salt and pepper	
1½ tbsp	oil	1½ tbsp
1 tbsp	vinegar	1 tbsp
½ tbsp	German mustard	½ tbsp
3 tbsp	finely chopped mixed herbs	3 tbsp
3 to 4 tbsp	soured cream	3 to 4 tbsp

Mash the egg yolks finely, season with salt and pepper and mix in the oil, vinegar and mustard. Stir the herbs in well. Then add the soured cream, judging the amount according to how thick the cream is. Press the sauce through a sieve before serving; discard the herbs that remain in the sieve.

FRAU RATH SCHLOSSER
URGROSSMUTTERS KOCHBUCH

A Cold Green Sauce for Fish, Game and Poultry

Eine Kalte Grüne Sauce zu Fisch, Wildpret, auch zu Geflügel zu Geben

The herbs for this recipe should include borage, sorrel, salad burnet and tarragon.

To make 35 cl (12 fl oz)

250 g	butter	8 oz
4	egg yolks	4
2	hard-boiled eggs, chopped	2
1 tbsp	olive oil	1 tbsp
1 tbsp	vinegar	1 tbsp
½	lemon, rind grated	½
1 tbsp	mustard	1 tbsp
60 g	mixed herbs, parboiled for a few seconds, squeezed dry in a towel and finely chopped	2 oz
	salt and pepper	

Cream the butter until it is very smooth. Whisk in the egg yolks and hard-boiled eggs. Add the oil, vinegar, lemon rind and mustard. Stir in the herbs and then press the sauce through a sieve. Season with salt and pepper.

FRAU RATH SCHLOSSER
URGROSSMUTTERS KOCHBUCH

Frankfurt Green Sauce

Grüne Sauce

To make about 45 cl (¾ pint)

60 g	mixed parsley, chervil and tarragon, finely chopped	2 oz
1 tsp	finely chopped fresh marjoram	1 tsp
3	hard-boiled egg yolks	3
1 tsp	mustard	1 tsp
	salt and pepper	
1 tbsp	wine vinegar	1 tbsp
¼ litre	olive oil	8 fl oz

Blend the parsley, chervil, tarragon and the marjoram with the egg yolks and press through a fine sieve. Season this purée with mustard, salt and pepper. Add the vinegar and mix well. Add the oil in a thin stream, stirring constantly.

THEODORE BÖTTIGER
SCHALEN UND KRUSTENTIERE

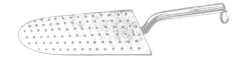

Gherkin Sauce

Gurkensosse

This is a sauce to serve with dishes of boiled beef.

To make 45 cl (¾ pint)

175 g	gherkins, finely chopped	6 oz
2 tbsp	chopped parsley	2 tbsp
1 tbsp	chopped fresh dill	1 tbsp
1	very small onion, finely chopped	1
1	anchovy fillet, chopped	1
1	tomato, skinned, seeded and finely chopped	1
2	hard-boiled eggs, sieved through a fine food mill	2
½ tsp	mustard	½ tsp
	salt and freshly ground pepper	
	sugar	
About 3 tbsp	olive oil	About 3 tbsp
About 3 tbsp	vinegar	About 3 tbsp

Stir the chopped gherkins, parsley, dill, onion, anchovy and tomato into the sieved eggs. To this mixture add the mustard, a good pinch of salt, a little pepper and a pinch of sugar. Stir in the olive oil, not quite as gingerly as for making mayonnaise, but with care. Thin down the sauce with a little vinegar. Taste and adjust the seasoning, if necessary. Keep in a cool place.

ROSL PHILPOT
VIENNESE COOKERY

Cambridge Sauce

This sauce should be kept about the same degree of thickness as a reduced velouté sauce. Salt must be used in moderation, owing to the presence of anchovies in the composition.

To make about ¼ litre (8 fl oz)

6	hard-boiled egg yolks	6
4	salt anchovies, soaked, filleted, rinsed and drained	4
1 tbsp	capers	1 tbsp
6	tarragon leaves	6
6	sprigs chervil	6
1 tsp	chopped chives	1 tsp
12	salad burnet leaves, blanched in boiling water for 1 minute, refreshed in cold water, then drained	12
1 tsp	English mustard	1 tsp
1 tsp	French mustard	1 tsp
	salt and pepper	
About 10 cl	oil	About 3½ fl oz
About 3 tbsp	tarragon vinegar	About 3 tbsp
1 tsp	chopped parsley	1 tsp

Take the egg yolks and anchovy fillets and put them into a mortar with the capers, tarragon, chervil, chives and blanched salad burnet. Pound these well together with the English and French mustards and some pepper and salt. Moisten with good salad oil and a little tarragon vinegar, taking care that the sauce be kept rather thick.

Having sufficiently moistened the sauce, take it out of the mortar into a drum sieve placed over a dish and proceed to rub the sauce through the sieve in the same manner as a purée. Pass the back part of a knife along the under part of the sieve, in order to detach therefrom any adhesive particles. Collect the sauce in a small basin and keep it on ice or in the refrigerator till wanted for use. Just before sending the sauce to table, add some chopped parsley.

CHARLES ELMÉ FRANCATELLI
THE MODERN COOK

Crab Sauce

Sauce Crabe à l'Huile

To extract crab meat from the shell, first break off the claws and legs by twisting them in the opposite direction to the way they face. Holding the crab underside up on a work surface, twist free the bony tail flap on the underside. Insert the tip of a rigid knife between the main shell and the section of shell to which the legs were attached. Loosen the rim of the underside, then twist the knife to prise it upwards. Pull the underside free of the shell and set it aside. Using a teaspoon, scoop out the meat from inside the shell and reserve it; but remove and discard the small, bag-like stomach sac and its appendages, which are just behind the crab's mouth. Pull away the soft, elongated gills along the edges of the underside and discard them. Split the underside down the middle with a heavy knife and use a skewer to remove the flesh from the crevices. Turn the underside over and prise the scraps of meat from the leg sockets. Crack the claw shells with a mallet and peel away the shell to extract the meat from the claws and pincers. Break apart the legs and remove the flesh similarly.

To make 45 cl (¾ pint)

1	female crab, boiled	1
2	salt anchovies, soaked, filleted, rinsed and dried	2
2	hard-boiled egg yolks	2
1 tsp	mustard powder	1 tsp
1	lemon, juice strained	1
	salt and pepper	
15 cl	oil	¼ pint
2 tbsp	chopped parsley	2 tbsp
2 tbsp	chopped chervil	2 tbsp

Remove the crab eggs and body meat and mix them with the claw meat. Pound the crab meat in a mortar, then incorporate the anchovies, egg yolks, mustard powder, lemon juice and salt and pepper. Sieve the paste into a bowl and stir in the oil, bit by bit. Lastly, add the parsley and chervil. Clean the crab shell and serve the sauce in it.

MANUEL PRATIQUE DE CUISINE PROVENÇALE

Herring Sauce

Haringsaus

Serve with cold meat or beetroot salad. Nowadays, chopped hard-boiled egg whites are often included. The sauce will be milder if a spoonful of yogurt or soured cream is added.

To make about 35 cl (12 fl oz)

1	pickled herring, filleted	1
3	hard-boiled egg yolks	3
1	onion	1
About 10 cl	oil	About 3½ fl oz
About 5 tbsp	vinegar	About 5 tbsp
	salt and pepper	

Chop the herring very finely together with egg yolks and the onion. Using your judgment, mix in enough oil and vinegar to make a thick sauce. Season with salt and pepper.

RIA HOLLEMAN
UIT GROOTMOEDERS KEUKEN

Sauce for Cold Fowl or Partridge

The author suggests that shallot vinegar can be used instead of the shallot, in which case 1 tablespoon of the wine vinegar should be omitted. To make shallot vinegar, chop four shallots and place them in a 60 cl (1 pint) bottle of white wine vinegar. Cover and leave in a warm place for three weeks, then strain the flavoured vinegar and bottle it.

To make 12.5 cl (4 fl oz)

2	hard-boiled egg yolks	2
1	salt anchovy, soaked, filleted, rinsed and dried	1
3 tbsp	white wine vinegar	3 tbsp
1	shallot, chopped	1
	cayenne pepper (optional)	
1 tsp	mustard	1 tsp
2 tbsp	oil	2 tbsp
	salt	

Pound the egg yolks in a mortar with the anchovy fillets, vinegar, shallot, cayenne pepper (if used) and mustard. When these are well pounded, add the oil. Strain the sauce and season with salt to taste.

MRS. RUNDELL
MODERN DOMESTIC COOKERY

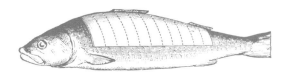

Provençal Garlic Mayonnaise

Aïoli

The technique of making aïoli *using boiled potato instead of egg yolks is shown on page 24.*

A good *aïoli* is made with good olive oil. It is traditionally prepared in a marble mortar with a wooden pestle; the weight of the mortar prevents it from slip-sliding around as one turns the pestle with one hand while dribbling the oil with the other. Avoid any garlic cloves that are not firm and crisp or at the heart of which a green germ has begun to form. The oil and the egg yolks should both be room temperature to discourage the *aïoli*'s breaking.

Some people pound a lump of crustless bread, soaked and squeezed dry, into the garlic and egg-yolk mixture before beginning to add the oil. A more easily digestible but less silken *aïoli* may be prepared by substituting boiled potato—about 90 g (3 oz), cooled until only tepid—for the egg yolks.

To make about 60 cl (1 pint)

3 or 4	garlic cloves	3 or 4
	salt	
2	egg yolks	2
About ½ litre	olive oil	About 16 fl oz
1	lemon, juice strained	1
About 2 tsp	tepid water	About 2 tsp

Place the garlic cloves in a mortar and reduce them to a paste with a pestle. Add a pinch of salt and the egg yolks and turn them with the pestle until their yellow pales. Then start to add the oil, pouring it in a thin thread while turning the mixture with the pestle. Take care to add the oil very slowly and, during this time, never stop turning. You should obtain a thick *pommade*. After having added about 3 to 4 tablespoons of oil, add the lemon juice and a teaspoonful of tepid water. Continue to add oil, little by little, and, when the *pommade* again becomes too thick, add another few drops of water, without which the mixture falls apart, so to speak, the oil separating itself from the rest.

If, despite all precautions, this accident should occur, remove everything from the mortar, put into it another egg yolk and a few drops of lemon juice and, little by little, spoonful by spoonful, add the unsuccessful *aïoli* while turning the pestle constantly.

RICHARD OLNEY
SIMPLE FRENCH FOOD

Garlic Mayonnaise

L'Aïoli

Aïoli, the triumph of Provençal cooking, is served with a variety of foods that have been simply cooked in salted water and it is alone responsible, with its penetrating bouquet, for strongly seasoning everything that it accompanies—cod, carrots, turnips, hard-boiled eggs, artichokes, and all kinds of Mediterranean seafood.

To make 45 cl (¾ pint)

6	garlic cloves	6
3	egg yolks	3
¼ tsp	salt	¼ tsp
35 cl	olive oil	12 fl oz
1	lemon, juice strained	1
1 tbsp	boiling water	1 tbsp

Pound the garlic in a mortar until reduced to a paste. Add the egg yolks, season with salt, then proceed as for mayonnaise: pour a thin thread of oil into the mortar while, with the other hand, mixing the ingredients together with the pestle, working it constantly. From time to time, add a few drops of the lemon juice. The *aïoli* should be thick and well-mixed. Finish by stirring in the boiling water, to prevent separation.

PAUL BOUILLARD
LA GOURMANDISE À BON MARCHÉ

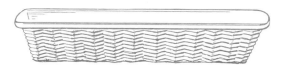

Garlic and Basil Sauce

Sauce Pistou à l'Ail

To make 30 cl (½ pint)

5 or 6	garlic cloves, cooked for 10 minutes in boiling water and drained	5 or 6
15	basil leaves	15
2	egg yolks	2
	salt and white pepper	
	lemon juice	
20 cl	olive oil	7 fl oz

Crush the garlic cloves and the basil in a mortar. Add the egg yolks, salt and pepper and a little lemon juice. Pour in the oil slowly, in a thin stream, pounding it in with the pestle so that the sauce thickens into a mayonnaise.

JEAN AND PAUL MINCHELLI
CRUSTACÉS, POISSONS ET COQUILLAGES

Fish Liver and Garlic Sauce

Rouille

This sauce is served with bouillabaisse and fish soups. For the sauce, use the liver of an angler-fish or red mullet, and use the fish itself as part of the ingredients for the fish soup. Angler-fish liver, which is large, delicate in flavour and smooth in texture, is usually discarded by the fishmonger unless it is requested. Red mullet is usually sold with the liver inside.

To make 30 cl (½ pint)

1	fish liver, poached in court-bouillon (*page 159*) until slightly firm, about 1 minute	1
2	garlic cloves	2
	salt	
1	egg yolk	1
1 tsp	cayenne pepper	1 tsp
15 cl	olive oil	¼ pint
1 tbsp	fish fumet (*page 159*)	1 tbsp
	powdered saffron	

Crush the garlic cloves in a mortar with a pinch of salt. Add the egg yolk, the fish liver and the cayenne pepper and stir together well. Pour in the olive oil, a little at a time, in a thin trickle, stirring all the time with the pestle. Finally, stir in the fish fumet and a pinch of saffron.

LUCETTE REY-BILLETON
LES BONNES RECETTES DU SOLEIL

Cold Provençal Sauce

Sauce Provençale Froide

Serve this cold sauce with grills, cold meats or fish.

To make 30 cl (½ pint)

2	garlic cloves	2
3	salt anchovies, soaked, filleted, rinsed and dried	3
2	egg yolks	2
1 tbsp	water	1 tbsp
	salt	
About ¼ litre	olive oil	About 8 fl oz
1	lemon, juice strained	1

In a mortar, pound the garlic cloves and anchovy fillets together to make a smooth purée. Add the egg yolks, water, and a little salt. Pound the mixture vigorously, adding the oil little by little. To finish, add the lemon juice. The sauce should be fairly light in colour.

MICHEL BARBEROUSSE
CUISINE PROVENÇALE

Cucumber Sauce

Kurkkukastike

Serve this cucumber sauce with dishes of cold meats.

	To make about 1 litre (1¾ pints)	
1	large cucumber, peeled and finely diced	1
¼ litre	mayonnaise (*page 167*)	8 fl oz
¼ litre	double cream, whipped	8 fl oz
1 to 2 tbsp	lemon juice	1 to 2 tbsp
¼ tsp	salt	¼ tsp
2 tsp	chopped fresh dill	2 tsp

Whip the mayonnaise until it is fluffy and fold in the cream. Stir in the lemon juice and salt. Just before serving, fold in the cucumber and the dill.

BEATRICE A. OJAKANGAS
THE FINNISH COOKBOOK

Mallorcan Sauce

Salsa Mallorquina

Anisette or pastis may be substituted for the absinthe.

This sauce is served with fish, crustaceans and shellfish.

	To make ¾ litre (1¼ pints)	
1	ripe tomato, lightly oiled	1
1	small sweet apple, lightly oiled	1
1	garlic clove, unpeeled	1
8	almonds, blanched and toasted	8
½ tsp	paprika	½ tsp
1 tbsp	absinthe	1 tbsp
½ litre	mayonnaise (*page 167*)	16 fl oz
	stock (*page 158*) (optional)	

Roast the tomato, apple and garlic on a baking sheet in a preheated 200°C (400°F or Mark 6) oven. Remove the tomato and garlic after 10 minutes and the apple after 20 minutes. Skin and seed the tomato, peel and core the apple and peel the garlic clove. Pound the garlic in a mortar with the almonds to form a fine paste. Then add the tomato, the apple pulp and the paprika and pound them very finely. Mix this paste and the absinthe into the mayonnaise. Thin the sauce with a few tablespoons of stock if desired.

ENCICLOPEDIA SALVAT DE LA COCINA: TOMO 8

Farmer's Wife Mayonnaise

Mayonnaise Fermière

	To make 45 cl (¾ pint)	
20 cl	mayonnaise (*page 167*)	7 fl oz
250 g	curd cheese	8 oz
2 or 3	sweet red peppers, grilled, peeled, seeded and chopped	2 or 3
2	small spring onions, quartered	2
	salt and freshly ground black pepper	
	cayenne pepper or paprika	
	lemon juice	

Place the cheese in a bowl, stir in the sweet peppers, then work in the mayonnaise, a spoonful at a time, beating with a whisk. Press the juice of the onions into the sauce, using a garlic press. Season to taste with salt, pepper and cayenne pepper or paprika. Mix in a few drops of lemon juice. Transfer the sauce to a sauceboat for serving.

LOUISETTE BERTHOLLE
LA CUISINE DES SAISONS

Tuna Fish Mayonnaise

Salsa Tonnata

This sauce is used in the classic Italian dish vitello tonnato, *where it accompanies cold poached veal.*

	To make about 1.25 litres (2 pints)	
200 g	tuna fish, flaked	7 oz
½ litre	mayonnaise (*page 167*)	16 fl oz
1	stick celery, sliced	1
1	onion, sliced	1
2	salt anchovies, soaked, filleted, rinsed, dried and finely chopped	2
½ litre	dry white wine	16 fl oz
12.5 cl	water	4 fl oz
30 g	butter (optional)	1 oz
	salt and pepper (optional)	

Put the celery, onion, tuna fish and anchovies into a saucepan. Add the wine and the water, bring the liquid to a simmer and let it cook for 45 minutes. Purée the contents of the pan by pushing them through a metal sieve. If the purée is very liquid, whisk in the butter while the purée is still hot. Pour the purée into a bowl and leave it to cool. When it is cold, fold in the mayonnaise and add salt and pepper if necessary.

ARMIDO FERRANDINI
ONESTÀ IN CUCINA

Butterless Béarnaise Sauce

Sauce Béarnaise Maigre

To make 45 cl (¾ pint)

2	shallots, finely chopped	2
About 6 tbsp	wine vinegar	About 6 tbsp
6	egg yolks	6
About 20 cl	olive oil	About 7 fl oz
10 cl	tomato purée (*page 164*), reduced and strained	3½ fl oz

Place the shallots and 4 tablespoons of the vinegar in a small saucepan over a low heat and reduce the mixture by simmering until no more than 1 tablespoon of liquid remains. Allow it to cool. Add the egg yolks and whisk them in, then mix in 15 cl (¼ pint) of the olive oil. Whisk the mixture over a very gentle heat until the sauce is thick and frothy, then pass it through a sieve into another saucepan. Whisk in the tomato purée, a little at a time, alternating it with a few more spoonfuls of olive oil. The sauce should be very thick. Complete the sauce by whisking in a little more vinegar to taste in a thin stream.

URBAIN DUBOIS AND ÉMILE BERNARD
LA CUISINE CLASSIQUE

Costelloise Sauce

Sauce Costelloise

This sauce may be used to accompany poached fish, hot or cold, asparagus or grilled meat.

To make 60 cl (1 pint)

15 cl	groundnut oil	¼ pint
8 cl	walnut oil	3 fl oz
15 cl	olive oil	¼ pint
2	strips thinly pared orange rind, finely chopped	2
4 tbsp	white wine vinegar	4 tbsp
8	white peppercorns, coarsely crushed	8
3 tbsp	cold water	3 tbsp
3	egg yolks	3
	salt	

Put the three different oils in a saucepan, stir them together and let them get lukewarm on the side of the stove.

Blanch the orange rind in a generous quantity of boiling water, refresh under cold running water and drain in a sieve.

Put the vinegar and the peppercorns in a saucepan, preferably of tinned copper, and reduce until the liquid has all but evaporated. Remove the pan from the heat and add the cold water and then the egg yolks.

Place the pan over a very low heat and whisk for about 3 minutes, gradually incorporating the oil in a thin trickle. Add the blanched orange rind and salt lightly. If you have to prepare the sauce in advance, keep it warm in a bain-marie.

JEAN AND PIERRE TROISGROS
THE NOUVELLE CUISINE

Hot Provençal Sauce

Sauce Provençale Chaude

The authors suggest that this sauce can be served plain with fish or poultry, or you can add a plain sauce ravigote *(recipe, page 162) to it, or the chopped garnish for a ravigote, or colour it green with spinach juice or chopped blanched parsley, depending on the dish you wish it to accompany.*

To make ¼ litre (8 fl oz)

2	egg yolks	2
1 tsp	sauce allemande (*page 162*) or leftover white sauce (*page 160*) (optional)	1 tsp
1	garlic clove, pounded to a purée	1
	cayenne pepper	
2	lemons, juice strained	2
15 cl	olive oil	¼ pint

Put the egg yolks, *sauce allemande* or white sauce (if using), garlic, a pinch of cayenne pepper and the lemon juice in a small pan. Place the pan in a bain-marie and cook over a moderate heat for 2 to 3 minutes. As soon as the sauce begins to thicken, remove it from the heat and stir in the oil, a little at a time so the sauce does not curdle. Serve immediately.

VIARD AND FOURET
LE CUISINIER ROYAL

Tyrolean Sauce

Sauce Tyrolienne

Make sure that you do not over-season this sauce.

To make about 60 cl (1 pint)

100 g	shallots, finely chopped	3½ oz
55 cl	olive oil	18 fl oz
2	garlic cloves, unpeeled	2
15 cl	dry white wine	¼ pint
2	tomatoes, skinned, seeded and coarsely chopped	2
1	sweet red or green pepper, seeded and chopped	1
2 tbsp	white wine vinegar	2 tbsp
4	egg yolks	4
1 tsp	French mustard	1 tsp
	salt and pepper	
1 tbsp each	chopped parsley, chervil and tarragon	1 tbsp each

Fry the shallots gently in 4 tablespoons of the olive oil, without letting them brown. Add the garlic and deglaze the pan deposits with the white wine. Add the tomatoes and the sweet pepper, and cook gently for 10 minutes to reduce the mixture. It should not be at all liquid, as this might cause the emulsion to separate.

Meanwhile, reduce the vinegar to half its original volume in an open pan. Away from the heat, whisk in the egg yolks. Place the pan in a larger pan of gently simmering water and gradually whisk in the remaining olive oil. The sauce should not be allowed to get hot.

Add the mustard and adjust the seasoning. Finish the sauce by stirring in as much of the sieved tomato mixture as you want. Add the parsley, chervil and tarragon.

LA CUISINE NATURELLE À L'HUILE D'OLIVE

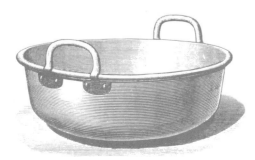

Béarnaise Sauce

Sauce Béarnaise

Should the sauce curdle whilst the pieces of butter are being blended into it, here is a method of rescuing it: put half a teaspoonful of cold lemon juice into a chilled bowl, then pour the sauce very slowly into the bowl whilst stirring and beating it constantly with a wooden spoon. The sauce should regain its emulsified consistency.

To make 30 cl (½ pint)

¼ litre	white wine vinegar	8 fl oz
5 or 6	shallots, very finely chopped	5 or 6
1 tbsp	coarsely chopped tarragon	1 tbsp
1 tbsp	coarsely chopped *fines herbes*	1 tbsp
4	egg yolks	4
250 g	butter, cut into small pieces	8 oz

Start by boiling the vinegar, shallots, tarragon and *fines herbes* in a small saucepan until the liquid has reduced to about 3 tablespoons. Strain the liquid through a fine-meshed sieve set over a small pan. Stir the egg yolks into the strained liquid and place the pan in a larger pan of warm water, over a gentle heat. Stir the mixture with a wooden spoon. Add the pieces of butter, a few at a time, stirring constantly in the same direction.

Once all the butter has been blended in, remove the sauce from the heat, pour it into a warmed sauceboat and serve.

IRÈNE LABARRE
LA CUISINE DES TROIS B

Bavarian Sauce

Sauce Bavaroise

This sauce is appropriate for several fish, particularly to the pike-perch which is often found in the north of France.

To make 30 cl (½ pint)

4 tbsp	white wine vinegar	4 tbsp
3 or 4	egg yolks	3 or 4
125 g	butter, cubed	4 oz
15 g	horseradish, sliced	½ oz
	salt	
	grated nutmeg	
100 g	crayfish butter (*page 163*)	3½ oz

Place the vinegar in a saucepan and boil until it is reduced by half. Off the heat, add 3 or 4 egg yolks, depending on the strength of the vinegar, 25 g (1 oz) of butter and the horseradish. Beat all together, add a little salt and nutmeg, and stir over a low heat until the sauce thickens slightly. Sieve the sauce into a clean saucepan, add the remaining butter and beat over a low heat until the sauce is foamy. Do not allow it to boil. Finally, beat in the crayfish butter.

ALEXANDRE DUMAS
LE GRAND DICTIONNAIRE DE CUISINE

Dijon Mustard Sauce

La Mousseline Dijonnaise

This sauce admirably complements all poached or grilled fish as well as fried or soft-boiled eggs.

To make 20 cl (7 fl oz)		
1½ tbsp	Dijon mustard	1½ tbsp
3	egg yolks	3
1	lemon, juice strained	1
1 tsp	cold water	1 tsp
	salt and pepper	
125 g	butter, chilled and diced	4 oz

Put the egg yolks, lemon juice, water, salt, a pinch of pepper and the butter into a medium-sized saucepan. Put the pan in a larger pan containing some boiling water. With a whisk, stir the egg yolks and butter together briskly. The sauce will very quickly become foamy and lightly thickened. At this stage the sauce is ready: add the Dijon mustard, adjust the seasoning, if necessary, and serve.

PAUL BOUILLARD
LA GOURMANDISE À BON MARCHÉ

Auscitaine Sauce

La Sauce Auscitaine

Auch—whence "Auscitaine"—is the capital of the Armagnac-producing region of Gascony.

This sauce would be a béarnaise if it were made with butter.

Take care not to make scrambled eggs by heating the yolks too much, nor to make an unstable sauce by beating the yolks up before they are warm enough.

To make ½ litre (16 fl oz)		
4	shallots, finely chopped	4
1	large sprig tarragon, stemmed and finely chopped	1
12	mint leaves, chopped	12
20 cl	red wine vinegar	7 fl oz
	salt	
6	white peppercorns, crushed	6
1 tbsp	red wine	1 tbsp
6	egg yolks	6
250 g	goose fat	8 oz

Place the shallots, tarragon, mint, vinegar, a little salt and the peppercorns in a saucepan. Boil for 10 minutes or until reduced to a quarter of the original volume. Add the wine and allow the mixture to cool to lukewarm.

Add the egg yolks to the tepid reduction. Put the goose fat to melt in another pan. Heat the egg yolk mixture in a heavy copper saucepan over a low heat, making sure that the pan does not become so hot that it burns your hand when you touch it. Beat for a long time, until the yolk mixture is very foamy and tends to collect around the wires of the whisk. Continuing to beat, add the melted goose fat little by little. You will have a smooth, creamy sauce with a very intense flavour.

ANDRÉ DAGUIN
LE NOUVEAU CUISINIER GASCON

Sea Urchin Hollandaise

Sauce à la Crème d'Oursins

The technique of opening sea urchins to remove the coral is shown on page 54.

To make 30 cl (½ pint)		
100 g	sea urchin coral, sieved	3½ oz
20 cl	thick hollandaise sauce (page 165)	7 fl oz

Whisk the sea urchin purée into the warm hollandaise sauce. Serve the flavoured hollandaise immediately.

MICHAEL BARBEROUSSE
CUISINE PROVENÇALE

Anchovy Sauce with Port

La Sauce aux Anchois

This sauce is to be served with pan-fried veal chops.

To make 20 cl (7 fl oz)

50 g	salt anchovies, soaked, filleted, rinsed and drained	2 oz
15 cl	port	¼ pint
125 g	butter	4 oz
2	shallots, thinly sliced	2
2	egg yolks	2
	cayenne pepper	
	pepper	

Melt the butter in a pan and add the shallots. Cook over a gentle heat for 15 minutes, then add the port and cook to reduce the liquid by about half.

Meanwhile, pound together the egg yolks and the anchovies. Add this paste to the port reduction, off the heat, then place the pan in another pan of boiling water and whisk the sauce until it becomes light and frothy. Season to taste with cayenne pepper and pepper.

ÉDOUARD DE POMIANE
LE CODE DE LA BONNE CHÈRE

Heavenly Sauce from Metz

Divine Sauce Messine

This sauce should accompany a fine fish cooked in a court-bouillon. It is very important that you should not start to heat the sauce until just before you want to serve it.

To make about 60 cl (1 pint)

½ litre	double cream	16 fl oz
15 g	butter, mashed with 1 tbsp flour	½ oz
2	egg yolks, beaten	2
½ tsp	mustard	½ tsp
1 tbsp	finely chopped chervil	1 tbsp
2 tbsp	finely chopped parsley	2 tbsp
1½ tsp	finely chopped tarragon	1½ tsp
1	shallot, finely chopped	1
1	lemon, juice strained, rind of ½ grated	1

Place all the ingredients except the lemon juice together in a pan over a very low heat. Cook, whisking all the time, for about 15 minutes, until the sauce is almost boiling, but on no account let it boil. Stir in the lemon juice and serve.

E. AURICOSTE DE LAZARQUE
CUISINE MESSINE

Sauce for Chicken or Veal

Sos Pentru Pui or Vitel

If you do not serve the sauce immediately, place the pan in hot water until you are ready to serve it. If you think the sauce is too thick, thin it with a little more wine.

To make 30 cl (½ pint)

6	egg yolks	6
2 tbsp	flour	2 tbsp
1 tbsp	finely chopped shallot or chives	1 tbsp
15 g	butter	½ oz
15 cl	dry white wine	¼ pint
1	lemon, juice strained	1

In a small saucepan, mix the egg yolks and flour, and then stir in the shallot or chives, butter, wine and lemon juice. Mix them well together and place the saucepan over a low heat. Stir the sauce gently until it begins to thicken, about 10 minutes, but do not let it boil. Serve immediately.

ANISOARA STAN
THE ROMANIAN COOK BOOK

Royal "Grey" Sauce for Fish

Ryba w Szarym Sosie po Krolewsku

The "grey" sauce is in fact brown in colour. In the present century, and no doubt in earlier ones too, it has been customary for Poles to serve carp with a grey sauce. The version below constitutes an unusual sauce which lends interest to most fish, especially the richer ones. In the instructions which follow, it is assumed that you have prepared separately enough fish for four people, preferably by poaching it.

To make 30 cl (½ pint)

2	egg yolks, lightly beaten	2
50 g	gingerbread, crumbled	2 oz
½ tsp	ground white pepper	½ tsp
½ tsp	ground cinnamon	½ tsp
20 cl	dry red wine	7 fl oz
1 tbsp	lemon juice	1 tbsp
30 g	sugar or 1 tbsp honey	1 oz
½	lemon, rind grated (optional)	½
40 g	sultanas	1½ oz
30 g	blanched almonds, finely slivered	1 oz
30 g	stoned olives, finely chopped	1 oz

Combine the egg yolks with the gingerbread. Add the pepper and cinnamon, followed by the wine, lemon juice, sugar or honey and lemon rind, if used. Mix well and heat slowly until the mixture comes to boiling point. Then remove from the heat and add the sultanas, almonds and olives. Let the sauce rest for at least 2 minutes, then pour it over the fish.

ALAN DAVIDSON
NORTH ATLANTIC SEAFOOD

Portobello Sauce

This is a rich and strongly flavoured sauce. Depending on the proportions of the main ingredients, the colour varies between a velvety brown and a macabre purplish black. This funereal garb is at the last minute relieved by the addition of chopped sweet red pepper. It makes an excellent dip to be eaten with chunks of bread, but its main duty lies with the more powerfully flavoured fish such as skate, conger, dogfish and other members of the shark family (monkfish, porbeagle) as well as tunny, squid and octopus.

To serve hot, put the cooled mixture of egg yolks and sauce into a double saucepan or bain-marie and stir over a gentle heat until the sauce is hot enough. Then garnish with the sweet red pepper and serve.

To make ½ litre (16 fl oz)

12	large black olives, stoned	12
1	small ripe avocado, peeled and stoned	1
2	garlic cloves	2
2	salt anchovies, soaked, filleted, rinsed and dried	2
½	lemon, juice strained	½
15 cl	dry red wine	¼ pint
15 cl	olive oil	¼ pint
1 tsp	freshly ground black pepper	1 tsp
2	egg yolks, well beaten	2
1 tbsp	finely chopped sweet red pepper	1 tbsp

Pound the olives with the avocado flesh, garlic cloves and anchovy fillets. Add the lemon juice and wine and purée in a blender. Place the mixture in a small, heavy saucepan, add the olive oil and cook for 7 to 8 minutes, stirring well. Season with the pepper. Let the mixture cool and then add it to the egg yolks, beating it in gradually with a wooden spoon. Before serving, garnish with the sweet red pepper.

GEORGE LASSALLE
THE ADVENTUROUS FISH COOK

Integral Sauces

Bolognese Meat Sauce

Ragù alla Bolognese

The technique of preparing this sauce is shown on page 84.

To serve 6

300 g	lean beef, minced	10 oz
100 g	butter	3½ oz
½	onion, finely chopped	½
1	carrot, finely chopped	1
60 g	lean ham or prosciutto, chopped (optional)	2 oz
1	strip lemon rind	1
	grated nutmeg	
1 tbsp	tomato purée (*page 164*)	1 tbsp
About 30 cl	veal stock (*page 158*)	About ½ pint
	salt	
2 tbsp	double cream	2 tbsp

Melt the butter in a casserole. Add the onion and carrot and fry them gently in the butter until they are soft but not coloured. Add the minced beef and cook it, stirring, until it is well browned. Then stir in the chopped ham or prosciutto, if used, and add the lemon rind and a pinch of grated nutmeg. Stir in the tomato purée and pour in enough stock to cover the meat. Add salt to taste, then cover the casserole and simmer gently for at least 1 hour.

A few minutes before the end of the cooking time, remove the lemon rind from the sauce and stir in the cream.

GIUSEPPE OBEROSLER
IL TESORETTO DELLA CUCINA ITALIANA

Brisket of Beef in Red Wine Sauce

Gedünstete Rinderbrust

For the soup greens, use a mixture of celery, onion, carrot and leek. A very little chopped lovage leaf may be added to them.

Serve this dish with dumplings, potatoes or pasta.

To serve 4

1 kg	brisket of beef	2 to 2½ lb
	salt and pepper	
15 g	lard	½ oz
200 g	soup greens, chopped	7 oz
1	bay leaf	1
1 tbsp	chopped thyme	1 tbsp
1 tbsp	chopped marjoram	1 tbsp
60 g	green bacon rind, in one piece	2 oz
¼ litre	stock (*page 158*)	8 fl oz
1 tbsp	flour	1 tbsp
12.5 cl	red wine	4 fl oz
2	tomatoes, skinned and quartered	2

Salt and pepper the beef on all sides. Fry the meat quickly in the lard. Add the soup greens, bay leaf, thyme, marjoram, bacon rind and 4 tablespoons of the stock, and cook gently, in a covered pot, until the vegetables are slightly roasted and the stock has almost completely reduced, about 12 minutes.

Stir in the flour and let it soak in for 2 minutes. Pour on the remaining stock and the red wine, add the quartered tomatoes and cook slowly until the meat is tender, about 1½ hours. Remove the meat to a warm serving dish; pass the sauce through a sieve and serve it with the meat.

HANS GUSTL KERNMAYR
SO KOCHTE MEINE MUTTER

Meat Sauce for Pasta

Il Sugo di Carne

To serve 4

100 g	lean beef, minced	3½ oz
8 cl	olive oil	3 fl oz
1	onion, chopped	1
	salt	
20 g	pine-nuts, pounded	⅔ oz
½ tsp	dried mushrooms, softened in hot water for 20 minutes, drained and chopped	½ tsp
1	sprig rosemary tied with 1 bay leaf	1
500 g	tomatoes, skinned, seeded and roughly chopped	1 lb

Heat the oil in a pan, add the onion and cook over a medium heat until the onion is golden, about 10 minutes. Add the meat, season with salt and continue cooking for 5 minutes or until the meat is brown. Add the pine-nuts, mushrooms, rosemary and bay leaf and the tomatoes. Cook over a low heat for 30 minutes, stirring often.

LUCETTO RAMELLA
RICETTE TRADIZIONALI DELLA LIGURIA

Calf's Sweetbreads in Butter Sauce

Ris de Veau au Beurre Blanc

To serve 4

4	calf's sweetbreads	4
	salt and pepper	
75 g	butter	2½ oz
1 tbsp	finely chopped shallots	1 tbsp
¼ litre	Muscadet or other dry white wine	8 fl oz
4 tbsp	double cream	4 tbsp

Soak the sweetbreads in several changes of cold water for 1½ hours. Blanch them in boiling, salted water for 10 minutes. Drain them and refresh them in cold water, then remove the membranes and the tendons. Cut the meat into escalopes and season with salt and pepper. Melt 30 g (1 oz) of the butter in a deep frying pan and brown the escalopes on both sides in it. Add the shallots and the wine. Allow the wine to reduce by half, then add the cream and simmer gently for 10 minutes.

Place the sweetbreads in a hot serving dish. Remove the

pan from the heat and whisk the remaining butter into the liquid, a little at a time. Be careful not to let the sauce boil. Pour the sauce over the sweetbreads and serve at once.

ALEXANDER WATT
PARIS BISTRO COOKERY

Calf's Head en Tortue

To serve 6

$\frac{1}{2}$	calf's head, boned, meat kept intact, bones broken up and browned in a preheated 200°C (400°F or Mark 6) oven for 15 minutes	$\frac{1}{2}$
125 g	beef dripping	4 oz
500 g	shin of beef, cubed	1 lb
500 g	stewing veal, cubed	1 lb
275 g	lean bacon, 175 g (6 oz) chopped, the rest finely minced	9 oz
350 g	onions, half finely chopped, half coarsely chopped	12 oz
60 g	celery, finely chopped	2 oz
2½ litres	stock (*page 158*)	4 pints
	salt	
12	black peppercorns	12
1	bunch marjoram, thyme and basil	1
250 g	turnips, finely chopped	8 oz
250 g	carrots, finely chopped	8 oz
	freshly ground pepper	
	ground allspice	
100 g	butter, or 30 g (1 oz) butter and 75 g (2½ oz) suet	3½ oz
15 g	parsley, chopped	½ oz
250 g	mushrooms, peeled, stalks and peel finely chopped, caps cut up neatly if large	8 oz
1 tsp	dried basil	1 tsp
30 g	*glace de viande* (*page 158*)	1 oz
30 g	flour	1 oz
15 cl	tomato purée (*page 164*)	¼ pint
1 tbsp	Marsala	1 tbsp

Blanch the meat from the calf's head for 10 minutes in boiling water, then drain and cool it. Choose a small stock-pot and put the beef dripping into it with the shin of beef, veal, chopped bacon, finely chopped onion and half the celery. Fry over a medium heat till the meat and vegetables start to take colour, then add the stock, together with 15 g (½ oz) of salt, the peppercorns and the mixed herbs. Bring slowly to the boil, skimming carefully, and then put in the calf's head, the bones and half the turnips and carrots. Bring back to the boil after this addition, but immediately afterwards reduce the heat to gentle simmering and continue to simmer for 3 hours. Now strain off the broth and set the head in the larder under a weight. When cold, take off the fat from the broth.

The next day, take the meat from beneath the weight, cut it into neat squares about 3 cm (1½ inches) in measurement, and season them with pepper, salt and allspice. Now take a sauté pan with high sides; put into it 75 g (2½ oz) of the butter or use the suet, melt this over a moderate heat and then stir in the finely minced bacon, the remaining onion, turnip, carrot and celery, the parsley and the peelings and stalks of the mushrooms. Season with salt and allspice and put in the dried basil. Fry over a low heat until the vegetables soften and turn colour, then put in the *glace de viande* and moisten with 90 cl (1½ pints) of the broth from cooking the calf's head; bring slowly to the boil and simmer till the vegetables are done, then strain off the broth into a bowl and let it get cold, so that the fat may be taken off. Now turn the broth to a sauce *à la tortue* in the following way.

Prepare a roux by melting the remaining butter—or 30 g (1 oz) of butter, if you have used the suet earlier—stirring in the flour and cooking over a low heat for 2 minutes. Then add the broth, bring to the boil, stirring, put in the mushroom caps, and simmer for 15 minutes. After this, empty the contents of the pan into a fine-meshed sieve with a bowl beneath it; pick out the pieces of mushroom, placing them on a plate aside, and pass the sauce through the sieve. Lastly, put the strained sauce into a stew-pan, stir in the tomato purée and the Marsala; mix well, add the mushrooms and the pieces of head, warm up gently without boiling and serve.

COL. A. F. (WYVERN) KENNEY-HERBERT
FIFTY DINNERS

Lamb in Curry Sauce

Shahi Korma

	To serve 4	
500 g	shoulder of lamb, boned, trimmed of fat, cubed	1 lb
60 g	*ghee*	2 oz
350 g	curd cheese	12 oz
	salt	
2	sticks cinnamon	2
1	bay leaf	1
2	cloves	2
2	cardamom pods	2
10	almonds, blanched and halved	10
	Masala	
3	medium-sized onions, chopped	3
2.5 cm	fresh ginger root, peeled and sliced	1 inch
3	garlic cloves	3
4	red chili peppers	4
1½ tbsp	poppy seeds	1½ tbsp
1 tsp	ground coriander	1 tsp

Grind together all the *masala* ingredients to make a smooth paste. Melt the *ghee* in a saucepan and add the *masala*. Stir well and cook until the *ghee* separates. Add the curd cheese and cook until well blended, stirring, for about 5 minutes. Then add the lamb and salt to taste. Add about 4 tablespoons of water, the cinnamon, bay leaf, cloves and cardamom pods and keep cooking over a low heat. Add a little more water from time to time, until the meat becomes a rich brown colour. Then add 30 cl (½ pint) of water and cook, covered, until the meat is tender and the gravy is a rich brown, about 1½ hours. Just before serving, heat well and add the almonds.

VIMLA PATIL (EDITOR)
KASHMIR TO KANYAKUMARI

Royal Roast Leg of Lamb with Saffron Raisin Sauce

Shahi Raan

Mughal garam masala *is made by grinding together the seeds of about 60 g (2 oz) of black or green cardamom pods, two 7.5 cm (3 inch) sticks of cinnamon, 1 tablespoon of cloves, 1 tablespoon of black peppercorns and 1½ teaspoons of grated nutmeg to a fine powder. The powder can be stored in an airtight container in a cool place.*

To bone the leg of lamb, hold it with the top side down on a chopping board. With a sharp boning knife held at the tip of the hip bone, cut the leg all the way down from the butt end to the shank end, thus opening the leg and exposing the bone. Separate the bones from the meat by working round them, scraping and pushing the meat away from the bones with the knife. When the bones are removed, re-form the leg into a cylinder, making sure to tuck in the meat at the shank tip. Secure the leg by tying it with string at several places.

	To serve 8 to 12	
3.25 to 4 kg	leg of lamb, all fat removed, boned, re-formed and tied with string	7½ to 9 lb
2 tsp	saffron threads	2 tsp
2 tbsp	flour or cornflour, mixed with 3 tbsp water	2 tbsp
	Marinade	
1 tbsp	chopped garlic	1 tbsp
2 tbsp	chopped fresh ginger root	2 tbsp
1 tsp	black or white cumin seeds	1 tsp
About 1 tsp	cayenne pepper	About 1 tsp
1½ tsp	Mughal *garam masala*	1½ tsp
4 tsp	coarse salt	4 tsp
100 g	seedless raisins	3½ oz
60 g	pistachio nuts or walnuts	2 oz
1	lemon, juice strained	1
45 g	light brown sugar	1½ oz
17.5 cl	yogurt	6 fl oz
4 tbsp	soured cream	4 tbsp

Prick the top of the lamb with a fork or thin skewer and place it in a large, fireproof, non-metal 4.5 litre (8 pint) casserole that can hold the lamb snugly. Set aside.

Put all the ingredients for the marinade into the container of a food processor or electric blender, and process until the ingredients are reduced to a fine, thick paste. If the machine begins to clog, add 2 to 3 tablespoons of water. Pour the marinade all over the lamb and spread it to coat the lamb thoroughly. Cover and let it marinate in the refrigerator for three days. Take the casserole from the refrigerator about 1 hour before cooking (or 4 hours before serving) and let it come to room temperature.

Put the saffron threads in a small bowl or saucer and, using your fingers, powder them as finely as possible. Add 2 tablespoons of hot water and let the saffron soak for 15 minutes. Sprinkle the dissolved saffron over the lamb. Place the casserole over a medium heat and bring the contents to the boil. Pour ¼ litre (8 fl oz) of boiling water down the sides of the casserole. Place a piece of aluminium foil on top of the casserole and cover tightly with the lid. Cook the lamb in the middle of a preheated 180°C (350°F or Mark 4) oven for 1½ hours. Lower the heat to 100°C (200°F or Mark ¼) and continue cooking for 45 minutes. Turn off the heat and let the casserole remain in the oven, with the door shut, for another 45 minutes. The cooking process is now completed, but keep the casserole in the oven until you are ready to serve the lamb. The lamb will remain warm for 45 minutes in the oven.

To serve, take the casserole from the oven, uncover and carefully place the lamb on a carving board. Cut off and discard the trussing strings. Heat the contents of the casserole to a gentle simmer over a low heat, skimming off the fat floating on the surface. Add the flour and water paste and cook, stirring rapidly, for 1 to 2 minutes, until the sauce is thickened. Check for salt. (The lamb may be returned to the casserole and kept warm, covered, over an electric warming tray or in a very low oven.) Slice the meat in 3 to 5 mm (⅛ to ¼ inch) thick slices and arrange them on a warm serving platter. Spoon some of the sauce over the slices of meat and serve the rest of it in a heated bowl or sauceboat.

JULIE SAHNI
CLASSIC INDIAN COOKING

Blanquette of Lamb with Saffron Sauce

Blanquette d'Agneau au Safran

To "turn" carrots and turnips, cut them into chunks about 2.5 cm (1 inch) long, then pare them with a sharp vegetable knife into the shape of olives. To glaze pearl onions, place the peeled onions in a pan with a little butter and sugar—in the proportions of 30 g (1 oz) of butter and 1 tablespoon of sugar for every

500 g (1 lb) of onions. Season with salt and pour in enough cold water to cover the onions partially. Bring the water to the boil, cover the pan and simmer until the onions are tender and the liquid is reduced to a glaze, about 15 minutes.

	To serve 4	
800 g	lamb breast and shoulder, boned, trimmed of fat and connective tissue, cut into 40 g (1½ oz) pieces	1¾ lb
60 cl	lamb stock (*page 158*), well seasoned	1 pint
10 cl	white wine	3½ fl oz
150 g	bouquet garni, consisting of onions, carrots, celery, ¼ bay leaf, 1 clove and some parsley stalks	5 oz
⅛ tsp	powdered saffron, dissolved in 1 tsp cold water	⅛ tsp
2	egg yolks	2
30 cl	double cream	½ pint
50 g	butter, cut into small pieces	2 oz
1 tbsp	lemon juice	1 tbsp
	salt and freshly ground pepper	
	Garnish	
50 g	"turned" carrots, cooked in boiling salted water for 5 minutes	2 oz
50 g	"turned" turnips, cooked in boiling salted water for 5 minutes	2 oz
50 g	fine green beans, cooked in boiling salted water for 2 minutes	2 oz
30 g	glazed pearl onions	1 oz

Blanch the lamb pieces in boiling, salted water; cool and wash them immediately under running water. Place the meat in a large pan, add the lamb stock and the white wine, bring to the boil and skim. Add the bouquet garni and the saffron, and simmer until the meat is tender, about 1½ hours, occasionally removing the fat and skimming. Remove the meat and keep it warm. Strain the stock into a clean pan through a fine-meshed sieve and boil it to reduce it to half its original volume.

Mix the egg yolks with the cream. Stir in a few spoonfuls of the stock, then add this mixture to the stock and heat it gently, without boiling, until it is thick. Strain the sauce through a piece of fine muslin, then carefully whisk in the butter. Add the lemon juice and season with salt and pepper.

Arrange the meat on a suitable serving dish and cover with the sauce. Garnish with the carrots, turnips, green beans and the freshly glazed pearl onions.

ANTON MOSIMANN
CUISINE À LA CARTE

Lamb Cutlets Bourdaloue

Noix d'Agneau des Landes Bourdaloue

Accompany this dish with a rice pilaff served separately.

	To serve 6	
18	small lamb cutlets, boned, fat trimmed	18
12	2.5 cm (1 inch) slices of eye of loin of lamb, fat trimmed	12
12	eggs	12
	salt and pepper	
¼ litre	double cream	8 fl oz
125 g	peas, boiled for 5 minutes and puréed	4 oz
125 g	butter	4 oz
12	button mushrooms, stalks discarded	12
4 tbsp	port	4 tbsp
12.5 cl	*glace de viande (page 158)*	4 fl oz
3 tbsp	Madeira	3 tbsp

Thickly butter a 25 cm (10 inch) ring mould. Beat the eggs thoroughly with a pinch each of salt and pepper. Beat in 2 tablespoons of the double cream and all the pea purée. Pour this mixture into the mould. Cover with buttered greaseproof paper and put the mould in a bain-marie. Cook in a preheated 170°C (325°F or Mark 3) oven for 45 minutes or until set.

Melt half the butter in a frying pan and sauté the cutlets, in batches if necessary, over a high heat for 5 minutes on each side or until lightly browned. Remove the cutlets from the pan and keep them warm.

Blanch the 12 rounds of lamb in boiling water for 1 minute. Drain them and pat them dry. Heat 30 g (1 oz) of butter in another frying pan. When it has melted, add the rounds of lamb and the mushrooms. When the meat is light beige in colour, add the port and cover the pan tightly, so that the vapour from the port condenses and falls back into the mixture to impregnate it. Cook for 5 minutes then add the rest of the cream and 5 tablespoons of the *glace de viande*. Simmer very gently, uncovered, until the liquid forms a thick glaze over the meat and mushrooms, about 20 minutes.

Unmould the egg mixture on to a round serving dish. Arrange the lamb cutlets round the outer edge of this border. Pile the meat and mushroom mixture into the centre of the dish in a pyramid. Keep the dish warm while you deglaze the pan in which the cutlets were cooked with the Madeira and the rest of the *glace de viande*. Let the sauce simmer for a few seconds. Remove the pan from the heat and whisk in the remaining butter. Pour the sauce round the border.

ÉDOUARD NIGNON
ÉLOGES DE LA CUISINE FRANÇAISE

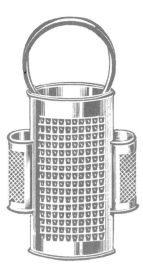

Fried Lamb Pieces with Mint and Shallot Sauce

Goujonettes d'Agneau

You can substitute softened butter for the clarified butter, whisking it in after the sauce has been thickened with egg yolks. Other herbs can be used instead of mint.

	To serve 4	
400 g	boned leg of lamb, cut into pieces 7 cm (2½ inches) long, 1 cm (½ inch) wide and 1 cm thick	14 oz
	salt and pepper	
1	egg	1
1 tbsp	cold water	1 tbsp
100 g	fresh white breadcrumbs	3½ oz
	groundnut oil for deep frying	
	Mint and shullot sauce	
10	fresh mint leaves, washed and dried, half finely chopped, half coarsely chopped	10
2	shallots, finely chopped	2
135 g	butter	4½ oz
10	peppercorns, coarsely crushed	10
4 tbsp	sherry vinegar	4 tbsp
4 tbsp	white wine	4 tbsp
2	egg yolks	2

Season the pieces of lamb with salt and pepper. Break the egg into a shallow dish, season it, add the cold water and beat well. Put the breadcrumbs in another shallow dish. Dip each piece of lamb into the beaten egg mixture, then roll it in the breadcrumbs, shaking any excess breadcrumbs back into the second dish. When all the lamb pieces have been coated in the egg and breadcrumbs, set them aside.

To make the sauce, first melt 125 g (4 oz) of the butter in a heavy pan over a very low heat. When the butter starts to foam, use a spoon to skim off the scum; continue skimming until no more scum rises, about 8 minutes. Set aside.

Melt the remaining butter in a heavy pan over a low heat and stir in the finely chopped mint and the shallots with a wooden spoon. Cook for 5 minutes until the shallots are translucent but not coloured. Add the crushed peppercorns, sherry vinegar and white wine; stir the mixture together well and reduce it for about 5 minutes until only about 3 tablespoons of liquid are left in the pan. Remove the pan from the heat and leave the liquid to get cold.

Put the egg yolks into a heavy pan and beat them together well. When the reduced mint mixture is cold, strain it through a fine-meshed sieve into the pan containing the egg yolks and whisk the mixture well. Place the pan over a low heat, whisking the mixture constantly for 4 minutes; use a circular motion, making figures-of-eight with the whisk so that all the mixture is beaten. Do not allow the mixture to boil. When the mixture has increased in volume and is thick and foamy, remove the pan from the heat and whisk in the clarified butter, a little at a time, until the sauce is very smooth. Add the coarsely chopped mint, season the sauce with salt and pepper, pour it into a heated sauceboat and set it aside. The sauce is meant to be served warm and must not be reheated.

Pour groundnut oil into a deep fryer to a depth of at least 2 cm (¾ inch) and set it over a moderate heat. When the oil reaches 190°C (375°F), fry the lamb pieces in it for 1 to 2 minutes. The meat should be pink and rare inside its coating of breadcrumbs. Remove the cooked lamb pieces from the deep fryer and leave them to drain on a paper towel for 1 to 2 minutes. Place the meat on a warmed serving dish. Whisk the sauce once more and serve it with the lamb.

ALAIN AND EVENTHIA SENDERENS
LA CUISINE RÉUSSIE

Pappardelle with Hare Sauce

Pappardelle sulla Lepre

Pappardelle *are strips of egg pasta about 1.5 cm (⅝ inch) wide, often with fluted edges. The technique of jointing a hare and reserving the blood is shown on page 54. The saddle and*

hindquarters of the hare may be reserved for another dish.

Instead of the hare's blood, you can use 100 g (3½ oz) of skinned tomatoes. The original Etruscan recipe does not include tomatoes, which were introduced from America after 1500.

	To serve 6	
400 g	pappardelle	14 oz
1	hare, forequarters and head (eyes removed) cut into pieces, heart, lungs and liver chopped, blood reserved	1
60 g	parsley, finely chopped	2 oz
1	stick celery, finely chopped	1
1	carrot, finely chopped	1
10 cl	olive oil	3½ fl oz
10 cl	red wine	3½ fl oz
	hot water	
10 cl	milk	3½ fl oz
	salt and pepper	
4 tbsp	Parmesan cheese, grated	4 tbsp

Place the pieces of hare in a pan with the chopped heart and lungs, the parsley, celery, carrot and oil. Cook over a high heat, stirring, until the hare is lightly browned and the vegetables have softened. Pour in the wine and cook until the liquid is syrupy. Dilute the reserved hare's blood with about half of its volume of hot water. Off the heat, pour the blood into the pan. Simmer gently for 10 minutes, then add the milk and season with salt and pepper. Cover and simmer for about 20 minutes more or until the pieces of hare are tender. Bone the hare and return the meat to the pan, with the chopped liver. Correct the seasoning.

Allow the sauce to simmer very gently. Meanwhile, bring a large pot of salted water to the boil and cook the *pappardelle* in it for about 12 minutes or until they are tender but still slightly firm to the bite. Drain the pasta and put it in a deep serving dish. Pour the hare sauce over the pasta and sprinkle with the cheese. Serve immediately.

FIAMMA NICCOLINI ADIMARI
IL LIBRO DELLA CACCIAGIONE

Rabbit with Snails

Conejo con Caracoles

Live snails should be soaked for about 5 minutes in coarse salt and wine vinegar, then rinsed in cold water. Place them in a large saucepan and pour boiling court-bouillon (recipe, page 159) over them. Bring the liquid to the boil again, remove the scum that forms on the surface, then lower the heat and simmer, with the pan partially covered, for about 2 hours or until the snails are tender. The snails are served in their shells.

To serve 4 to 6		
1 kg	tender rabbit, cleaned and cut into 10 to 12 serving pieces, liver reserved	2 to 2½ lb
72	snails, cooked and well drained	72
	salt and freshly ground pepper	
	flour	
20 cl	oil	7 fl oz
1	large onion, chopped	1
1	bouquet garni, consisting of bay leaf, thyme, oregano, 1 small piece dried orange rind and 1 small stick cinnamon	1
3	ripe medium-sized tomatoes, skinned, seeded and chopped	3
17.5 cl	wine vinegar	6 fl oz
8 cl	anise-flavoured liqueur	3 fl oz
	stock (*page 158*) or hot water	
¼ tsp	powdered saffron	¼ tsp
1	large garlic clove	1
2	dry plain sweet biscuits	2
12	pine-nuts	12
8	almonds, blanched and toasted	8
3 tbsp	chopped parsley	3 tbsp

Season the rabbit pieces with salt and a little pepper, coat them with flour and fry in the oil in a cast-iron casserole over a medium heat. When they are half done, after about 20 minutes, add the onion and bouquet garni. When the onion is browned, add the tomatoes. Stir and, when the tomato is soft, add the vinegar and the anise liqueur. Cover the casserole and cook until the liquid has reduced by half, about 15 minutes. Then pour in stock or hot water to cover the pieces of rabbit. Simmer, covered, for 20 minutes.

Meanwhile, fry the rabbit liver. In a mortar, pound the saffron, garlic, biscuits, pine-nuts, almonds and 1 tablespoon of the parsley to a fine paste. Add the rabbit liver and pound again. Dilute with a little of the rabbit cooking juices and then pour into the casserole. Add the snails.

Adjust the seasoning with salt and pepper. Simmer slowly for a further 15 minutes until the rabbit is tender and ready. Just before serving, remove the bouquet garni and sprinkle over the remaining parsley. Serve from the casserole.

NESTOR LUJAN AND JUAN PERUCHO
EL LIBRO DE LA COCINA ESPAÑOLA

Stewed Rabbit with Tarragon and Garlic

Fricassée de Lapin à l'Estragon et à l'Ail

Order a small rabbit or rabbit joint (thighs and backs). A whole rabbit should be cut into eight joints weighing about 100 g (3½ oz) each; the thighs should be cut in half and the back into three pieces. Instead of straining the sauce into a sauceboat, it can be poured directly over the rabbit.

You can substitute any kind of poultry or veal for the rabbit. Shallots can be used instead of garlic, and basil, fennel, curry powder or paprika instead of tarragon.

To serve 4		
1	small rabbit, jointed	1
	salt and pepper	
1 tbsp	groundnut oil	1 tbsp
25 g	butter	¾ oz
3 tbsp	tarragon vinegar	3 tbsp
250 g	tomatoes, skinned, seeded and chopped	8 oz
60 g	fresh tarragon, leaves removed and reserved, stalks tied in a bunch	2 oz
12 to 14	garlic cloves, unpeeled	12 to 14
¼ litre	milk	8 fl oz
½ litre	*crème fraîche* or double cream	16 fl oz
	sugar	

Season each rabbit joint with salt and pepper. In a cast-iron frying pan, heat the oil and sauté the rabbit joints on all sides, turning them occasionally with a fork, for about 17 minutes. Add half the butter to the pan. When the rabbit joints are well browned, put them on a dish and keep them warm.

Pour off any fat left in the frying pan and wipe the pan out with an absorbent cloth. Return it to the heat and add the tarragon vinegar. Scrape the bottom of the pan with a wooden spoon to dislodge the caramelized juices and let the liquid reduce for 2 to 3 minutes. Then add the tomatoes. Add the bunch of tarragon stalks to the pan and simmer for 4 minutes.

Put the garlic cloves into a saucepan and cover them with the milk. Bring the milk to the boil and simmer for 4 minutes, then drain the cloves in a conical sieve. Peel the cloves.

Pour the *crème fraîche* or double cream into the pan containing the tomatoes. Season with salt and pepper. Bring the mixture to just below boiling point, then add the rabbit joints. Cover the pan and simmer for another 15 minutes.

Put the remaining butter into a saucepan and melt it over a low heat. Add the drained garlic cloves. Add salt, pepper and a pinch of sugar. Cook the garlic over a low heat for 15 to 16 minutes, stirring gently from time to time with a wooden spoon, so that the cloves colour evenly.

When the rabbit is cooked, arrange the joints on a warm serving dish. Taste the sauce and adjust the seasoning. Whisk the sauce again, then strain it through a conical sieve into a warmed sauceboat. Sprinkle the rabbit with the tarragon leaves and arrange the caramelized garlic cloves round it. Serve immediately.

ALAIN AND EVENTHIA SENDERENS
LA CUISINE RÉUSSIE

Chicken Liver Sauce

Salsa di Fegatini

To serve 4

4	chicken livers, finely chopped	4
50 g	butter	2 oz
100 g	prosciutto, finely chopped	3½ oz
1	onion, chopped	1
30 g	parsley, chopped	1 oz
1 tbsp	flour	1 tbsp
20 cl	chicken broth (*page 159*)	7 fl oz
8 cl	Marsala	3 fl oz
	ground mixed spices or grated nutmeg (optional)	
	salt	

Melt the butter in a pan, add the chicken livers, prosciutto, onion and parsley and fry lightly. Stir in the flour and cook, stirring, until the mixture colours a little. Dilute the sauce with the chicken broth and Marsala. Add a pinch of mixed spices or nutmeg, if desired. Add salt if necessary.

GIUSEPPE OBEROSLER
IL TESORETTO DELLA CUCINA ITALIANA

Chicken Makhni

Silver varkh is edible silver leaf. It can be obtained from specialist Indian food shops.

To serve 4

1	small chicken	1
2 tbsp	vinegar	2 tbsp
	salt	
250 g	curd cheese	8 oz
½	small papaya, finely chopped	½
1 tsp	chili powder	1 tsp
3 tbsp	tomato purée (*page 164*)	3 tbsp
2	large onions, finely chopped	2
30 g	butter	1 oz
¼ tsp	turmeric	¼ tsp
¼ tsp	*garam masala*	¼ tsp
4	tomatoes, skinned, seeded and finely chopped	4
4 tbsp	double cream, lightly whipped	4 tbsp
12.5 cl	water	4 fl oz
25 g	cashew nuts	¾ oz
25 g	pistachio nuts	¾ oz
25 g	raisins	¾ oz
1	sheet silver varkh (optional)	1

Make deep cuts all over the chicken. Marinate it for 15 minutes in a mixture of the vinegar and 2 teaspoons of salt.

Mix together half the curd cheese, the papaya, ½ teaspoon of the chili powder and 2 tablespoons of the tomato purée. Rub this mixture into the chicken and leave it for 2 hours.

Roast the chicken in a preheated 200°C (400°F or Mark 6) oven for 45 minutes. Fry the onions in the butter until they start to brown. Then add the turmeric, the remaining chili powder, the *garam masala* and the tomatoes. When the tomatoes are almost cooked, after about 5 minutes, add the cream, the remaining curd cheese and tomato purée, and the water. Season with salt. Add the chicken and cook over a medium heat for 10 minutes. Serve garnished with the nuts and raisins, and the silver varkh if used.

VIMLA PATIL (EDITOR)
KASHMIR TO KANYAKUMARI

Chicken in Onion Tomato Gravy

Murgh Masala

This is a classic dish from Punjab, a state in the north of India. Like all stews, it improves with keeping. It can be kept in the refrigerator for up to two days, or it can be frozen. Defrost thoroughly before reheating. To reheat, gently simmer the chicken over a low heat until it is warmed through. Taste, and if necessary add salt. Fold in the ground, roasted cumin seeds and chopped coriander leaves before serving.

To serve 8

Two 1.5 kg	chickens, cut into 8 to 10 pieces each, wing tips discarded	Two 3 lb
15 cl	light vegetable oil	$\frac{1}{4}$ pint
600 g	onions, thinly sliced	$1\frac{1}{4}$ lb
2 tbsp	finely chopped garlic	2 tbsp
3 tbsp	finely chopped fresh ginger root	3 tbsp
Two 7.5 cm	sticks cinnamon	Two 3 inch
4	black or 8 green cardamom pods	4
1 tbsp	turmeric	1 tbsp
1 tsp	cayenne pepper	1 tsp
250 g	ripe tomatoes, skinned, seeded and puréed	8 oz
1 tbsp	coarse salt	1 tbsp
$\frac{1}{2}$ litre	boiling water	16 fl oz
$1\frac{1}{2}$ tbsp	cumin seeds, roasted in a dry pan for a few minutes, then finely ground	$1\frac{1}{2}$ tbsp
3 to 4 tbsp	chopped fresh coriander leaves or 2 tbsp dried coriander leaves	3 to 4 tbsp

Pull the skin away from the chicken pieces, using kitchen paper to get a better grip. Heat 2 tablespoons of the oil in a large, 4.5 litre (8 pint) heavy-bottomed pan, preferably one with a non-stick surface, over a high heat. When the oil is very hot, add the chicken pieces, a few at a time, and sear them for about 3 to 4 minutes, until they lose their pink colour and get nicely browned on all sides. Remove them with a slotted spoon and reserve them in a bowl. Continue with the rest of the chicken pieces until all of them are seared.

Add the remaining oil to the pan, along with the sliced onions. Reduce the heat to medium and fry the onions until they turn light brown, about 30 minutes, stirring constantly to prevent them burning. Add the chopped garlic and ginger, and fry for an additional 5 minutes. Add the cinnamon and cardamom, and continue frying for about 2 minutes more, until the spices are slightly puffed and beginning to brown. Add the turmeric and cayenne pepper, and stir rapidly for 10 to 15 seconds. Add the puréed tomatoes, the chicken pieces, the salt and boiling water. Stir to mix, reduce the heat and simmer, covered, for about 45 minutes until the chicken is cooked and very tender and the gravy has thickened. If the

gravy has not thickened adequately, increase the heat and boil rapidly, uncovered, until it thickens. If, on the other hand, the evaporation is too fast, add a little water. Check frequently during cooking to ensure that the sauce is not burning. The finished dish should have plenty of thick, pulpy gravy. Turn off the heat and let the dish rest, covered, for at least 1 hour, preferably 2 hours, before serving.

When ready to serve, heat thoroughly, fold in the ground cumin and chopped coriander, check for salt and serve.

JULIE SAHNI
CLASSIC INDIAN COOKING

Circassian Chicken

Çerkes Tavuğu

To remove the slightly bitter brown skin from shelled walnuts, blanch them in a little boiling water for 2 to 3 minutes, so that the skin is loosened and can be peeled off. The walnuts can be ground in a food processor.

To serve 6 to 8

One 1.75 kg chicken		One $3\frac{1}{2}$ lb
1	thick slice bread	1
250 g	shelled walnuts, skinned and ground to a paste	8 oz
1	garlic clove, crushed	1
1 tbsp	walnut oil	1 tbsp
2 tbsp	paprika	2 tbsp
	black olives (optional)	
	Court-bouillon	
1	sprig parsley	1
1	bay leaf	1
1	strip lemon rind	1
1	carrot, sliced	1
1	onion, sliced	1
1	stick celery, sliced	1
	salt and pepper	
About 2 litres	water	About $3\frac{1}{2}$ pints

Make your court-bouillon with the parsley, bay leaf, lemon rind, carrot, onion, celery, salt and pepper and enough cold water just to cover the chicken. Poach the chicken in this for about 1 hour or until it is tender, then allow it to cool in the liquid. Lift out the chicken, remove the skin and as many bones as possible and lay the meat in neat pieces, slightly heaped, in a large dish. Strain the stock.

Soak the bread in some of the chicken stock, squeeze the bread and add it to the walnut paste together with the crushed garlic. Blend in a food processor until the mixture forms a smooth paste. Now add to the paste as much of the stock as is necessary to make a thick, creamy sauce, blend well and pour it over the chicken, covering it completely.

In a small pan, heat together very gently the walnut oil and paprika, until the oil becomes a beautiful red colour. Take it off the heat to cool and let the pepper settle at the bottom of the pan. Carefully pour off the coloured oil. Indent a pattern in the surface of the walnut sauce with your finger—traditionally a big curly "S" and a couple of smaller wiggles at the side—and pour as much as you need of the oil into the pattern.

Serve the chicken lukewarm if possible. If it has been refrigerated, bring it to room temperature before serving. Garnish the chicken, if you like, with a few black olives.

DOROTHY BROWN (EDITOR)
SYMPOSIUM FARE

Royal Chicken in Silky White Almond Sauce

Shahi Murgh Badaami

In this recipe, the word "silky" refers to the appearance of the sauce, not to its texture, which is indeed grainy. If you want a hotter taste, add all eight chili peppers, as suggested.

This dish can be made a day ahead and then refrigerated. This prolonged resting allows the flavours to penetrate the chicken, and makes it taste even better. The dish can be kept in the refrigerator for up to two days, or frozen. Defrost it thoroughly before reheating. To reheat, simmer gently until it is warmed through. Check for salt before serving.

To serve 4		
One 1.5 kg	chicken, cut into 8 to 10 pieces, wing tips discarded	One 3 lb
15 cl	light vegetable oil	$\frac{1}{4}$ pint
400 g	onions, thinly sliced	14 oz
45 g	almonds, blanched and slivered	$1\frac{1}{2}$ oz
4 tbsp	coriander seeds	4 tbsp
About 50	green cardamom pods	About 50
4 to 8	red chili peppers, seeded and chopped, or 1 to 2 tsp cayenne pepper	4 to 8
$\frac{1}{4}$ litre	water	8 fl oz
$\frac{1}{2}$ litre	yogurt	16 fl oz
$2\frac{1}{2}$ tsp	coarse salt	$2\frac{1}{2}$ tsp

Pull the skin away from all the chicken pieces, using kitchen paper to get a better grip. Heat 2 tablespoons of the oil over a medium heat in a wide, heavy-bottomed pan. When the oil is hot, add the chicken pieces, a few at a time, and cook, turning constantly, until they lose their pink colour and begin to sear, about 2 minutes. Do not allow them to brown or the sauce will turn dark. Take them out with a slotted spoon and reserve them in a bowl. Continue with the rest of the chicken pieces until all are seared and set aside.

Add the remaining oil to the pan, along with the sliced onions. Fry the onions, stirring constantly to keep them from colouring unevenly, for about 10 minutes, until they are wilted and pale golden. Do not let the onions over-brown. Add the slivered almonds, coriander, cardamom pods and chopped red chili peppers (if you are using cayenne pepper, do not add it at this stage), and cook for an additional 3 to 5 minutes, or until the almonds are lightly coloured and the cardamom pods are puffed up. If you are using cayenne pepper, add it now and stir. Turn off the heat.

Put the entire mixture, with the water, into the container of an electric blender or food processor, and run the machine until the mixture is reduced to a fine, smooth purée. Return the purée to the pan, along with the chicken pieces, yogurt and salt, and bring to the boil. Reduce the heat and simmer, covered, for about 45 minutes, until the chicken is meltingly tender and the sauce has thickened nicely. At this point the oil will begin to separate from the sauce, and a thin glaze will form over both the sauce and the chicken. Turn off the heat and let the dish rest, covered, for 30 minutes before serving. When ready to serve, reheat the dish until piping hot, check for salt and serve.

JULIE SAHNI
CLASSIC INDIAN COOKING

Chicken with White Wine

Coq au Riesling

Coq au Riesling, cooked in the aromatic white wine of Alsace, is lighter and more delicate than the better known *coq au vin* from Burgundy. Be sure to use a white wine that is not too acidic. The chicken is good served with home-made noodles.

To serve 4

One 1.5 kg	chicken, cut into 4 pieces	One 3 lb
	salt and pepper	
2 tbsp	oil	2 tbsp
60 g	butter	2 oz
4	shallots, chopped	4
1½ tbsp	cognac	1½ tbsp
37.5 cl	dry white wine, preferably Alsatian Riesling	14 fl oz
1	bouquet garni	1
	grated nutmeg	
150 g	mushrooms, quartered	5 oz
½	lemon, juice strained	½
8 cl	*crème fraîche* or double cream	3 fl oz
1	egg yolk	1

Season the chicken pieces with salt and pepper. Heat the oil and half the butter over a medium heat in a large pot, add the chicken pieces and brown them on all sides. Lower the heat, add the chopped shallots and continue cooking for 2 minutes. Pour in the cognac and light it; when the flame dies, stir the chicken quickly and add the wine, bouquet garni, salt, pepper and a pinch of nutmeg. Bring to the boil, cover and cook over a low heat for 30 to 40 minutes, or until the chicken is nearly tender when pierced.

While the chicken is cooking, prepare the mushrooms: heat the remaining butter in a frying pan and add the mushrooms with the lemon juice. Cook slowly for 10 minutes or until the mushrooms are tender. Add the mushrooms with any liquid to the chicken and continue to simmer for 10 minutes, or until the chicken is tender.

Discard the bouquet garni and transfer the chicken and mushrooms to a warmed serving platter. Skim any fat from the cooking liquid. Mix the cream and egg yolk together in a bowl, then slowly add the cooking liquid, stirring constantly. Return the sauce to the pan and heat gently until it thickens slightly. Do not boil the sauce or it will curdle. Remove it from the heat and taste for seasoning. Strain the sauce over the chicken pieces and serve.

ANNE WILLAN AND L'ÉCOLE DE CUISINE LA VARENNE, PARIS
FRENCH REGIONAL COOKING

Chicken in Red Wine Sauce

Poulet Sauté au Brouilly

The author suggests serving this dish with a gratin of noodles and cheese, and a salad. Brouilly is a Beaujolais wine.

To serve 4

One 1.25 to 1.5 kg	chicken, cut into serving pieces, including the back, neck, gizzard and liver	One 2½ to 3 lb
	salt and pepper	
30 g	butter	1 oz
125 g	mushrooms, left whole if very small, otherwise halved, quartered or sliced	4 oz
30 g	shallots, chopped	1 oz
1 tsp	finely chopped garlic	1 tsp
2 tbsp	flour	2 tbsp
35 cl	dry red wine, preferably Brouilly	12 fl oz
15 cl	chicken stock (*page 158*)	¼ pint
1	bay leaf	1
1	sprig parsley	1
2	sprigs fresh thyme or ¼ tsp dried thyme	2

Sprinkle the chicken pieces with salt and pepper. Heat the butter in a frying pan large enough to hold the chicken pieces in one layer without crowding. Add the chicken pieces, skin side down. Cook the chicken over a moderately high heat until golden-brown—about 6 to 7 minutes. Turn the pieces over and cook about 5 minutes longer.

Stir in the mushrooms, shallots and garlic. Cook for about 1 minute, then sprinkle evenly with the flour. Add the wine and 12.5 cl (4 fl oz) of the stock and bring to the boil. Add the bay leaf, parsley and thyme. Season with salt and pepper to taste and cover. Cook for 15 to 20 minutes.

Using a slotted spoon, transfer the meaty parts of the chicken to a fireproof casserole. Add the mushrooms, but leave the back, gizzard, neck and liver in the frying pan. Strain the sauce over the chicken, pressing with a wooden spoon to extract the juices. Add the remaining stock to the frying pan and swirl it round to thin the sauce remaining in the pan. Strain this over the chicken. Reheat before serving.

PIERRE FRANEY
THE NEW YORK TIMES 60-MINUTE GOURMET

Malay Satay

Blachan *is a paste made of dried and salted shrimps; it can be bought from Oriental grocers. To make coconut milk, infuse the grated flesh of one coconut in scalded milk or boiling water for 1 hour, then strain through a muslin-lined sieve and squeeze the flesh in the muslin to extract all the liquid. To make tamarind water, soak a piece of tamarind until soft in 8 cl (3 fl oz) of water, then strain off the water through a fine sieve, pressing the tamarind with a spoon to extract all the liquid.*

To serve this dish, arrange the skewers of grilled meat on a plate, pour the sauce over them and accompany them with cubes of fresh, unpeeled cucumber. The Malays eat *satay* with pieces of rice cake made from glutinous rice boiled and then cooled under a press, which they dip in the sauce, but plain rice is just as acceptable.

To serve 4

500 g	fillet steak, rump steak or chicken breast, cut into 1 cm (½ inch) cubes	1 lb
8 cl	peanut oil	3 fl oz
	Satay sauce	
2 tsp	coriander seeds	2 tsp
1 tsp	fennel seeds	1 tsp
1 tsp	ground cumin	1 tsp
½ to 1 tsp	chili powder	½ to 1 tsp
2 tbsp	peanut oil	2 tbsp
2	onions, finely chopped	2
1	garlic clove, finely chopped	1
5 mm	cube *blachan*, chopped	¼ inch
100 g	peanuts, roasted and roughly ground	3½ oz
17.5 cl	coconut milk	6 fl oz
4 tbsp	tamarind water, made from a piece of tamarind the size of a hazelnut	4 tbsp
1 tsp	brown sugar	1 tsp
½	lemon, juice strained	½
	salt	

Thread the cubes of meat on to skewers about 15 cm (6 inches) long, leaving about 7.5 cm (3 inches) at the holding end. Grill the meat over a charcoal fire or under the grill, basting occasionally with the oil.

To make the sauce, grind the coriander, fennel, cumin and chili powder in a blender. Heat the oil in a saucepan and fry the onions, garlic, *blachan* and ground spices until they are well cooked and aromatic. Add the ground peanuts and coconut milk, tamarind water and sugar and stir well. Allow to simmer for 10 minutes and, just before serving, stir in the lemon juice and salt to taste.

ROSEMARY BRISSENDEN
SOUTH EAST ASIAN FOOD

Courtesan's Sardines

Sardines à la Courtisane

The technique of preparing duxelles *is shown on page 9.*

Just before serving this dish, surround the sardines with a crown of little potato croquettes.

To serve 4

12	sardines, boned	12
175 g	*duxelles*	6 oz
10 cl	white wine	3½ fl oz
	salt and pepper	
60 g	butter	2 oz
4	slices firm white bread, each cut into 3 pieces the same size and shape as the sardines	4
125 g	spinach, boiled in salted water for 2 minutes, drained and puréed	4 oz
20 cl	fish velouté sauce (*page 162*), reduced to the consistency of thick cream	7 fl oz
40 g	Cheddar or Gruyère cheese, grated	1½ oz

Spread the sardines out on a board, skin side down. Put a tablespoonful of the *duxelles* on each, and fold the sardines over. Then arrange the filled sardines on a buttered fireproof dish, sprinkle them with the wine, and season with salt and pepper. Bring the liquid gently to the boil and poach the sardines for 10 minutes or until they are cooked through.

Melt the butter in a frying pan and fry the bread pieces in it over a high heat until they are nicely browned. Set them to drain on kitchen paper.

Arrange the fried bread croûtons on a dish. Put a sardine on each one. Mix the spinach purée into the velouté sauce and pour the sauce over the sardines. Dredge with the cheese and place under a hot grill to melt and brown the cheese topping.

A. CAILLAT
150 MANIÈRES D'ACCOMODER LES SARDINES

Sardines with Leeks and Mussels

Sardines à la Cettoise

The technique of cooking mussels is shown on page 10.

To serve 4

12	sardines, filleted, each fillet rolled up tightly	12
2	leeks, sliced into *julienne*	2
2	sticks celery, sliced into *julienne*	2
125 g	ceps, thinly sliced	4 oz
60 g	butter	2 oz
60 cl	mussels, cooked, removed from their shells, cooking liquid reserved	1 pint
	salt and pepper	
1	angler-fish liver, mashed	1
	cayenne pepper	
1	lemon, juice strained	1
2 tbsp	chopped chervil	2 tbsp

Put the leeks, celery and ceps in a pan with the butter and cook over a low heat for 10 minutes or until the vegetables are soft. Moisten with the cooking liquid from the mussels.

Arrange the sardines on the vegetable mixture, season, cover with a piece of buttered paper and cook in a preheated 180°C (350°F or Mark 4) oven for 20 minutes. When the sardines are cooked, remove them from the pan and arrange them in a ring on a serving dish. Add the mussels to the vegetable mixture, bring to the boil and thicken by stirring in the angler-fish liver. Season with a pinch of cayenne pepper and the lemon juice. Strain out the vegetables and put them in the centre of the ring of sardines, coat the sardines with the remaining sauce and sprinkle chervil over all.

A. CAILLAT
150 MANIÈRES D'ACCOMODER LES SARDINES

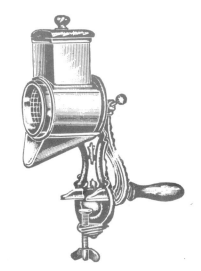

Cod in Garlic and Pepper Sauce

Rumesco

If Spanish dried romesco peppers are not available, substitute dried red chili peppers.

To serve 4

1 kg	salt cod, cut into serving pieces and soaked for 36 hours to desalt it	2 to 2½ lb
2	slices white bread	2
6	garlic cloves	6
¼ litre	olive oil	8 fl oz
4	dried *romesco* peppers, soaked in hot water for 2 hours	4
1	sweet pepper, grilled, peeled, seeded and chopped	1
2	tomatoes, skinned, seeded and chopped	2
30 g	blanched almonds	1 oz
1 tbsp	flour	1 tbsp

Fry the bread and garlic in the oil until golden. When they are fried, pound them in a mortar with the dried peppers, sweet pepper and tomatoes. Add the almonds and continue to pound all the ingredients to a paste. Thin the paste down with 8 cl (3 fl oz) of water and put it into a casserole with the cod and the flour. Cook gently for a minute or two, then stir in ½ litre (16 fl oz) of water and simmer for 15 minutes.

COCINA REGIONAL ESPAÑOLA

Cod with Green Sauce

Småtorsk med Gronn Saus

To serve 6

1	small cod, cleaned, head and fins removed	1
1.5 litres	fish fumet (*page 159*)	2½ pints
30 g	butter	1 oz
3 tbsp	flour	3 tbsp
4	tomatoes, skinned, seeded and chopped	4
2	hard-boiled eggs, chopped	2
1 tbsp	chopped dill	1 tbsp
1 tbsp	chopped chives	1 tbsp
	salt and pepper	
45 g	cheese, grated	1½ oz

Poach the fish whole in the fish fumet for 20 minutes or until tender. Remove the fish to an ovenproof dish. Melt the butter in a saucepan, add the flour and cook it gently for a few minutes. Whisk in 60 cl (1 pint) of the fish fumet, bring the sauce to the boil and leave it to cook gently for 2 minutes. Stir in the tomatoes, the hard-boiled eggs and the herbs. Season with salt and pepper.

Pour the sauce over the fish, sprinkle it with the grated cheese and cook it in a preheated 190°C (375°F or Mark 5) oven for 5 to 6 minutes to allow the flavours in the juices to mingle together to make a delicious dish.

HROAR DEGE
FRA NEPTUNS GAFFEL

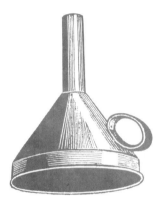

Chicken Turbot with Leeks

Turbotin aux Poireaux

Chicken turbot is the name given to small turbot weighing about 1 to 1.5 kg (2 to 3 lb). Use the head and trimmings from the fish to prepare the fumet.

	To serve 4	
850 g	chicken turbot, skinned, filleted and cut into small strips of equal size	1¾ lb
6	small leeks, cut into 2 cm (¾ inch) pieces	6
About ¾ litre	fish fumet (*page 159*)	About 1¼ pints
	salt and pepper	
3 tbsp	*crème fraîche* or double cream	3 tbsp
	sugar	
2 tbsp	dry French vermouth	2 tbsp

Arrange the leeks in a shallow pan and cover them with the fish fumet. Season and cook, covered, over a gentle heat, for 15 minutes, until cooked but still firm. Do not overcook. Drain the leeks, reserving the cooking liquid. Distribute them among four individual dishes and keep them hot.

Put 4 tablespoons of the fish fumet in a small sauté pan with the *crème fraîche* or double cream, a pinch of sugar, pepper and the vermouth. Poach the fish in this sauce for 5 to 6 seconds. Arrange the fish pieces on the leeks.

Reduce the sauce in which the fish cooked until it is thick

enough to coat the back of a spoon, then add the reserved cooking liquid from the leeks. Pour the sauce over the fish and leeks and serve immediately.

JEAN AND PAUL MINCHELLI
CRUSTACÉS, POISSONS ET COQUILLAGES

Trout with Leeks

Truites aux Poireaux

	To serve 6	
6	trout, cleaned, split down the back to within 1 cm (½ inch) of either end of the spine, spine broken and removed	6
3	large leeks, white parts only	3
4	shallots, finely chopped	4
¼ litre	dry white wine	8 fl oz
200 g	butter	7 oz
3 tbsp	cream	3 tbsp
	salt and pepper	
	Stuffing	
3	whiting, skinned and filleted	3
3	egg yolks	3
3 tbsp	double cream	3 tbsp
1	small onion, finely chopped	1
	grated nutmeg	
30 g	butter	1 oz

First prepare the stuffing. Pound the whiting fillets in a mortar, add the egg yolks, cream, onion and a pinch of nutmeg, and mix well. Melt the butter and gently heat the stuffing in it. Stuff the bellies of the trout.

Blanch the leeks in boiling salted water for 15 minutes. Separate the leaves, select the tender inner ones and wrap them, in ribbon fashion, round each of the trout.

Make a bed of the shallots on the bottom of a shallow pan or ovenproof dish. Pour in the wine and place the trout on top of the shallots. Cover with a piece of buttered greaseproof paper and poach in a preheated 180°C (350°F or Mark 4) oven for 15 minutes or until tender. Remove the trout and arrange them on a hot, heatproof serving dish. Pour the juice from the pan into a saucepan and reduce it quickly until there is about 8 cl (3 fl oz) of liquid left. Remove from the heat and whisk in the butter and cream, a little at a time. Adjust the seasoning. Pour the sauce over the fish and brown under a preheated grill. Be careful that the sauce does not get so hot as to boil, otherwise it will separate.

ALEXANDER WATT
PARIS BISTRO COOKERY

Burbot in Leek, Coriander and Saffron Sauce

Lotte aux Blancs de Poireaux,
Coriandre Frais et Safran

The burbot can be replaced by any white fish of your choice, the leeks by cucumbers, the coriander by fresh mint leaves and the sauce flavoured with curry powder instead of saffron.

To serve 4

600 g	burbot, cleaned, cut into 4 equal pieces and trimmed	1¼ lb
2	sprigs fresh coriander, leaves plucked	2
	powdered saffron	
10 g	butter	⅓ oz
2	medium-sized shallots, finely chopped	2
30 g	mushrooms, finely chopped	1 oz
	salt and pepper	
15 cl	dry white wine	¼ pint
200 g	leeks, white parts only, or 4 leeks, each abo : 12 cm (4½ inches) long, cut lengthwise into 4 cm (1½ inch) sections	7 oz
35 cl	*crème fraîche* or double cream	12 fl oz

Put the coriander leaves in a heavy pan with a pinch of saffron and set the pan aside.

Melt the butter in a large, wide, ovenproof pan over moderate heat; add the shallots, stirring them well with a wooden spoon. Cook the shallots for about 1 minute without letting them colour. Stir in the mushrooms. Season the fish slices on both sides, then place them on top of the shallot and mushroom mixture, making sure that the slices do not overlap. Sprinkle over the wine; bring to the boil and put the pan into a preheated 220°C (425°F or Mark 7) oven for 6 minutes.

Pour 1 litre (1¾ pints) of water into a pan, add 1 teaspoon of salt and bring to the boil over a high heat. Plunge in the leeks and cook them for 5 minutes, keeping the water at a gentle boil. Remove the leeks from the pan and leave them to drain on kitchen paper.

Take the pan out of the oven and place the fish on kitchen paper to drain. Reduce the liquid in which the fish was cooked over a high heat until there are only about 2 tablespoons left. Whisk in the cream, then bring the mixture to the boil. Lower the heat and leave the sauce for several minutes to thicken to a smooth, creamy consistency. Season with salt and pepper.

Tip the leeks into the pan containing the coriander and saffron; set a very fine-meshed sieve over this pan and strain the sauce into it, pushing the sauce through with a wooden spoon. Place the pan on the heat and simmer the sauce gently for 3 to 4 minutes, or until it has thickened slightly.

Place a slice of fish on each of four heated plates and put the plates in the oven, leaving the oven door slightly ajar, until the sauce is cooked. Coat each piece of fish with the sauce and arrange the leek slices round the fish. Serve immediately.

ALAIN AND EVENTHIA SENDERENS
LA CUISINE RÉUSSIE

Salmon in Basil Sauce

Escalope de Saumon au Basilic

Salmon roe is available, canned, from delicatessens. Escalopes are slices cut from the filleted tail piece of a salmon.

This sauce must be served on ovenproof plates at room temperature so that it does not separate. Since the salmon is so easy to overcook, watch it carefully during the cooking.

To serve 6

18	salmon escalopes, each weighing about 60 g (2 oz)	18
150 g	butter cut into 10 equal pieces	5 oz
3	shallots, sliced	3
2	mushrooms, sliced	2
½ litre	dry white wine	16 fl oz
60 g	basil, 30 g (1 oz) sliced	2 oz
½ litre	fish fumet (*page 159*)	16 fl oz
½ litre	double cream	16 fl oz
	salt (optional)	
	salmon roe (optional)	

Melt two of the pieces of butter in a saucepan. Add the shallots and mushrooms and sweat over a low heat for 10 minutes. Add the wine and sliced basil. Reduce the liquid by half over a moderate heat. Add the fish fumet and again reduce by half. Pour in the cream and continue to reduce the sauce, over a medium heat, until it has thickened. (It will coat a spoon rather heavily.) Strain the sauce into a clean saucepan.

In a blender or food processor, purée the remaining basil (saving a few nice leaves for a garnish) with 12.5 cl (4 fl oz) of the sauce. Whisk the purée into the remaining sauce and, over a low heat, whisk in the remaining pieces of butter, one at a time. Season with salt if necessary. Strain and reserve.

Cover the bottom of each plate with sauce. Place the salmon escalopes on top of the sauce and cook in a preheated 230°C (450°F or Mark 8) oven or under the grill for 1 minute, or until just cooked. Garnish each plate with fresh basil leaves or salmon roe and serve immediately.

WOLFGANG PUCK
WOLFGANG PUCK'S MODERN FRENCH COOKING FOR THE
AMERICAN KITCHEN

John Dory with Red Wine

Saint-Pierre au Vin Rouge

If John Dory is unavailable, red snapper and sea bass are suitable substitutes.

To serve 6

Three 1 kg	John Dory, skinned and filleted, bones reserved	Three 2 to 2½ lb
3	shallots, sliced	3
30 g	parsley, leaves finely chopped, stems reserved	1 oz
1	stick celery, sliced	1
3	leeks (white part only), 1 sliced in rounds, 2 cut into *julienne*	3
½ tsp	black peppercorns	½ tsp
½ litre	dry red wine	16 fl oz
175 g	butter	6 oz
½ litre	double cream	16 fl oz
12	large white mushrooms, very finely sliced, sprinkled with lemon juice	12
	salt and pepper	
	lemon juice	

Prepare a fish fumet using the reserved fish bones, shallots, parsley stems, celery, sliced leek, peppercorns and wine, with enough water to cover. Bring to the boil and simmer for 20 minutes. Strain and set aside.

To make leek ragout, sauté the leek *julienne* in 15 g (½ oz) of the butter until wilted. Add half the cream and reduce over a medium heat until the ragout has thickened, about 5 minutes. Reserve and keep warm.

Sauté the mushrooms lightly in 15 g (½ oz) of the butter. Reserve and keep warm.

Reduce the fish fumet to ¼ litre (8 fl oz) by boiling it over a medium heat. Add the remaining cream and continue to reduce the sauce until it is thick enough to coat the back of a spoon. Whisk in 125 g (4 oz) of the butter, a small piece at a time. Season to taste with salt, pepper and lemon juice. Strain the sauce and keep it warm.

Heat a heavy sauté pan and melt the remaining butter. Season the fish fillets with salt and pepper. Sauté the fillets slowly over a low heat until they feel springy to the touch.

To serve, place a spoonful of the leek ragout in the centre of each warmed dinner plate. Cover the ragout with a fish fillet. Cover each fillet with sauce, top with the mushrooms and sprinkle lightly with the chopped parsley leaves.

WOLFGANG PUCK
WOLFGANG PUCK'S MODERN FRENCH COOKING FOR THE
AMERICAN KITCHEN

Fillets of John Dory in White Wine Sauce with Tomatoes

Filets de Saint-Pierre sans Nom

The technique of making a savoury sabayon is on page 64.

To serve 4

Two 1.5 kg	John Dory, skinned and filleted	Two 3 lb
	salt and freshly ground pepper	
12.5 cl	dry white wine	4 fl oz
4 tbsp	fish fumet (*page 159*)	4 tbsp
1	lemon, juice strained	1
5 tbsp	French dry vermouth	5 tbsp
2	egg yolks	2
1 tbsp	finely chopped chives	1 tbsp
	cayenne pepper	
30 cl	tomato purée (*page 164*), well seasoned	½ pint

Take an ovenproof dish large enough to contain the fish fillets and butter it. Season the fillets with salt and pepper and place them in the dish. Add 4 tablespoons of the wine and the fish fumet and sprinkle on 2 tablespoons of the lemon juice. Cover with buttered greaseproof paper, bring the liquid to the boil, then poach the fish in a preheated 200°C (400°F or Mark 6) oven for 3 to 4 minutes, until it is just tender. Remove the fish fillets from the dish and keep them warm.

Reduce the fish fumet a little and strain it. Add the vermouth and the remaining white wine and reduce the liquid to half its original volume. Allow it to cool a little, then stir in the egg yolks. Put the mixture in the top of a double boiler over gently simmering water and whisk it until it is very stiff, like a sabayon. Flavour the sauce with lemon juice to taste, stir in the chives and season well with salt, pepper and cayenne pepper.

Arrange the hot tomato purée on a plate. Place the fillets on top and cover them with the sauce. Serve immediately.

ANTON MOSIMANN
CUISINE À LA CARTE

Lucien's Mussels

Moules, Façon Lucien

The technique of preparing mussels is shown on page 10.

To serve 4

2.25 litres	mussels, scrubbed	4 pints
1	onion, finely chopped	1
1	shallot, finely chopped	1
6	stalks parsley, finely chopped	6
12.5 cl	dry white wine	4 fl oz
1 tbsp	double cream	1 tbsp
3	tomatoes, skinned, seeded and coarsely chopped	3
20 cl	hollandaise sauce *(page 165)*	7 fl oz
1	lemon, juice strained	1
	freshly ground pepper	
1 tbsp	*fines herbes* (use a mixture of parsley, chives, chervil and tarragon)	1 tbsp

Place the mussels in a stew-pan. Add the onion, shallot, parsley stalks and wine. Cover the pan tightly and put it on a high heat. After 2 minutes, shake the pan vigorously. Do this three more times during the cooking of the mussels, which should take only 5 to 6 minutes in all. The mussels should then be cooked and their shells wide open. Lift the mussels out of the stew-pan and keep them hot.

Pass the cooking juices through a fine-meshed sieve. Rinse out the stew-pan and return the juices to it; heat and pour in the cream. Bring the liquid to the boil gently, whisk and allow to reduce by half. Heat the tomatoes in a small pan to evaporate their water, then add them to the reduced liquid in the stew-pan. Remove the pan from the heat and pour in the hollandaise sauce. Reheat, but be careful the sauce does not approach boiling point, otherwise it will separate. Add the lemon juice and a pinch of pepper.

Remove the upper shell from each of the mussels and place the mussels flat on four hot plates. Pour the sauce over the mussels and sprinkle with the *fines herbes*. Serve at once.

ALEXANDER WATT
PARIS BISTRO COOKERY

Mussel and Courgette Gratin

Gratin de Moules aux Courgettes

To serve 6

2 litres	mussels, scrubbed	3½ pints
1 kg	courgettes, cut into 2 mm (⅛ inch) slices	2 to 2½ lb
1	bay leaf	1
5 tbsp	groundnut oil	5 tbsp
	salt and pepper	
15 g	butter	½ oz
1 tbsp	flour	1 tbsp
2	egg yolks	2
2 tbsp	*crème fraîche* or double cream	2 tbsp
75 g	Gruyère cheese, grated	2½ oz

Place a large, heavy-bottomed casserole over a high heat and tip in the cleaned mussels. Add the bay leaf and cover the casserole. After about 5 minutes, steam will start to pour out from under the lid of the casserole, indicating that the mussels have opened. Place a large sieve over a large mixing bowl and strain the mussels into this. In this way, you can drain the mussels without losing any of their liquor, which you will need to make the sauce.

Heat the groundnut oil in a large frying pan over a high heat. When the oil is hot, add the sliced courgettes and a little salt and pepper. Cook them for about 6 minutes, turning them from time to time with a skimmer. Meanwhile, take the mussels from their shells and reserve them on a plate.

When the courgettes are cooked, take them from the pan with the skimmer and drain them of as much oil as possible. Distribute them evenly over the bottom of a shallow gratin dish. Scatter the mussels over the bed of courgettes.

Melt the butter in a small saucepan over a gentle heat. When it begins to foam, add the flour, stir it in and leave to cook for 1 minute. Then add the mussels' cooking liquor and a little salt and pepper to taste. Turn the heat to high and whisk the mixture continuously for about 3 minutes, until the sauce thickens. Take the pan from the heat.

Place the egg yolks in a bowl and add the *crème fraîche* or double cream. Mix them together and then pour this mixture into the thickened sauce, whisking all the time.

Pour the sauce evenly over the mussels in the gratin dish, then sprinkle the grated cheese over the top. Cook the dish in a preheated 240°C (475°F or Mark 9) oven for 5 minutes, then place it under a hot grill for a further 5 minutes to form an even, crisp crust over the dish.

MICHEL OLIVER
MES RECETTES À LA TÉLÉ

Mussels in Fennel Sauce

Cassolette de Moules au Fenouil

To serve 4

2.25 litres	mussels, scrubbed	4 pints
90 g	butter, softened	3 oz
1 tbsp	finely chopped shallots	1 tbsp
20 cl	dry white wine	7 fl oz
100 g	fennel, finely sliced	3½ oz
10 cl	court-bouillon (*page 159*)	3½ fl oz
30 cl	double cream	½ pint
	salt and freshly ground pepper	
	cayenne pepper	
1 tbsp	finely chopped chives	1 tbsp
1 tbsp	finely chopped fennel leaves	1 tbsp

Melt 30 g (1 oz) of the butter in a large pan and sweat the finely chopped shallots in it. Add the mussels. Add the white wine, fennel and court-bouillon, cover the pan and bring the liquid to the boil. Cook, shaking the pan from time to time, for 3 to 5 minutes until all the mussel shells have opened. Strain off the liquid into another pan and reduce it over a gentle heat to half its original volume.

Meanwhile, take the mussels out of their shells, remove and discard the beards and keep the mussels warm. Add the cream to the reduced cooking liquid and let the sauce reduce further until it becomes smooth and thick. Take the sauce from the heat and gradually whisk in the remaining butter. Return the mussels to the sauce and season with salt, pepper and cayenne pepper to taste. Add the chopped chives and fennel leaves. Arrange the mussels in their sauce on a serving dish and serve immediately.

ANTON MOSIMANN
CUISINE À LA CARTE

Prawns Poached in Coconut Milk with Fresh Herbs

Yerra Moolee

To make coconut milk, pour ¾ litre (1¼ pints) of scalded milk or boiling water over the grated flesh of a coconut and leave to soak for 1 hour. Strain through muslin, then bring the edges of the muslin together and squeeze out all the liquid from the coconut flesh before discarding it. Use the resulting coconut milk as required.

This dish comes from Kerala, a state on the south-western coast of India. It can be made to taste much hotter by increasing the quantity of green chili peppers. The dish may be prepared a day ahead, refrigerated and reheated just before serving. However, it is not suitable for freezing.

	To serve 6	
1 kg	prawns, peeled and washed thoroughly	2 to 2½ lb
10 cl	light vegetable oil	3½ fl oz
200 g	onions, finely chopped	7 oz
2	garlic cloves, finely chopped	2
1½ tbsp	ground ginger or 10 cm (4 inch) fresh ginger root, finely chopped and crushed	1½ tbsp
About 2	green chili peppers, seeded and finely chopped	About 2
¼ tsp	turmeric	¼ tsp
2 tbsp	ground coriander	2 tbsp
About ¾ litre	coconut milk	About 1¼ pints
1½ tsp	coarse salt	1½ tsp
2 tbsp	finely chopped fresh coriander leaves or 1 tbsp dried coriander leaves	2 tbsp

Heat the oil in a large heavy-bottomed pan and add the onions. Fry the onions over a high heat until they turn golden-brown (about 10 minutes), stirring constantly to prevent them burning. Reduce the heat to medium, add the garlic, ginger and chili peppers to taste and fry for an additional 2 minutes. Add the turmeric and ground coriander, stir rapidly for 15 seconds and add the coconut milk and salt. Cook the sauce, uncovered, for about 10 minutes until it thickens, stirring frequently to ensure that it does not stick or burn.

Add the prawns, mix, reduce the heat to low and simmer, covered, for 5 to 7 minutes or until the prawns are cooked through. Do not overcook the prawns or they will become tough and chewy. Check the seasoning, stir in the coriander leaves and serve.

JULIE SAHNI
CLASSIC INDIAN COOKING

Dublin Bay Prawns with Herbs and Crayfish Sauce

Grosses Langoustines de Petits Bateaux aux Herbes à Soupe en Civet

The soup herbs might include a little garden cress or purslane, some leaves from celery sticks, parsley, a young nettle top, some new leek leaves—anything you might pick, while going round your garden, to put into the day's soup.

To serve 4

24	very large Dublin Bay prawns	24
½ litre	white wine court-bouillon (*page 159*)	16 fl oz
1	orange, rind grated	1
30 g	aniseeds or fennel seeds	1 oz
	pepper	
15 cl	*sauce bâtarde* (*page 166*)	5 fl oz
30 g	assorted soup herbs	1 oz
1	garlic clove, unpeeled	1
100 g	butter	3½ oz
125 g	pork back fat, sliced into strips and blanched	4 oz
	Crayfish sauce	
300 g	crayfish, shelled and roughly chopped	10 oz
50 g	butter	2 oz
50 g	celery, finely diced	2 oz
60 g	carrots, finely diced	2 oz
120 g	shallots, finely diced	4 oz
1	garlic clove	1
50 g	mushrooms, finely diced	2 oz
20 g	parsley, finely chopped	⅔ oz
3 tbsp	*fine champagne*	3 tbsp
1 litre	red wine, cooked over a medium heat until reduced by half	1¾ pints
½ tsp	peppercorns, coarsely crushed	½ tsp
	salt	
1 tsp	reduced fish fumet (*page 159*)	1 tsp

To make the sauce, quickly fry the crayfish in 20 g (⅔ oz) of the butter until they colour, about 3 minutes. Sweat the vegetables and parsley in the same pan over a gentle heat for 7 minutes, deglaze the pan with the *fine champagne* and add the reduced red wine. Season with the crushed peppercorns and salt to taste, and add the reduced fish fumet. Strain the sauce through a fine-meshed conical sieve and reduce over a gentle heat until only 8 tablespoons remain. Whisk in the remaining butter, a little at a time.

To cook the prawns, bring the court-bouillon to the boil in a large, round, flat-based pan, with the orange rind and the aniseeds or fennel seeds. Season well with pepper. Throw in as many of the prawns as will fit in the pan in a single layer. Keep the liquid at a brisk boil and cook the prawns for 3 minutes. Take the cooked prawns from the pan and cook the next batch of prawns. Continue until all the prawns are cooked. Shell the tails and keep them hot in the *sauce bâtarde* mixed with a few spoonfuls of the court-bouillon.

Cook the soup herbs and the garlic in the butter in a sauté pan over a high heat to dry them well.

In a small frying pan, cook the strips of pork fat until they colour. Arrange the herbs on a dish, place the prawn tails in the centre and encircle them with the crayfish sauce. Sprinkle the prawns with the *sauce bâtarde* and strew the pork fat strips over them.

ALAIN CHAPEL
LA CUISINE C'EST BEAUCOUP PLUS QUE DES RECETTES

Cardoons with Beef Marrow Sauce

Cardons à la Moelle

If cardoons are not available, fennel or celery can be substituted. The technique of extracting bone marrow from beef shin bones and poaching the marrow is shown on page 11.

To serve 4

1 kg	cardoons, trimmed and cooked in boiling salted water for 40 to 50 minutes	2 to 2½ lb
100 g	beef marrow, poached and sliced	3½ oz
30 g	butter	1 oz
1 tbsp	flour	1 tbsp
4 tbsp	*glace de viande* (*page 158*) or jellied roasting juices	4 tbsp
About ½ litre	stock (*page 158*)	About 16 fl oz
1 tbsp	lemon juice	1 tbsp
	salt and pepper	
	chopped parsley	

Melt the butter in a saucepan, stir in the flour and then the *glace de viande* or roasting juices and enough stock to make a light sauce. Start on the liquid side and then boil it down steadily. Add the lemon juice and then the marrow to reheat. Check the seasoning and stir in a little chopped parsley.

Put the cardoons into a hot serving dish, pour over the sauce and serve immediately.

JANE GRIGSON
JANE GRIGSON'S VEGETABLE BOOK

add the mushrooms and stir so that they do not stick. Add salt and the chopped parsley.

When all the liquid that the mushrooms give out has evaporated, moisten them with the white wine. Continue cooking the mushrooms, adding the broth, a little at a time. When only 2 tablespoons of broth remain, stir this into the flour, then add this paste to the mushrooms and leave them to cook for about 1 hour.

Boil the macaroni in salted water for 10 to 15 minutes, then drain. Season with salt and pepper, add the Parmesan cheese and toss. Put the macaroni into a serving dish and place the curls of butter here and there.

Remove the garlic cloves from the mushroom sauce and serve the sauce with the macaroni.

GIUSEPPE OBEROSLER
IL TESORETTO DELLA CUCINA ITALIANA

Macaroni with Mushrooms

Maccheroni coi Funghi

Dried boletus mushrooms, also known as ceps or by their Italian name, porcini, *can be bought at delicatessens and specialist grocers' shops.*

To serve 4

350 g	macaroni	12 oz
	salt and pepper	
30 g	Parmesan cheese, finely grated	1 oz
8	butter curls	8
	Mushroom sauce	
125 g	dried boletus mushrooms, soaked in tepid water for 1 hour, then drained	4 oz
4 tbsp	olive oil	4 tbsp
40 g	butter	1½ oz
3	garlic cloves	3
1	small onion, chopped	1
	salt	
6 tbsp	chopped parsley	6 tbsp
5 tbsp	white wine	5 tbsp
About 17.5 cl	chicken broth (*page 159*)	About 6 fl oz
2 tsp	flour	2 tsp

Clean the mushrooms in two or three changes of water, removing the "spines" that are under the cap if they are green and soft. If the "spines" are firm, leave them. Cut the mushrooms into small pieces or thin slices.

Put a casserole over a medium heat and put in the olive oil, butter, garlic and chopped onion. When they begin to colour,

Spaghetti with Tomato Sauce

Spaghetti all'Amatriciana

Pecorino *is an Italian cheese made from ewe's milk. If it is not available, use Parmesan cheese instead.*

To serve 4

300 g	spaghetti, boiled in plenty of salted water for 7 to 10 minutes and drained	10 oz
500 g	tomatoes, skinned, seeded and coarsely chopped	1 lb
1	garlic clove	1
15 g	lard	½ oz
1	onion, finely chopped	1
100 g	lean green bacon, cut into cubes	3½ oz
10 cl	dry white wine	3½ fl oz
	salt	
	chili powder	
30 g	*pecorino* cheese, grated	1 oz

Fry the garlic in the lard. When it is golden, remove and discard it and add the onion and bacon to the pan. Then add the wine. Cook until the liquid is reduced by half, about 3 minutes, then add the tomatoes, season with salt and chili powder, and heat through. Mix the sauce with the spaghetti and sprinkle with the cheese before serving.

FRANCA FESLIKENIAN
CUCINA E VINI DEL LAZIO

Artichoke Bottom Soufflés

Fonds d'Artichauts Soufflés

The technique of preparing artichoke bottoms for cooking is demonstrated on page 78.

To serve 12

24	artichoke bottoms	24
30 cl	veal stock (*page 158*)	½ pint
30 cl	double cream	½ pint
	salt	
300 g	butter	10 oz
12	egg yolks, lightly beaten	12
400 g	Parmesan cheese, grated	14 oz
10 g	Gruyère cheese, grated	⅓ oz
	sugar	
10	egg whites, very stiffly beaten	10

Butter a sauté pan and place the artichoke bottoms in it. Cover the pan and put it over a very gentle heat. Leave the artichokes to cook for 15 minutes, then pour over them the veal stock and the double cream. Season with a little salt, and leave the pan over the heat so that the sauce reduces and envelopes the artichokes in a creamy coating . This will take about 15 minutes.

Meanwhile, melt the butter in a fireproof earthenware casserole. When the butter is hot, stir in the beaten egg yolks, a little at a time. Cook the eggs for a few seconds only, over a gentle heat, just so that they thicken slightly, then remove the casserole from the heat and stir in the grated cheeses and a pinch of sugar. Heat the mixture gently, watching it all the time. As soon as the cheese has melted and the mixture has become a delicious paste, remove it from the heat and fold in the beaten egg whites gently.

Remove the artichoke bottoms from the sauce in the sauté pan and place them on a round, flat, ovenproof dish. Transfer the cheese soufflé mixture to a piping bag with a plain nozzle and pipe a large blob of the mixture into each artichoke bottom. Bake the artichokes in a preheated 200°C (400°F or Mark 6) oven for 20 minutes or until the soufflés are risen and golden-brown. Serve them as soon as they come out of the oven, accompanied by the sauce in which the artichokes were cooked, which will be creamy and coloured light brown.

ÉDOUARD NIGNON
ÉLOGES DE LA CUISINE FRANÇAISE

Dessert Sauces

Merton Sauce

To make 35 cl (12 fl oz)

125 g	butter	4 oz
125 g	sugar	4 oz
8 cl	sherry	3 fl oz
8 cl	brandy	3 fl oz

Work the butter with a wooden spoon to a cream, adding first the sugar and then the sherry and the brandy by degrees.

MASSEY AND SON'S COMPREHENSIVE PUDDING BOOK

Apricot Butter with Rum

The author suggests that this sauce could be substituted for brandy butter, which is traditionally served with Christmas pudding and mince pies. The apricot butter can be kept for up to one month in the refrigerator.

To make about 500 g (1 lb)

90 g	dried apricots, cut into eighths with scissors	3 oz
250 g	butter, softened	8 oz
1 tbsp	rum	1 tbsp
30 g	ground almonds	1 oz
½	lemon, rind finely grated	½
½ tsp	vanilla extract	½ tsp

Put the apricots in a small bowl, just cover them with water and leave to soak overnight.

Drain the apricots and combine them with all the other ingredients in a small deep bowl or blender. Blend at the lowest speed until a smooth paste is obtained or mash with a fork. Pack the flavoured butter into small pots, cover with plastic wrap or foil and refrigerate.

PATRICIA HOLDEN WHITE
FOOD AS PRESENTS

Sauce for His Serene Highness's Puddings

This is an entry in the author's old family recipe book. She suggests that "His Serene Highness" must have been Prince Edward of Saxe Weimar, a noted gourmet. The sauce can be served with most puddings, especially steamed puddings.

To make 250 g (8 oz)

125 g	butter	4 oz
125 g	icing sugar	4 oz
2 tbsp	brandy	2 tbsp
1 tbsp	sherry	1 tbsp

Beat the butter and sugar together till they are quite white and very light; this takes time. Add the brandy and sherry, very slowly, by degrees, and beat until thoroughly mixed.

LADY MURIEL BECKWITH
SAUCES, SWEET AND SAVOURY

Moulded Tapioca Pudding, Apricot Sauce

Pudding Moulé au Tapioca, Sauce aux Abricots

The technique for making apricot sauce is demonstrated on page 37. If you wish to serve the pudding hot, heat the sauce until it is warmed through, remove it from the heat and stir in 15 g (½ oz) of butter; alternatively, the author suggests that the hot pudding may be served with a sweet sabayon sauce (recipe, page 166). If the pudding is to be served cold, a raspberry purée can be substituted for the apricot sauce.

To serve 4

125 g	tapioca	4 oz
½ litre	milk	16 fl oz
60 g	sugar	2 oz
	salt	
½	vanilla pod or ½ tsp vanilla extract	½
90 g	butter	3 oz
3	eggs, yolks separated from whites, whites stiffly beaten	3

Apricot sauce

500 g	ripe apricots, halved, stones removed	1 lb
10 cl	Madeira or port (optional)	3½ fl oz
15 cl	sugar syrup (*page 164*)	¼ pint

To make the tapioca pudding, combine the milk, sugar, a small pinch of salt, vanilla and 45 g (1½ oz) of the butter in a casserole, bring to the boil and slowly pour in the tapioca, stirring the while. Stir over direct heat for 1 minute, then put the casserole, covered, into a preheated 150°C (300°F or Mark 2) oven for about 20 minutes. Turn it out into a mixing bowl, remove the vanilla pod, if used, stir in the rest of the butter and the yolks of the eggs. Gently fold in the stiffly beaten whites. Butter a 1 litre (1¾ pint) mould generously and sprinkle the inside lightly with tapioca. Pour the mixture into the mould and poach it in a bain-marie in hot, but not boiling, water in a preheated 170° to 180°C (325° to 350°F or Mark 3 to 4) oven for about 30 minutes or until the centre of the pudding is elastic to the touch. Remove the mould from the hot water and allow the pudding to settle for about 10 minutes before unmoulding it. If the pudding is to be served chilled, leave the mould over it to protect the surface from the air until just before serving.

To make the sauce, put the apricots in a pan with the Madeira or port, if used, and the syrup. Poach them for 5 minutes or until tender. Remove the apricots to a nylon sieve set over a bowl. Reserve the poaching liquid. Rub the apricots through the sieve and discard the skins. If you wish, add a little of the poaching liquid to the sauce to thin it.

Coat the pudding with some of the sauce and send the rest of the sauce to table in a separate dish.

RICHARD OLNEY
THE FRENCH MENU COOKBOOK

Raspberry Sauce

Coulis de Framboises

To ensure that this sauce has a fresh taste, it is very important to use only the freshest and ripest raspberries.

To make ¼ litre (8 fl oz)

250 g	ripe raspberries	8 oz
80 g	castor sugar	2½ oz
1	lemon, juice strained	1
1 tbsp	raspberry liqueur	1 tbsp

Purée the raspberries in a blender. Stir in the sugar. Flavour with the lemon juice and the raspberry liqueur. Strain the purée through a fine nylon sieve to remove the pips.

ANTON MOSIMANN
CUISINE À LA CARTE

Rhubarb Sauce

Rhabarber-Sauce

This sauce is served with puddings and sweet dumplings.

To make ¾ litre (1¼ pints)

500 g	rhubarb, cut into 5 cm (2 inch) lengths	1 lb
¼ litre	water	8 fl oz
2 tbsp	potato flour	2 tbsp
30 cl	sweet white wine	½ pint
60 g	currants	2 oz
5 cm	stick cinnamon	2 inch
2	strips thinly pared lemon rind	2
About 125 g	sugar	About 4 oz

Boil the rhubarb in 10 cl (3½ fl oz) of the water for about 20 minutes, until it is soft. Press it through a sieve. Whisk the potato flour with 15 cl (¼ pint) of the white wine, stir this into the rhubarb purée and add the remaining wine. Bring the mixture gently to the boil and simmer for 5 minutes, stirring continuously until it thickens.

Meanwhile, boil the currants with the cinnamon and lemon rind in the rest of the water for 10 minutes or until the currants are plump. Remove the cinnamon and lemon rind, and add the currants, with their cooking liquid, to the rhubarb mixture. Add sugar to taste.

LOUISE RICHTER AND SOPHIE CHARLOTTE HOMMER
ILLUSTRIRTES HAMBURGER KOCHBUCH

Apricot Jam Sauce

To make ½ litre (16 fl oz)

500 g	apricot jam	1 lb
1	lemon, juice strained	1
20 cl	sherry	7 fl oz
2 tbsp	sugar syrup (*page 164*)	2 tbsp

Pass the jam through a sieve. Add the lemon juice, sherry and syrup. Make the sauce hot and serve.

MASSEY AND SON'S COMPREHENSIVE PUDDING BOOK

Cherry Sauce in the French Style

Sauce de Cerise à la Française

This is served hot with hot desserts and cold, flavoured with a little kirsch, to accompany cold desserts. If you use black cherries, substitute red wine for white and vanilla for the cinnamon and lemon rind.

To make ½ litre (16 fl oz)

500 g	red cherries, stoned	1 lb
15 cl	water	¼ pint
8 cl	white wine	3 fl oz
60 g	sugar	2 oz
½ tsp	ground cinnamon	½ tsp
½	lemon, rind grated	½

Cook the cherries with the water, wine, sugar, cinnamon and lemon rind for about 15 minutes. When they are soft, press them through a very fine sieve into another pan, and continue to cook the purée until it has a thick consistency and a perfect flavour, about 10 more minutes.

JOSEPH FAVRE
DICTIONNAIRE UNIVERSEL DE CUISINE PRATIQUE

Butterscotch Ice Cream Sauce

The technique of making butterscotch ice cream sauce is demonstrated on page 38.

To make about ¼ litre (8 fl oz)

230 g	soft brown sugar	7½ oz
2½ tbsp	liquid glucose	2½ tbsp
4 tbsp	water	4 tbsp
75 g	butter	2½ oz
5 tbsp	double cream	5 tbsp
	salt (optional)	
½ tsp	vanilla extract (optional)	½ tsp

Combine the brown sugar, liquid glucose, water and butter in a saucepan. Bring to the boil over a medium heat and cook, stirring occasionally, until the soft-ball stage is reached—112° to 116°C (234° to 240°F) on a sugar thermometer. This takes about 4 minutes. Remove the pan from the heat and let the mixture cool slightly.

Add the cream and also a pinch of salt and the vanilla, if used. Mix well. Serve warm or cold.

ELISE W. MANNING (EDITOR)
HOMEMADE ICE CREAM AND CAKE

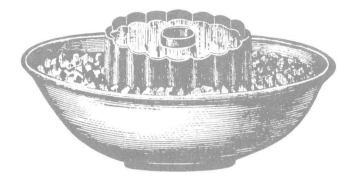

Vanilla Cream

Crème à la Vanille

To make about 1.4 litres (2¼ pints)

1	vanilla pod	1
1 litre	milk	1¾ pints
125 g	sugar	4 oz
4	eggs	4
5	egg yolks	5

Bring the milk to the boil with the sugar and the vanilla pod, then cover it and leave it to cool. Remove the vanilla pod.

Beat together the eggs and the egg yolks and stir in the milk. Put the mixture in a saucepan over a very low heat or in a bain-marie and cook it, stirring vigorously. When the custard is thick enough to coat the spoon, strain it through a fine-meshed sieve into a large bowl and leave it to get cold.

ALFRED CONTOUR
LE CUISINIER BOURGUIGNON

Foamy Vanilla Sauce

Sauce Mousseuse à la Vanille

To make 45 cl (¾ pint)

½	vanilla pod	½
125 g	sugar	4 oz
10 cl	water	3½ fl oz
7	egg yolks, lightly beaten	7
	double cream, whipped	

Dissolve the sugar in the water over a low heat, then bring to the boil and cook the syrup for 1 minute. Add the half vanilla pod and set the syrup aside for 20 minutes to allow the flavour of the vanilla to infuse.

Remove the vanilla pod from the syrup and pour the syrup

on to the egg yolks, stirring. Strain the egg and syrup mixture into a pan. Place the pan over a very low heat and whisk the mixture until it is very thick and frothy. Take the pan from the heat and continue to whisk the mixture while it cools. When it is cold, fold in several spoonfuls of whipped cream.

URBAIN DUBOIS AND ÉMILE BERNARD
LA CUISINE CLASSIQUE

Aniseed Cream Sauce

Sauce Crème à l'Anisette

This sauce is served with cold or frozen desserts. By replacing the aniseeds with cumin or ginger, coffee extract, a vanilla pod, strawberry or raspberry purée, rose-water, crushed crystallized violets, grated chocolate, etc., and proceeding in the same way as directed here, you can obtain infinite variations on this exquisite cream.

To flavour it with a fruit purée, add the purée at the same time as the cream, when the preparation is on the ice. You can also, more economically, omit the egg yolks and instead mix 2 tablespoons of cornflour with 2 tablespoons of water and add this to the milk with the sugar and the flavouring. Bring to the boil to thicken the sauce. When the sauce is thick, colour it, if you wish, cool it and add the cream.

To make ¾ litre (1¼ pints)

2 tsp	aniseeds	2 tsp
¼ litre	double cream, whipped	8 fl oz
½ litre	milk	16 fl oz
60 g	sugar	2 oz
8	egg yolks, lightly beaten	8
10 cl	kirsch	3½ fl oz

Simmer the milk, sugar and aniseeds together for 10 minutes. Pour the boiling mixture on to the egg yolks, a little at a time, whisking all the time. Then place the sauce over a gentle heat and continue to whisk the mixture until it thickens. Do not let it boil. Press the custard through a sieve, then add the kirsch. Set the pan on ice and stir the custard until it is cool. Lastly, fold in the whipped cream.

JOSEPH FAVRE
DICTIONNAIRE UNIVERSEL DE CUISINE PRATIQUE

Peach Leaf Custard

Creme à la Feuille de Pêcher

Scented geranium leaves can be substituted for peach leaves.

	To make 1 litre (1¾ pints)	
6	peach leaves	6
¾ litre	milk	1¼ pints
5	egg yolks	5
250 g	castor sugar	8 oz
	cornflour	

Bring the milk to the boil with the peach leaves, then set it aside to infuse for 15 minutes. In a large bowl, beat together the egg yolks and the sugar vigorously until the mixture is very pale and light. Stir in a pinch of cornflour.

Bring the milk to the boil again, then pour it on to the egg and sugar mixture, a little at a time, stirring all the time. Return the mixture to the saucepan and place it over a gentle heat. Cook the custard, stirring it all the time with a wooden spoon. As soon as the custard reaches boiling point and thickens, take the pan from the heat. Remove the peach leaves and leave the custard to cool.

ANNICK MARIE
LE GRAND LIVRE DE LA CUISINE BOURGUIGNONNE

Foamy Sauce

	To make about ½ litre (16 fl oz)	
125 g	butter, at room temperature	4 oz
150 g	icing sugar	5 oz
1	egg, well beaten	1
2 tbsp	brandy or sherry	2 tbsp
12.5 cl	double cream, whipped	4 fl oz

Cream the butter and gradually add the sugar. Add the beaten egg. Place the mixture in the top part of a double boiler over boiling water and add the brandy or sherry. Beat constantly with a whisk until the mixture thickens and becomes hot and foamy, about 10 minutes. Remove from the heat and fold in the whipped cream. Place in a serving bowl and serve at once while the sauce is still warm.

JUNE PLATT
JUNE PLATT'S NEW ENGLAND COOK BOOK

Almond Custard

Mandelsauce

	To make ¾ litre (1¼ pints)	
30 g	almonds, including 2 bitter almonds, blanched and chopped	1 oz
1	vanilla pod	1
15 cl	milk	¼ pint
½ litre	double cream	16 fl oz
2 tsp	flour	2 tsp
2 tsp	sugar	2 tsp
3	egg yolks, beaten	3

Cook the chopped almonds slowly with the vanilla pod in the milk for 15 minutes. Pass this through a sieve and stir in the cream, flour and sugar. Cook this sauce, stirring constantly, over a very low heat for about 10 minutes, or until it is very thick, then whisk in the egg yolks and continue to cook for a few minutes more.

HENRIETTE DAVIDIS
PRAKTISCHES KOCHBUCH

Almond Cream Sauce

The egg white in this recipe prevents the almonds from becoming oily when they are pounded.

Serve this sauce as hot as possible with any hot pudding.

	To make about 35 cl (12 fl oz)	
30 g	almonds, blanched	1 oz
6	bitter almonds, blanched	6
12.5 cl	double cream	4 fl oz
2	eggs, yolks separated from whites, whites lightly beaten, yolks well beaten	2
125 g	sugar	4 oz
1 tbsp	orange-flower water	1 tbsp

Pound the almonds in a mortar (or put them twice through a food processor, using the finest blade), adding in turn a little of the egg white, the sugar and the orange-flower water. Put this mixture in a saucepan (or the top of a double boiler).

Mix the beaten egg yolks with the cream. Pour the cream into the almond mixture and beat with a whisk over a very low heat until the mixture is smooth, thick and frothy.

LOUIS P. DE GOUY
THE GOLD COOK BOOK

Chocolate Cream

Crème au Chocolat

To make about 1.5 litres (2½ pints)

45 g	chocolate	1½ oz
4 tbsp	water	4 tbsp
1 litre	milk	1¾ pints
125 g	sugar	4 oz
4	eggs	4
5	egg yolks	5

Melt the chocolate in the water over a very gentle heat, stirring all the time. Stir in the milk and sugar, bring the mixture to the boil, then leave it to cool.

Beat together the eggs and the egg yolks, then pour in the chocolate-flavoured milk. Put the mixture in a saucepan over a very low heat or in a bain-marie and cook it, stirring vigorously as it thickens. When the custard is thick enough to coat the spoon, strain it through a fine-meshed sieve into a large bowl and leave it to cool.

ALFRED CONTOUR
LE CUISINIER BOURGUIGNON

Tea Sauce

To make ½ litre (16 fl oz)

10 cl	strong black tea	3½ fl oz
3 tbsp	brandy	3 tbsp
	sugar	
	Custard	
4	egg yolks	4
2 tbsp	milk	2 tbsp
30 cl	double cream	½ pint

First prepare the custard. Mix the egg yolks with the milk. Stir the cream over a gentle heat until it boils. Off the heat, quickly stir in the egg mixture.

Pour the tea and brandy into a bowl and stir in the custard. Sweeten to taste with sugar.

MASSEY AND SON'S COMPREHENSIVE PUDDING BOOK

Standard Preparations

Vinaigrette

The proportion of vinegar to oil may be varied according to the strength of the vinegar or the tartness of the food to be sauced, but one part vinegar to four or five parts oil is a good ratio. If desired, lemon juice may be substituted for the vinegar.

To make about 15 cl (¼ pint)

1 tsp	salt	1 tsp
¼ tsp	freshly ground pepper	¼ tsp
2 tbsp	wine vinegar	2 tbsp
12.5 cl	olive oil	4 fl oz

Put the salt and pepper into a small bowl. Add the vinegar and stir until the salt has dissolved. Then stir in the olive oil.

Garlic vinaigrette: Pound half a garlic clove to a purée with the salt and pepper before adding the vinegar.

Green vinaigrette: Soak, fillet, rinse and dry two salt anchovies and pound them in a mortar with a garlic clove, 1 teaspoon of coarse salt and some freshly ground pepper. When the mixture is a smooth paste, stir in the vinegar, then about 10 cl (3½ fl oz) of oil. Stir in 2 tablespoons of parboiled, squeezed and finely chopped or puréed spinach, together with 1 tablespoon of chopped capers and 2 tablespoons of chopped mixed parsley, chives, tarragon, basil and chervil.

Mustard vinaigrette: Mix 1 teaspoon (more or less to taste, and depending on the food to be sauced) of Dijon mustard with the salt and pepper. Add the vinegar and stir until the mustard is dissolved before adding the oil.

Ravigote: Make 15 cl (¼ pint) of vinaigrette. Stir in 1 tablespoon of chopped capers, 1 tablespoon of finely chopped onion and 2 tablespoons of finely chopped mixed chives, parsley, chervil and tarragon. (See also page 162.)

Tomato vinaigrette: Peel and halve one large, ripe tomato; squeeze out the seeds and water and press the flesh through a sieve. Stir together the salt and pepper and vinegar, then mix in the puréed tomato. Gradually stir in 15 cl (¼ pint) of olive oil. If tomatoes are not in season, use puréed canned tomatoes.

Vinaigrette with egg: Before adding the oil, stir in the yolk of a soft-boiled egg. The cooked part of the egg white may be chopped and added to the prepared vinaigrette. *Fines herbes* and chopped shallot may also be added to taste.

Other variations: Any vinaigrette may be combined with chopped fresh herbs (such as parsley, *fines herbes*, basil, mint, majoram or hyssop), capers, chopped shallots or finely sliced gherkins. Alternatively, the juice from roasted sweet peppers or, if the dressing is to be used for a meat salad, 1 to 2 tablespoons of degreased roasting juices may be added.

Lemon and Cream Sauce

To flavour the sauce with mint, lightly crush six to eight mint leaves and macerate them in the lemon juice for 15 minutes.

To make about 35 cl (12 fl oz)

1	large lemon, juice strained	1
30 cl	double cream	½ pint
	salt and pepper	

Put salt and pepper to taste in a bowl and pour the strained lemon juice on them. Stir until the salt has dissolved. Pour in the cream in a thin stream, stirring all the time, until the sauce has thickened. Serve at once.

Red pepper and cream sauce: Dissolve salt and pepper to taste in the juice of half a lemon, then stir in 2 to 3 tablespoons of sweet red pepper purée (*page 9*). Gradually pour in about 30 cl (½ pint) of single cream, stirring all the time, until the sauce has the consistency and colour required.

Veal Stock

A very gelatinous stock which is suitable for use in *chaud-froid* sauce (*recipe, page 163*) or as aspic can be made by adding two split, blanched calf's feet to the ingredients. The finished stock should be reduced briefly after cleansing so that it sets to a firm jelly.

Chicken stock can be made by adding another 1 kg (2 to 2½ lb) of chicken carcasses, necks, feet, wings, gizzards and hearts to the quantity given below. To make game stock, add 1 kg (2 to 2½ lb) of game carcasses and trimmings to the veal stock ingredients. For lamb or pork stock, use 3 kg (7 lb) of meaty bones and trimmings of the appropriate meat instead of the veal, beef and chicken; lamb and pork stock are only used in dishes made with their respective meats.

To make about 3 litres (5 pints)

1 kg	shin of veal, including meaty veal knuckle	2 to 2½ lb
1 kg	shin or leg of beef	2 to 2½ lb
1 kg	chicken backs, necks and wing tips	2 to 2½ lb
About 5 litres	water	About 9 pints
1	bouquet garni, including leek and celery	1
1	garlic head	1
2	onions, 1 stuck with 2 cloves	2
4	large carrots	4
	salt	

Place a round wire rack in the bottom of a large stock-pot to prevent the ingredients from sticking. Fit all the meat, bones and chicken pieces into the pot and add enough water to cover

them by about 4 cm (1½ inches). Bring very slowly to the boil, using a spoon to skim off the scum that rises. Keep skimming, occasionally adding a glass of cold water to retard the boil, until no more scum rises—10 to 15 minutes. Add the bouquet garni, garlic, onions, carrots and a little salt, and skim once more as the liquid returns to the boil. Reduce the heat to very low, cover the pot with the lid ajar and simmer for at least 5 and preferably 7 hours. From time to time, skim off any fat that rises to the surface.

Strain the stock into a large bowl, then strain it again through a colander lined with dampened muslin. Leave the stock to cool, then refrigerate it. When the stock has set to a jelly, scrape off the solid layer of fat and discard it. Remove any remaining traces of fat by pressing a kitchen towel gently on to the surface of the stock.

Glace de viande: Prepare veal stock as above, but do not add salt to it. When it has been cleansed of all fat, put it into a saucepan just large enough to hold it and bring to the boil. Set the pan half off the heat and let the stock boil gently. From time to time, skim off the skin of impurities that collects on the cooler side of the pan. When the stock has reduced by about a third, after 1 hour or somewhat longer, strain it through a fine-meshed sieve into a smaller pan; continue to simmer the stock gently, skimming occasionally, for another hour or so, when it will again have reduced by about a third. Strain it again into a smaller pan and let it reduce for another hour. The liquid will now be thick and syrupy. Pour it into a bowl, leave it to cool, then refrigerate it. It will keep in the refrigerator almost indefinitely.

Coulis

To make about ¾ litre (1¼ pints)

2 tbsp	olive oil	2 tbsp
2 kg	boned shin of veal	4 lb
1	Parma ham knuckle	1
2	carrots, coarsely chopped	2
2	onions, coarsely chopped	2
30 cl	white wine	½ pint
About 2 litres	veal stock (*left*)	About 3½ pints
1	bouquet garni	1

Heat the olive oil in a heavy pan just large enough to hold all the meats. Add the meats and vegetables. Cook, covered, over a low heat, turning occasionally, for about 45 minutes, or until the juices exuded from the meats have evaporated and their deposits have caramelized. Pour in about half the wine and scrape the pan vigorously with a spatula so that the deposits dissolve in the liquid. Turn up the heat and evaporate the liquid completely. When the juices start to caramelize again, pour in the rest of the wine, deglaze the pan again and once more reduce the liquid completely.

Add enough veal stock to cover the meats and vegetables. Bring to a simmer and skim off the scum that rises to the surface. When no more scum rises, add the bouquet garni. Cover the pan with the lid slightly ajar and cook very gently for about 4 hours.

Remove the pieces of meat from the pan. Take out the bouquet garni, place it in a sieve and press out all the juices from it. Then strain the *coulis* through the sieve and press out all the juices from the vegetables.

Place the strained *coulis* in a pan and simmer gently, half off the heat. Occasionally remove the skin of impurities that collects on the cooler side of the pan. After about 1 hour or more, when the liquid has reduced by about half, remove the pan from the heat and pour the *coulis* through a very fine-meshed sieve into a bowl. Allow the *coulis* to cool, stirring it continuously to prevent a skin forming, then refrigerate.

Beef Broth

Broth is the liquid left over from poaching meats for a meal. It is less concentrated and less gelatinous than stock.

A chicken may be poached in the same way as beef. Use a 2.5 to 3 kg (5 to 7 lb) boiling fowl instead of the beef and cook it for 1 to $2\frac{1}{2}$ hours, depending on its age.

To make about 2.5 litres (4½ pints)

1 kg	shin or leg of beef	2 to 2½ lb
1 kg	plate or short ribs of beef	2 to 2½ lb
About 3 litres	water	About 5½ pints
300 g	carrots	10 oz
1	large onion, stuck with 3 cloves	1
1	large head of garlic	1
1	bouquet garni	1
	salt	

Place a wire rack in the bottom of a stock-pot to prevent the ingredients from sticking. Tie the meat into compact shapes with string. Fit all the meat into the pot and cover with water. Bring very slowly to the boil; it should take about 1 hour for the water to reach boiling point. With a skimming spoon, carefully lift off the surface scum as the liquid comes to the boil. Add the carrots, onion, garlic, bouquet garni and salt, and skim once more as the broth returns to the boil.

Turn the heat down, cover the pot with the lid ajar, and leave to simmer undisturbed for 3 to 3½ hours. Remove the beef from the pot, slice and serve.

Strain the broth through a colander lined with dampened muslin. Degrease thoroughly with kitchen paper, or allow the broth to cool completely and then remove the solidified fat from the top with a spoon.

Court-Bouillon

This is a general-purpose poaching liquid for most fish and shellfish. The amount of wine can be increased or decreased according to taste. For poaching crayfish, 2 sprigs of dill should be included instead of fennel

To make about 2 litres (3½ pints)

1 each	large onion, carrot and leek, sliced	1 each
1	stick celery, diced	1
60 g	parsley	2 oz
2	sprigs thyme	2
2	stalks fennel (optional)	2
1	garlic clove (optional)	1
1	bay leaf	1
1½ litres	water	2½ pints
	salt	
½ litre	red or white wine	16 fl oz
5 or 6	peppercorns	5 or 6

Put the vegetables, herbs and water into a large pan, and season with a pinch of salt. Bring to the boil, then lower the heat, cover and simmer for about 15 minutes. Pour in the wine and simmer for a further 15 minutes, adding the peppercorns for the last few minutes of cooking.

Fish Fumet

To make about 2 litres (3½ pints)

1 kg	fish heads, bones and trimmings, rinsed and broken into convenient pieces	2 to 2½ lb
1 each	onion, carrot and leek, sliced	1 each
1	stick celery, cut into pieces	1
1	bay leaf	1
2	sprigs thyme	2
2	sprigs parsley	2
½ litre	red or white wine	16 fl oz
About 2 litres	water	About 3½ pints
	salt	

Place the fish, vegetables and herbs in a large pan. Add the wine and enough water to cover the fish and season lightly with salt. Bring to the boil over a low heat. With a large shallow spoon, skim off the scum that rises to the surface as the liquid reaches a simmer. Keep skimming until no more scum rises, then cover and simmer for about 30 minutes. Strain through a colander lined with dampened muslin.

White Sauce

This recipe can be used whenever béchamel sauce is required. If the sauce is finished with cream, it is often known as *sauce crème* (cream sauce).

To make about 30 cl (½ pint)

30 g	butter	1 oz
2 tbsp	flour	2 tbsp
60 cl	milk	1 pint
	salt and pepper	
	grated nutmeg (optional)	
Up to 30 cl	double cream	Up to ½ pint

Melt the butter in a heavy saucepan. Stir in the flour and cook, stirring, over a low heat for 2 to 3 minutes. Pour in all the milk, whisking constantly to blend the mixture smoothly. Increase the heat and continue whisking while the sauce comes to the boil. Season with a very little salt. Reduce the heat and simmer for at least 45 minutes, stirring every so often to prevent the sauce from sticking to the bottom of the pan. Strain the sauce into another pan, set it over a low heat and whisk in enough double cream to give the required consistency. Add pepper and a pinch of nutmeg if desired.

Bohémienne: Make 15 cl (¼ pint) of stiff white sauce and stir until cold. Whisk in two egg yolks and 2 tablespoons of tarragon vinegar. Season with salt and pepper to taste. Whisk in 15 cl (¼ pint) of olive oil in a light trickle, as for mayonnaise. Finish with more tarragon vinegar to taste.

Cardinal: Make 30 cl (½ pint) of white sauce. Add 10 cl (3½ fl oz) of fish fumet (*recipe, page 159*) and 2 to 3 tablespoons of liquid from preserved truffles. Boil until the sauce has reduced to about three-quarters of its original volume. Off the heat, stir in 2 tablespoons of double cream, 30 cl (1 oz) of lobster butter and a little cayenne pepper. Serve this sauce with lobster, fish and shellfish.

Mornay: Make 60 cl (1 pint) of white sauce and stir in about 20 cl (7 fl oz) of cream. Add about 30 g (1 oz) each of grated Gruyère and Parmesan cheese, stirring until the cheese has melted. Finish, off the heat, with 30 g (1 oz) of butter, added in fragments. Serve with fish and cooked vegetables. If the sauce is to be used for a gratin, it should be thinner than usual and the butter may be omitted.

Nantua: Make 30 cl (½ pint) of white sauce and stir in 10 cl (3½ fl oz) of cream. Off the heat, stir in 40 g (1½ oz) of crayfish

butter (*recipe, page 163*) and, if you like, a garnish of crayfish tails. Serve with poached white fish, or use the sauce to make a gratin of crayfish tails.

Soubise: Make 30 cl (½ pint) of white sauce and about 30 cl (½ pint) of onion purée (*page 34*). Combine the white sauce and the onion purée. Reheat and stir in 10 cl (3½ fl oz) of cream. Serve this sauce with lamb.

Brown Sauce

Brown sauce is also known as *demi-glace*. With the addition of a little tomato purée (*recipe, page 164*), it becomes *sauce espagnole*, but plain brown sauce may be used in any recipe that calls for *sauce espagnole*.

If water rather than stock is used to moisten the meats, add a little salt, bearing in mind that the final sauce will be much reduced and concentrated.

Brown game sauce is made by substituting the bones and trimmings from game birds, rabbit, hare and venison for the beef and veal, and using either game stock or veal stock. About 10 cl (3½ fl oz) of wine vinegar can be used with the white wine for deglazing, and 4 or 5 juniper berries can be added.

To make about 60 cl (1 pint)

500 g	shin of beef, cubed	1 lb
1	veal knuckle bone, broken up	1
1 kg	lean veal, cubed	2 to 2½ lb
500 g	chicken wing tips, backs and necks	1 lb
1	sheet pork rind, 20 by 15 cm (8 by 6 inches), parboiled for 2 to 3 minutes, refreshed in cold water, drained and coarsely chopped	1
2 each	carrots, leeks and onions, coarsely chopped	2 each
1	stick celery, coarsely chopped	1
4 or 5	garlic cloves, crushed	4 or 5
2	sprigs thyme	2
1	bay leaf	1
About 4 tbsp	olive oil	About 4 tbsp
4 tbsp	flour	4 tbsp
75 cl	dry white wine	1¼ pints
About 2 litres	veal stock (*page 158*) or water	About 3½ pints
	salt	

In a large, shallow roasting pan, distribute the meats, chopped vegetables, garlic and herbs. Toss all the ingredients in the olive oil so that they are evenly coated with oil. Cook in a preheated 230°C (450°F or Mark 8) oven for about 30 minutes, until the meats are well and evenly browned, stirring them thoroughly about half way through the cooking time. Sprinkle in the flour, stir with a spatula, and return the pan to the oven for about 10 minutes to brown the flour.

Set the pan on a medium heat. Pour in the white wine and scrape the caramelized deposits on the bottom of the pan to dissolve them in the wine. Cook rapidly for about 10 minutes until most of the liquid has evaporated.

Transfer the contents of the pan to a large stock-pot and cover completely with veal stock. Partially cover the pot, bring to the boil, then simmer very gently for at least 3 hours, preferably 5 to 6 hours.

Ladle the meats into a sieve set over a deep bowl. Pick out and discard the bones. Using a wooden pestle, press out the juices from the meat, then strain the cooking liquid through the sieve. Let the sauce cool a little, then remove excess fat from the surface.

Pour the sauce, a ladleful at a time, through a very fine-meshed *chinois* into a saucepan. Set the pan to one side of a medium heat and let the sauce simmer and reduce for about 1 hour. From time to time, skim off the skin that forms on the cooler side of the pan. Towards the end of the cooking time, taste and add salt as required.

Bordelaise: Add 60 cl (1 pint) of red wine reduction (*page 10*) to the prepared brown sauce. Simmer over a medium heat until the sauce has reduced to about a third of its original volume. Stir in 1 tablespoon of *glace de viande* (*recipe, page 158*) and a little lemon juice.

Moelle: Add 125 g (4 oz) of poached bone marrow dice (*page 11*) to 60 cl (1 pint) of *bordelaise*. Alternatively, make a sauce in the same way as the *bordelaise*, using a white wine reduction. Add a little chopped parsley, if you like. This sauce is traditionally served with grilled beef.

Chasseur: Finely chop 125 g (4 oz) of mushrooms and fry them in 15 g (½ oz) of butter until golden. Add 1 tablespoon of chopped shallots, one or two skinned, seeded and chopped tomatoes and 30 cl (½ pint) of white wine, and simmer until the liquid has reduced by about half. Add 30 cl (½ pint) of brown sauce and return to the boil. Garnish with 1 teaspoon of chopped parsley. This sauce is usually served with sautés of chicken, rabbit or veal; you can add the pan deglazing juices to the sauce. Stews containing the same ingredients are also called *chasseur*.

Chateaubriand: Place 30 g (1 oz) of chopped shallots, a sprig of thyme, a bay leaf, 30 g (1 oz) of finely chopped mushrooms and 15 cl (¼ pint) of white wine in a pan and simmer until the liquid is reduced by two-thirds. Add 30 cl (½ pint) of brown sauce. Sieve and return to the boil. Off heat, swirl in 60 g (2 oz) of butter, cut into fragments, and a little tarragon and chopped parsley. This sauce can also be made using 30 cl (½ pint) of velouté (*recipe, page 162*) instead of brown sauce; it is usually served with grilled beef.

Lyonnaise: Cook 60 g (2 oz) of finely sliced onion in 15 g (½ oz) of butter until soft and yellowed. Add 15 cl (¼ pint) of white wine and 15 cl of wine vinegar, and simmer until the liquid has reduced by two-thirds. Add 60 cl (1 pint) of brown sauce and reheat. This sauce is usually served with grilled meats.

Madère: Boil 60 cl (1 pint) of brown sauce rapidly, stirring all the time, until it has reduced by about a quarter. Add 2 to 3 tablespoons of Madeira, or enough Madeira to bring it back to its original consistency. This sauce is served with braised ham and boiled tongue. Parboiled calf's head is sometimes braised in *sauce madère*.

Périgueux: Add 1 tablespoon of liquid from preserved truffles to 45 cl (¾ pint) of *sauce madère*. Garnish with 90 g (3 oz) of truffle dice (*page 11*). This sauce is sometimes known as *périgourdine* when the garnish is truffle slices; it is usually served with grilled beef.

Poivrade ordinaire: Prepare a brown sauce, substituting red wine vinegar for 10 cl (3½ fl oz) of the wine. After the sauce has been reduced, tie 10 crushed black peppercorns in a piece of muslin and drop them into the sauce. Cook for a further 5 to 10 minutes, then strain and serve.

Poivrade for venison or hare: Prepare in the same way as *poivrade ordinaire*, using a brown game sauce.

Chevreuil: Make in the same way as a *sauce bordelaise* (*left*), substituting game *poivrade* for brown sauce. Finish with a little cayenne pepper.

Diane: Make 60 cl (1 pint) of *poivrade* for venison or hare and finish it by stirring in 15 cl (¼ pint) of double cream (or more, to taste).

Grand-veneur: Make 60 cl (1 pint) of *poivrade* for venison or hare. Melt 1 tablespoon of redcurrant jelly over a low heat with a few drops of water and stir in 15 cl (¼ pint) of double cream. Stir this into the sauce, off the heat. This sauce is usually served with roast or grilled venison or hare.

Romaine: Cook 2 tablespoons of sugar until it caramelizes. Add 4 tablespoons of vinegar and stir until the caramel has dissolved. Add 60 cl (1 pint) of brown game sauce or *poivrade*. Cook until the liquid has reduced by about a quarter. Garnish with 2 tablespoons each of grilled pine-nuts, plumped sultanas and plumped currants. This sauce is usually served with roast or grilled venison.

Zingara: Mix 30 cl (½ pint) of tomato purée (*recipe, page 164*) with 60 cl (1 pint) of brown sauce. Add 2 tablespoons of Madeira and a little cayenne pepper. Garnish the sauce with 30 g (1 oz) each of mushrooms, ham and tongue, cut into *julienne*, and a small truffle also cut into *julienne*. This sauce is usually served with grilled chicken or veal.

Velouté Sauce

For a very fine and concentrated velouté, the sauce should be left to simmer very gently and reduce for several hours, with occasional skimming. For this, however, you will need to prepare the sauce with three times the quantities of ingredients given here to produce 60 cl (1 pint) of finished velouté.

To make about 60 cl (1 pint)

60 g	butter	2 oz
4 tbsp	flour	4 tbsp
1.25 litres	veal, chicken or game stock (*page 158*) or fish fumet (*page 159*)	2 pints
	double cream	

Melt the butter in a heavy saucepan over a low heat. With a whisk, stir in the flour to make a roux and cook, stirring, for a minute or two. Pour the stock or fumet into the pan, whisking constantly. Raise the heat and continue to whisk until the sauce comes to the boil. Reduce the heat to low and move the saucepan half off the heat so that the liquid simmers on only one side of the pan. A skin of impurities will form on the surface of the still side. Remove this skin periodically with a spoon. Cook the sauce for at least 45 minutes to reduce it and to eliminate the taste of flour. Stir in enough cream to give the required consistency.

Aurore: Make 60 cl (1 pint) of creamed velouté using veal or chicken stock or fish fumet. Add 10 cl ($3\frac{1}{2}$ fl oz) of very red tomato purée (*recipe, page 164*). Remove the pan from the heat and stir in 60 g (2 oz) of butter. This sauce is served with vegetables, chicken or fish. (See also *suprême.*)

Bercy: Make 60 cl (1 pint) of velouté using fish fumet. Toss 30 g (1 oz) of chopped shallots in butter and add 30 cl ($\frac{1}{2}$ pint) of white wine. Boil until the liquid has reduced to about a third of its original volume. Mix the reduced liquid with the fish velouté and reduce the sauce to a coating consistency. Off the heat, stir in a little lemon juice, 60 g (2 oz) of butter and some chopped parsley. This sauce is served with poached fish.

Marinière: Make 60 cl (1 pint) of *bercy.* Poach mussels (*page 10*) and add 15 cl ($\frac{1}{4}$ pint) of their cooking liquid to the sauce. Reduce the sauce to its original quantity and then garnish with the mussels.

Bonnefoy: Make 60 cl (1 pint) of velouté using veal stock. Boil 30 cl ($\frac{1}{2}$ pint) of white wine with 60 g (2 oz) of chopped shallots until only a little liquid remains. Mix the reduction with the velouté and simmer for a further 20 minutes. Sieve, reheat, then garnish with a little chopped parsley and tarragon. This sauce is served with fish and white meats.

Bretonne: Make 60 cl (1 pint) of velouté using fish fumet. Cut 30 g (1 oz) each of leeks, celery, spring onions and mushrooms into *julienne,* then gently sweat them in butter until they are soft. Mix the *julienne* with the fish velouté. This sauce is served with poached fish.

Chivry: This sauce is served with poached chicken. Make 60 cl (1 pint) of velouté using part of the chicken's poaching liquid. Put 4 tablespoons of coarsely chopped *fines herbes* and a pinch of young burnet, if available, into 30 cl ($\frac{1}{2}$ pint) of white wine. Cover and leave to infuse for at least 10 minutes. Strain, then mix the liquid with the chicken velouté. Reduce the sauce to three-quarters of its original volume. Off the heat, stir in 60 g (2 oz) of herb butter (*recipe, opposite page*).

Normande: This sauce, sometimes known as *sauce vin blanc,* usually accompanies sole poached in fish fumet and mushroom cooking liquid. The poaching liquid is added to the sauce and, classically, the dish is garnished with poached oysters and mussels, mushrooms and prawn tails and, often, sliced truffles, trussed crayfish and sometimes deep-fried smelts. The poaching liquid of the garnishes is often added to the sauce, and it may be finished with crayfish or other flavoured butters. A simpler garnish of mushrooms and mussels alone will suit today's tastes better. Any delicately flavoured fish can be prepared in this way—turbot or brill, for instance.

Make 60 cl (1 pint) of velouté with fish fumet. Add the fish's poaching liquid and 10 cl ($3\frac{1}{2}$ fl oz) of mussel cooking liquid. Reduce the sauce to its original consistency. Mix 2 tablespoons of the velouté with four egg yolks and 3 tablespoons of double cream, then stir this mixture into the velouté. Cook over a gentle heat, stirring continuously, until the sauce begins to thicken. Off the heat, stir in 60 g (2 oz) of butter.

Poulette: This sauce—also known as *allemande, blanquette* and thickened velouté—is made in the same way as *sauce normande,* except that the velouté is based on veal stock or poaching liquid from the meats to be sauced. If mushrooms are included in the sauce's garnish, their cooking liquid is added to the sauce.

Make 60 cl (1 pint) of velouté using veal or chicken stock. Mix 2 to 3 tablespoons of the velouté with four egg yolks, 3 tablespoons of cream and the strained juice of half a lemon. Off the heat, stir this mixture into the velouté. Return the pan to a low heat and stir until the sauce is lightly thickened, but do not let it approach the boil. Off the heat, stir in 60 g (2 oz) of butter to finish the sauce.

Ravigote: Make 60 cl (1 pint) of velouté using veal stock. Mix 15 cl ($\frac{1}{4}$ pint) of white wine with a couple of tablespoons of white wine vinegar. Boil the wine and vinegar mixture until it is about half its original volume. Add this liquid to the velouté. Off the heat, stir in 30 g (1 oz) of shallot butter prepared in the same way as herb butter (*recipe, opposite page*), and a little chopped chervil, tarragon and chives. This sauce is served with white meats. (See also page 157.)

Suprême: This sauce accompanies poached chicken and the chicken's poaching liquid is used to make the sauce. The richest sauce is made by poaching the chicken in veal stock, but in home kitchens it is often poached in water or a simple chicken broth (*recipe, page 159*). If mushrooms garnish the dish, their cooking liquid is added to the sauce. The sauce can be finished with herb or other flavoured butter.

Make 60 cl (1 pint) velouté with some of the chicken's poaching liquid. A little at a time, add 20 cl (7 fl oz) of double cream, reducing the sauce over a fairly high heat. Pass the sauce through a fine-meshed sieve and, off the heat, stir in 2 to 3 more tablespoons of cream and 30 g (1 oz) of butter.

Aurore: Add about 10 cl (3½ fl oz) of tomato purée (*recipe, page 164*) to the finished *sauce suprême* to give a pink colour.

Hongroise: Sweat one chopped onion seasoned with a large pinch of paprika in butter until it is soft but not coloured. Add 8 cl (3 fl oz) of white wine and a small bouquet garni. Boil until the liquid has reduced to about a third of its original volume, then add it to the finished *sauce suprême*. Simmer gently, skimming, for about 10 minutes, then strain.

Ivoire: Stir 2 tablespoons of *glace de viande* (*recipe, page 158*) into the finished *sauce suprême*. If this sauce is finished with sweet red pepper butter or if a sweet red pepper purée is added, it becomes *sauce albufera*.

Vénitienne: Make 60 cl (1 pint) of velouté using fish fumet. Boil 1 tablespoon of chopped shallots with 15 cl (¼ pint) of tarragon vinegar and white wine, mixed in equal proportions, until only a little liquid remains. Strain the reduction and add the liquid to the velouté. Off the heat, stir in 60 g (2 oz) of herb butter (*recipe, page 163*) and a little chopped chervil and tarragon. This sauce is served with poached fish.

White Chaud-Froid Sauce

To make a brown *chaud-froid* sauce, substitute brown sauce (*recipe, page 160*) for the double cream. Red *chaud-froid* sauce is made by stirring enough tomato purée (*recipe, page 164*) or sweet red pepper purée (*page 9*) into the finished white sauce to give the depth of colour required. A yellow sauce can be made by adding powdered saffron dissolved in a little hot water, and a green sauce is made by adding finely puréed, parboiled, squeezed spinach.

To make about 55 cl (18 fl oz)

60 cl	velouté sauce (*opposite page*)	1 pint
¼ litre	reduced, gelatinous veal stock (*page 158*) or 2 tbsp *glace de viande* (*page 158*) or *coulis* (*page 158*)	8 fl oz
20 cl	double cream	7 fl oz

Over a low heat, add the veal stock to the velouté sauce, a spoonful at a time. Cook, stirring, until the sauce has reduced to about 45 cl (¾ pint). Gradually stir in half the double cream and reduce again, then add the remaining cream and return to the boil. Pour the sauce into a metal bowl and stir over ice until it cools and starts to thicken.

Flavoured Butter

To make about 300 g (10 oz)

250 g	butter	8 oz

Soften the butter to room temperature, or beat it to make it pliable. Using a wooden spoon or a pestle, work it into the prepared flavouring of your choice. Using a flexible scraper, press the butter through a very fine-meshed drum sieve. Use the butter immediately, or cover and refrigerate.

Anchovy butter: Soak and fillet 100 g (3½ oz) of salt anchovies. Rinse and drain them, then pound them to a coarse paste. Add the butter and work it in, then sieve.

Crayfish butter: Poach 250 g (8 oz) of live crayfish in a court-bouillon (*recipe, page 159*) for 5 to 10 minutes, then let them cool in their cooking liquid. Pull off the tail of each crayfish, shell it and reserve the tail meat for a garnish or main dish. Place the shells and heads in a mortar and pound them to a creamy paste. Pass this paste through the medium or coarse disc of a food mill to remove fragments of shell, then pass this purée through a fine sieve. Work in the softened butter. Sieve the butter again if necessary.

Herb butter: Remove the stems from 60 g (2 oz) of mixed parsley, chives, tarragon and chervil. Blanch the leaves in boiling water for 1 minute, then drain and press them in a towel to dry. Blanch two finely chopped shallots for 1 minute, then drain and dry in the same way. Place the herbs and the shallots in a mortar and pound them with a little coarse salt to a fine purée. Pound in the butter and sieve.

Bread Sauce

To make the sauce thicker, whisk in more breadcrumbs after removing the onion and seasonings. If a thinner consistency is preferred, add more cream.

To make ½ litre (16 fl oz)

100 g	crustless, day-old white bread, crumbled	3½ oz
60 cl	milk	1 pint
1	onion, stuck with 2 cloves	1
	salt	
1	bay leaf	1
1 or 2	blades mace	1 or 2
15 cl	double cream	¼ pint
30 g	butter, cut into pieces	1 oz

Pour the milk into a saucepan, add the onion, a pinch of salt, the bay leaf and mace and bring the milk to the boil. Stir in the bread and reduce the heat. Simmer the milk over a low heat for about 20 minutes, stirring occasionally. Remove the onion and seasonings with a slotted spoon and whisk the cream into the sauce. Take the pan off the heat and whisk in the butter.

Carrot Sauce

To make 1 litre (1¾ pints)

600 g	carrots, peeled and trimmed, cored and cut into pieces if old	1¼ lb
100 g	butter, 60 g (2 oz) cut into small cubes	3½ oz
About 1 tbsp	sugar	About 1 tbsp
	salt	
About 30 cl	double cream	About ½ pint

Place the carrots in a saucepan with 40 g (1½ oz) of the butter, sugar to taste, a little salt and enough water to cover them half way. Bring the water to the boil, then partially cover the pan and simmer the carrots for 40 to 45 minutes or until they are very tender. Shake the pan occasionally during the cooking time. Remove the lid and reduce the cooking liquid over a high heat until it becomes a thick glaze—5 to 10 minutes.

Purée the carrots and their glaze together in a food processor. Return the purée to the pan and reheat it over a high heat, stirring continuously. Whisk in enough double cream to give the sauce a pouring consistency. Finally, off the heat, whisk in the remaining butter, a little at a time.

Tomato Purée

When fresh ripe tomatoes are not available, use canned Italian plum tomatoes. The sauce can be flavoured with herbs other than those given below; parsley, basil, oregano and marjoram are all suitable substitutes. If summer-ripened garden tomatoes are used, no sugar is necessary.

To make about 30 cl (½ pint)

750 g	very ripe tomatoes, chopped	1½ lb
1	onion, finely chopped	1
2	garlic cloves, chopped	2
1 tbsp	olive oil	1 tbsp
3 or 4	sprigs fresh thyme or 1 tsp dried thyme	3 or 4
1	bay leaf	1
1 to 2 tsp	sugar (optional)	1 to 2 tsp
	salt and freshly ground pepper	

In a large enamelled or tin-lined pan, gently fry the onion and garlic in the oil until they are soft but not brown. Add the other ingredients and simmer gently, uncovered, for about 30 minutes, stirring occasionally with a wooden spoon. When the tomatoes have been reduced to a thick pulp, press the mixture through a sieve, using a wooden pestle.

Return the purée to the pan and cook it, stirring frequently, over a low heat, for about 30 minutes. Season to taste just before serving.

Sugar Syrup

The proportions given below produce a light sugar syrup which is a suitable poaching medium for fruit. To make caramel, reduce the quantity of water to 15 cl (¼ pint) and, when the syrup has come to the boil, continue to cook it rapidly until all the water has evaporated and the syrup turns a rich amber colour. As soon as this happens, place the pan in a bowl of iced water to prevent the caramel from burning.

To make about 1.5 litres (2½ pints)

500 g	sugar	1 lb
1.25 litres	water	2 pints

Place the sugar and water in a saucepan and place the pan over a medium heat. Stir gently until the sugar has dissolved. Brush down the sides of the pan from time to time with a pastry brush dipped in water to dissolve any sugar crystals that may have stuck to the sides. When the sugar has dissolved, stop stirring and increase the heat to bring the syrup to the boil. Boil rapidly for a minute or two.

Beurre Blanc

To make 30 to 45 cl ($\frac{1}{2}$ to $\frac{3}{4}$ pint)

250to400g	cold butter, cut into small cubes	8 to 14 oz
10 cl	dry white wine	3$\frac{1}{2}$ fl oz
10 cl	white wine vinegar	3$\frac{1}{2}$ fl oz
3	shallots, very finely chopped	3
	salt and pepper	

In a heavy stainless steel, enamelled or tin-lined pan, simmer the wine and vinegar with the shallots over a low heat until only enough liquid remains to moisten the shallots. Remove the pan from the heat, season the mixture with salt and pepper, and allow it to cool for a few minutes. Place the pan on a fireproof mat over a very low heat and whisk in the butter cubes, a handful at a time, adding more as the preceding batch begins to disappear. Remove the pan from the heat as soon as all the butter has been incorporated and the sauce has the consistency of single cream.

Hollandaise Sauce

Melted clarified butter can be used instead of solid butter pieces to make a somewhat stiffer sauce. Pour the liquid butter, a small ladleful at a time, into the pan, whisking continually. Do not add more butter until the previous addition has been completely incorporated. If the sauce becomes too thick, thin it by whisking in 1 tablespoon of warm water or a little extra lemon juice.

Olive oil can be used in place of butter, but in this case the sauce cannot be called hollandaise.

To make about 30 cl ($\frac{1}{2}$ pint)

3	egg yolks	3
1 tbsp	cold water	1 tbsp
	salt and pepper	
250 g	cold butter, cut into small cubes	8 oz
1 tbsp	strained lemon juice	1 tbsp

In a large pan, heat some water until it simmers, then reduce the heat to low. Place a saucepan on a trivet inside the larger pan, to make a bain-marie. Put the egg yolks, cold water and a little salt and pepper in the saucepan, and beat until the yolks are smooth. Whisk a handful of butter cubes into the yolks and, as the butter is absorbed, add more until it is all used up. Beat the sauce until it becomes thick and creamy. Finally, whisk in the lemon juice.

Béarnaise: Put 15 cl ($\frac{1}{4}$ pint) of dry white wine, 4 tablespoons of wine vinegar, two finely chopped shallots and 15 g ($\frac{1}{2}$ oz) each of chopped tarragon and chervil into an enamelled or stainless steel saucepan. Boil until only about 2 tablespoons of syrupy liquid remain. Strain the reduction, discard the solids and add three egg yolks. Place the pan in a bain-marie and whisk until the mixture thickens slightly. Add about $\frac{1}{4}$ litre (8 fl oz) of oil, or 250 g (8 oz) of butter, as for hollandaise. Thin with water or lemon juice if necessary. Stir in a teaspoon each of finely chopped tarragon and chervil.

Choron: Make 30 cl ($\frac{1}{2}$ pint) of béarnaise sauce. Stir in 2 tablespoons of coarse tomato purée (*page 30, above*). If preferred, the tarragon and chervil may be omitted.

Foyot: Make 30 cl ($\frac{1}{2}$ pint) of béarnaise sauce. Whisk in 2 tablespoons of melted *glace de viande* (*recipe, page 158*). This sauce, also known as *valois*, is served with grilled beef.

Paloise: Make 30 cl ($\frac{1}{2}$ pint) of béarnaise sauce, using mint in place of the tarragon.

Maltaise: Make 60 cl (1 pint) of hollandaise sauce, mixing the egg yolks with a tablespoon of lemon juice instead of cold water. Instead of the final addition of lemon juice, whisk in the juice of a blood orange.

Noisette: Make 30 cl ($\frac{1}{2}$ pint) of hollandaise sauce. Heat 60 g (2 oz) of butter until it foams and, just as it begins to turn brown, remove it from the heat—it will give off a characteristic hazelnut odour. Leave the melted butter for a while to allow the solids in it to settle, then pour it into a sieve lined with dampened muslin set over a bowl. Discard any solids that cling to the cloth. Stir the strained clarified butter into the hollandaise sauce. This sauce is usually served with boiled fish, especially salmon and trout.

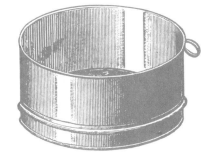

Sauce Bâtarde

This sauce is also known as butter sauce. The egg yolks may be mixed with a tablespoon of cream instead of water.

To make about 60 cl (1 pint)

2	egg yolks	2
1 tbsp	cold water	1 tbsp
250 g	butter	8 oz
3 tbsp	flour	3 tbsp
60 cl	warm water, slightly salted	1 pint
1 tbsp	strained lemon juice	1 tbsp
	salt and pepper	

Put the egg yolks and cold water into a bowl; beat the mixture until it is smooth, then set it aside.

Over a low heat, melt 60 g (2 oz) of the butter in a heavy saucepan, add the flour and stir until the mixture begins to bubble. Add the lightly salted warm water, whisking rapidly until the mixture boils. Remove from the heat, allow the mixture to cool for at least 1 minute, then whisk in the beaten egg yolks. Return the pan to a low heat and whisk until the sauce has thickened slightly. Do not allow it to boil.

Off the heat, pour in the lemon juice, then add the rest of the butter, cut into small cubes, and whisk steadily until it has amalgamated with the sauce. Adjust the seasoning and serve immediately.

Câpres: Make 60 cl (1 pint) of *bâtarde*. Stir in 2 tablespoons of capers. This sauce is usually served with boiled fish.

Sweet Sabayon

15 cl (¼ pint) of lightly whipped double cream or a stiffly beaten egg white can be folded into the sabayon if desired. If a simple dry white wine is used, a little grated lemon rind or a tablespoonful of vanilla sugar may be added for flavour; if a fine wine is used, no other flavouring should be added.

To make about 60 cl (1 pint)

200 g	castor sugar	7 oz
6	egg yolks	6
30 cl	dry white wine, Sauternes, champagne, Marsala or sherry	½ pint

Pour the sugar into a large saucepan and add the egg yolks. Place the pan in a larger pan of water heated to just below simmering point and whisk the egg yolks and sugar together until the sugar has completely dissolved and the mixture is pale and creamy. Pour in the wine, whisking all the time. The mixture will slowly froth up into an abundant mousse, doubling its volume after about 5 minutes. Continue to whisk

for another 5 to 10 minutes or until the sauce is very light and foamy. It is now ready to be served hot. To serve the sauce cold, set the pan in a bowl of ice cubes and continue to whisk the sauce until it is sufficiently chilled.

Savoury Sabayon

To make about 30 cl (½ pint)

30 cl	fish fumet (*page 159*)	½ pint
3	egg yolks	3
175 to 250 g	cold butter, diced	6 to 8 oz

In a small saucepan, boil the fish fumet until it has been reduced to about 5 to 6 tablespoons. Leave it to cool, then add the egg yolks. Place the pan in a larger one containing water at just below simmering point, set over a low heat. Whisk together the egg yolks and fumet and continue whisking for about 10 minutes or until the mixture is thick. Then whisk in the butter cubes, a handful at a time, making sure that each addition is completely incorporated into the sauce before the next is added. When enough butter has been incorporated to make a thick, foamy sauce, transfer it to a warmed sauceboat and serve.

Custard

To make about 60 cl (1 pint)

6	egg yolks	6
60 to 125 g	castor sugar	2 to 4 oz
60 cl	milk, scalded	1 pint

In a bowl, beat the eggs and sugar with a wire whisk until the mixture turns pale and forms a ribbon when dribbled on the surface. Slowly add the hot milk, stirring all the time.

Transfer the mixture to a heavy saucepan. Cook the custard over a very low heat, stirring continually in a figure-of-eight pattern with a wooden spoon. Do not let the custard boil. When the custard is thick enough to coat the back of a spoon, remove the pan from the heat and stand it briefly in a bowl of ice cubes to arrest the cooking. Stir gently so that a skin does not form on the surface.

To keep the custard warm, cover the pan and place it in a warm bain-marie. Strain the custard into a warmed serving bowl or sauceboat to serve.

If the custard is to be served cold, keep the pan on ice and stir the custard occasionally until it is sufficiently chilled. It can be kept, covered, in the refrigerator.

Caramel custard: Whisk about 8 cl (3 fl oz) of caramel sauce (*page 66*) into the prepared custard before serving.

Mayonnaise

To prevent curdling, the egg yolks and oil should be at room temperature and the oil should be added very gradually at first. Mayonnaise will keep for several days in a covered container in a larder or refrigerator. Stir it well before use. One to 2 teaspoons of Dijon mustard may be mixed in with the vinegar or lemon juice.

To make about ½ litre (16 fl oz)

3	egg yolks	3
	salt and pepper	
1 tbsp	wine vinegar or lemon juice	1 tbsp
½ litre	olive oil	16 fl oz

Put the egg yolks in a bowl. Season with salt and pepper and whisk until smooth. Add the vinegar or lemon juice and mix thoroughly. Whisking constantly, add the oil, drop by drop to begin with. When the sauce starts to thicken, pour the remaining oil in a thin, steady stream, whisking rhythmically. If the mayonnaise becomes too thick, thin it with a little more vinegar or lemon juice or warm water.

Andalouse: Make ½ litre (16 fl oz) of mayonnaise. Stir in 2 to 3 tablespoons of very red tomato purée (*recipe, page 164*). Garnish with one sweet red pepper, grilled, seeded, peeled and cut into fine *julienne.*

Chantilly: Make ½ litre (16 fl oz) of mayonnaise using lemon juice. Beat 3 tablespoons of double cream until foamy but not stiff. Fold the cream into the mayonnaise just before serving.

Gribiche: Hard boil five eggs. Remove the yolks and reserve three of the whites. Mash the yolks with one raw yolk and a teaspoon of Dijon mustard to form a smooth paste. Add lemon juice and oil as for plain mayonnaise. Stir in a tablespoon of mixed chopped tarragon, parsley and chervil and a tablespoon of mixed chopped gherkins and capers. Garnish with the reserved egg whites, cut into *julienne.*

Mousquétaire: Make ½ litre (16 fl oz) of mayonnaise. Boil two or three finely chopped shallots in 10 cl (3½ fl oz) of white wine until virtually no liquid remains. Stir the shallots into the mayonnaise. Garnish with a tablespoon of chopped chives and a little cayenne pepper.

Rémoulade: Make ½ litre (16 fl oz) of mayonnaise, adding a tablespoon of mustard. Stir in a large tablespoon each of chopped gherkins and capers, a tablespoon of chopped mixed parsley, chervil and tarragon, and two or three finely chopped anchovy fillets.

Suédoise: Make ½ litre (16 fl oz) of mayonnaise. Stir in 4 tablespoons of unsweetened apple purée and 1 tablespoon of finely grated horseradish. This sauce is served with cold beef.

Tartare (1): Make ½ litre (16 fl oz) of mayonnaise using hard-boiled egg yolks and one raw yolk, as for *gribiche* (*left*). Stir in 60 g (2 oz) finely chopped onion and a tablespoon of chopped chives. This sauce is served with fish.

   Tartare (2): Make ½ litre (16 fl oz) of mayonnaise. Stir in a mixture of finely chopped sour gherkins, capers and *fines herbes;* vary the proportions according to taste.

Verte: Make ½ litre (16 fl oz) of mayonnaise. Blanch in boiling water for about 2 minutes 30 g (1 oz) of parsley, chervil, tarragon, and chives in equal quantities, 30 g (1 oz) of watercress leaves and 60 g (2 oz) of spinach. Drain and refresh them in cold water, then squeeze them dry in a towel. Pound the blanched herbs to a paste, then pass the paste through a sieve. Stir the sieved paste into the mayonnaise.

Mousseline

To colour mousseline with spinach, boil 500 g (1 lb) of spinach in salted water for 1 to 2 minutes, then refresh the leaves in cold water, drain them well and squeeze them repeatedly in your hands. Press the leaves through a fine-meshed sieve or purée them in a food processor. Stir enough of the purée into the mousseline to give the required colour.

To make about 60 cl (1 pint)

250 g	skinned fillets of whiting, pike, salmon, hake, monkfish or John Dory, chopped	8 oz
	salt and pepper	
	cayenne pepper and grated nutmeg (optional)	
1	large egg white	1
¼ litre	double cream	8 fl oz

Work the fish to a smooth purée by pounding it in a mortar or blending it in a food processor. Season with salt and pepper and with cayenne pepper and nutmeg, if used. Add the egg white, pounding until it is completely incorporated. A little at a time, rub the purée through a fine-meshed sieve, using a plastic scraper for a drum sieve, or a wooden pestle for any other sieve. Pack the purée into a glass or metal bowl and press plastic film against the surface. Place the bowl in a larger bowl of crushed ice and refrigerate for at least 1 hour.

Using a wooden spoon, work a little of the cream into the mixture. Return the bowls to the refrigerator for 15 minutes. Continue beating in small quantities of cream, refrigerating for 15 minutes between each addition. Beat the mixture vigorously as soon as it becomes soft enough. When about half the cream has been incorporated, refrigerate for a few minutes. Lightly whip the remaining cream and incorporate it into the purée. Refrigerate until ready for use.

Recipe Index

English recipe titles are listed by categories such as "Anchovy Sauce", "Cream", "Fish and Shellfish, Sauces for" and "Wine Sauces", and within those categories appear alphabetically. Foreign recipe titles are listed alphabetically without regard to category.

General Index/Glossary

Included in this index are definitions of many of the culinary terms used in this book: definitions are in italics. The recipes in the Anthology are listed in the Recipe Index on page 168.

Almond sauce (Romesco), 22, 24-25
Allspice: *the dried berry—used whole or ground—of a member of the myrtle family. Called allspice because it has something of the aroma of clove, cinnamon and nutmeg combined;* 7
Anchovies, 5; butter flavoured with, 12; filleting, 12; pounding, 12; purée, 12; in salsa verde, 18
Apples, purée, 36; sauce, 36-37
Apricots, poaching, 37; purée, 36, 37; sauce, 36, 37
Aromatics: *all substances—such as vegetables, herbs and spices—that add aroma and flavour to food when used in cooking;* 7, 8, 42-43
Artichokes, 78-79
Asparagus, 63
Aspic, glazing with, 52, 53
Bain-marie: *a large pot or vessel in which water is heated so that a smaller pot can be placed inside and its contents cooked or heated. Used for custards, creams and other preparations that cannot tolerate direct heat or boiling;* 57, 60, 61, 64
Basil, 6; in pesto, 22-23; with tomatoes, 30
Bâtarde sauce, 5, 6, 57, 68-69
Bay leaves, 6, 7
Beans, haricot, and tomato sauce, 34-35
Béarnaise sauce, 6, 57, 60, 62-63
Béchamel, Marquis de, 5
Béchamel sauce, 5
Berries, to purée, 36
Beurre blanc, 5, 15, 26-27
Blanch: *to plunge food into boiling water for a short period. Done for a number of reasons: to remove strong flavours, such as the excess saltiness of some bacon; to soften vegetables before further cooking; to facilitate the removal of skins or shells. Another meaning is "to whiten";* herbs, 12; orange or lemon rind, 20; shallots, 12
Blanched almonds: *almonds that have been peeled by blanching (q.v.).*
Bones, extracting marrow from, 8, 11; marrow as garnish, 8; in stock, 41, 42
Bordelaise sauce, 46, 48
Bouquet garni, 6, 7
Braising, 71, 77; artichokes, 78-79; sweetbreads, 77
Bread sauce, 7, 19
Brill, 42, 50, 51
Broccoli, 63
Brown sauce, 5, 41, 46; with blood (for game), 54-55; garnishes for, 46; with truffles (Périgueux), 46, 48; with wine and aromatics (Bordelaise), 46, 48
Butter, anchovy, 12; clarified, 61; crayfish, 12, 13; herb, 6, 12
Butter sauces, 26-27
Buttermilk: *a by-product of churning cream to make butter, buttermilk is used in cheese-making and with leavening agents in baking. Nowadays, it is also made by thickening skimmed milk with a bacterial culture.*
Butterscotch sauce, 38-39
Caramel custard, 66
Caramel sauce, 38
Caramelize: *to heat sugar until it turns brown and syrupy. Also to evaporate meat or vegetable juices to leave a brown "caramel" residue on the bottom of the pan.*
Carrots, in mirepoix, 8; purée, 15, 32-33
Cauliflower, 63, 68-69
Cayenne pepper, 7, 19
Celeriac, 32
Celery, in bouquet garni, 7; in mirepoix, 8; with tomatoes, 30
Chaud-froid, 41, 52-53
Cheese sauce, see Mornay sauce
Chervil, 6, 17
Chicken, with chaud-froid in aspic, 52-53
Chicory, 16
Chili peppers: *numerous varieties of small finger-shaped hot peppers, native to tropical America and the West Indies.*

Chives, 6
Chocolate, to melt, 38, 39; sauce, 38, 39
Choron sauce, 57, 60, 62
Clarified butter: *butter from which the water, milk solids and salt have been removed;* 61
Cloves, 7, 19, 36
Coral (sea urchin roe), 54; extracting, 54; purée, 54; to thicken fish velouté, 54-55
Coulis, 41, 42, 44-45, 52, 77
Court-bouillon: *cooking liquid flavoured with aromatic vegetables and wine.*
Cranberry sauce, 19
Crayfish, butter, 12, 13; sauce, 28; shelling, 13; tails, 28
Cream sauce, with lemon, 16-17; with pepper purée, 18
Crème fraîche: *slightly ripened, sharp-tasting double cream widely available in France. The nearest equivalent is fresh double cream which can be substituted in most recipes where crème fraîche is required.*
Croûtons: *small cubes of bread fried in butter and used as garnish.*
Cumberland sauce, 19, 20-21
Custard, 57, 66-67; with caramel, 66; vanilla, 66
Dandelion leaves, 16
Deglaze: *to pour a liquid such as wine, stock, water or cream into a pan in which meat or vegetables have been fried or roasted in order to incorporate the particles remaining on the bottom of the pan in a sauce or soup;* 47, 71, 73, 74, 76
Demi-glace, 46
Desserts, sauces for, 15, 36-39, 64-65, 66-67
Duxelles, 8, 9, 19; velouté combined with, 51
Egg-based sauces, bâtarde, 6, 57, 68-69; béarnaise, 57, 60, 62-63; choron, 57, 60, 62; custard, 57, 66-67; gribiche, 58, 59; hollandaise, 5, 57, 60-61; maltaise, 57, 60, 63; mayonnaise, 57, 58-59; sabayon, 57, 64-65
Endive, 16-17
Fines herbes: *mixture of finely chopped fresh herbs that always incorporates parsley plus one or more other herbs, such as chives, tarragon and chervil;* 6
Fish, fumet, 41, 42, 49, 77; sabayon, 57, 64-65; sauces for, 22, 24-25, 26-27, 28, 49-51, 54, 61, 62-63, 64-65, 68-69, 80-81; velouté, 8, 49, 50, 54; see also individual fish
Fruit, purée, 36; sauces, 36; see also individual fruit
Fumet, fish, 41, 42, 49, 77; sabayon from, 64-65; velouté from, 49, 50; red wine in, 80-81
Game sauces, 7, 46, 49, 72; chaud-froid, 52-53; with blood, 54-55; with truffles (Périgueux), 46, 48
Garam masala: *mixture of ground spices, usually equal parts of cinnamon, cloves, cardamoms, black cumin seeds, nutmeg and mace, and sometimes also coriander seeds and bay leaves. Available from Indian grocers.*
Garlic, 15, 22; in vinaigrette, 16; sauce, 15, 22, 24-25
Gelatine, 41, 42, 77
Glace de viande, 41, 42, 44-45
Glaze, meat, 41, 42, 44-45, 77
Glazing, roast lamb, 78-79; with aspic, 52, 53
Gooseberry, purée, 36; in sauce bâtarde, 68
Gravy, 71
Green butter, 12
Green sauce (salsa verde), 16, 18
Gribiche, 58, 59
Gutting, hares and rabbits, 54
Hare, in chaud-froid, 54; skinning and gutting, 54
Herbs, 6; to blanch, 12; bouquet garni, 6, 7; butter flavoured with, 6, 12, 50; fines herbes, 6; mayonnaise with, 58
Hollandaise sauce, 5, 57, 60-61
Horseradish, 19
Julienne: *the French term for vegetables or other food cut into thin strips.*
Juniper berries, 7
Kidneys, 62, 74-75
Lamb, glazing, 78-79; larding, 78
Larding, 78
La Varenne, François Pierre, 5
"Le Cuisinier François", 5
Leeks, 7, 63
Lemon juice, and cream, 16-17, 18
Lettuce, dressing for, 16-17; purée, 32
Liquamen, 5
Mace, 7, 19
Madeira, 64, 78

Maltaise sauce, 57, 60, 63
Marinade, 5
Marjoram, 6
Marrow, bone, to extract, 11; as garnish, 8
Mayonnaise, 57, 58-59; gribiche, 58, 59; with herbs, 58; pink, 58
Meat glaze, 41, 42, 44-45, 77
Minced meat, 84
Mint, 6; salad dressing, 16-17
Mirepoix, 8, 19; in red wine, 10
Mixed spices: *mixture of spices and herbs; classically equal proportions of nutmeg, mace, cinnamon, cayenne pepper, white pepper, cloves, ground bay leaf, thyme, marjoram and savory.*
Monkfish, 28, 42
Mornay sauce, 28, 29
Mushrooms, as garnish, 8; to keep white, 11; see also Duxelles
Mussels, as garnish, 8; to open, 10
Mustard, in vinaigrette, 16
Nantua sauce, 28
Nuoc mam: *Vietnamese fermented fish sauce, available from speciality food stores.*
Nutmeg, 7, 36
Oil and vinegar, salad dressing, 16-17
Olive oil, 16
Onions, in mirepoix, 8; sauce (soubise), 34-35; with tomatoes, 30; see also Duxelles
Oregano, 6, 30
Oranges, 57, 60; in maltaise sauce, 63
Paprika, 16
Parsley, 6, 7, 9
Partridge, with chaud-froid in aspic, 52-53
Pasta, sauces for, 15, 22-23, 71, 84
Peaches, Peach Melba, 36; purée, 36
Peanut oil, 16
Pears, poached with sweet sabayon, 64-65; purée, 36
Pepper, cayenne, 7
Pepper mill, spices for, 7
Peppercorns, 7
Peppers, see Chili peppers, Sweet peppers
Périgueux sauce, 46, 48
Pestle and mortar, 11, 13, 22
Pesto, 6, 15, 22-23
Pineapple, purée, 36
Pine-nuts, 15, 22
Plums, purée, 36
Poaching, 71, 77; apricots, 37; prawns, 10; salmon, 80; sole, 80-81
Pork, 34-35, 36-37; sautéing, 72
Potatoes, 24; sauces for, 71, 84
Poultry, sauces for, 19, 52-53, 68-69, 71, 72
Prawns, 18, 30-31; as garnish, 8, 10; peeling, 10; poaching, 10
Prosciutto: *Italian unsmoked ham, here refers to prosciutto crudo (raw ham e.g. Parma ham);* 84
Purées, anchovy, 12; apple, 36-37; apricot, 36, 37; bean, 34-35; carrot, 15, 32-33; celeriac, 32; coral, 54; crayfish, 12, 13; gooseberry, 36; lettuce, 32; onion, 34-35; peach, 36; pear, 36; pineapple, 36; plum, 36; raspberry, 36; redcurrant, 36; sorrel, 32-33; spinach, 32; strawberry, 36; sweet pepper, 8, 9; tomato, 8, 30-31, 57, 62; turnip, 32
Ragù, 84
Raspberries, purée, 36; sauce, 36
Redcurrants, purée, 36; sauce, 19
Red pepper sauce, 18
Reduce: *to boil down a liquid to concentrate its flavour and thicken it to the consistency of a sauce;* braising and poaching liquids, 71; red wine, 10
Rice, sauces for, 30-31, 71
Rind, blanching, 20
Roasting, 71, 76; juices, 8
Rocket, 16
Romesco, 22, 24-25
Rosemary, 6, 7
Roux, 5, 15, 28, 41, 46, 57
Sabayon, savoury, 57, 64-65; sweet, 64-65
Saffron, 7; in velouté, 51
Salad dressing, 16; cream with pepper purée, 18; mint, 16-17; oil and vinegar, 16-17; see also Mayonnaise

Recipe Credits

The sources for the recipes in this volume are shown below. Page references in brackets indicate where the recipes appear in the Anthology.

Adimari, Fiamma Niccolini, *Il Libro della Cacciagione.* © Casa Editrice Sonzogno 1979. Published by Sonzogno, Milano. Translated by permission of Gruppo Editoriale Fabbri Bompiani—Sonzogno—Etas. S.p.A. *(page 137).*

Agulló, Ferran, *Llibre de la Cuina Catalana.* Published by Alta Fulla, Barcelona. Translated by permission of Alta Fulla *(pages 91, 97).*

Albert, B., *Le Cuisinier Parisien.* Published in Paris by Louis Tenré, Libraire, 1833 *(pages 101, 108 and 110).*

Alperi, Magdalena, *Tratado Completo de Comidas y Bebidas.* © Magdalena Alperi. First edition June 1977. Second edition December 1978. Translated by permission of the author, Gijon (Asturias) *(page 103).*

Barberousse, Michel, *Cuisine Provençale.* Published by Librairie de la Presse, Biarritz. Translated by permission of Librairie de la Presse *(pages 125, 129).*

Barthélémy, F., *Les Menus Expliqués de Cuisine Pratique.* Copyright by Le Cordon Bleu. Published by Bibliotheque du Journal "Le Cordon-Bleu", Paris. Translated by permission of Le Cordon Bleu *(pages 102, 104 and 117).*

Beckwith, Lady Muriel, *Sauces, Sweet and Savoury—How to Make Them.* Copyright Lady Muriel Beckwith. Published by Herbert Jenkins Limited, London, 1953. By permission of The Hutchinson Publishing Group, London *(pages 109, 153).*

Bertholle, Louisette, *La Cuisine des Saisons.* © Opera Mundi, Paris, 1980. Co-published by Albin Michel—Opera Mundi, Paris. Translated by permission of Editions Albin Michel *(page 126).*

Bickel, Walter and Kramer, René, *Wild und Geflügel*

in der Internationalen Küche. © 1974 by Kochbuchverlag Heimeran KG, München. Published by Wilhelm Heyne Verlag, München. Translated by permission of BLV Verlagsgesellschaft mbH, Munich *(page 94).*

Bontou, Aloïde, *Traité de Cuisine Bourgeoise Bordelaise.* 3rd edition. Published by Fëret et Fils, Éditeurs, Bordeaux 1910. Translated by permission of Éditions Feret et Fils *(pages 112, 115 and 118)*

Böttiger, Theodor, *Schalen- und Krustentiere.* © 1972 by Wilhelm Heyne Verlag, München. Published by Wilhelm Heyne Verlag. Translated by permission of Wilhelm Heyne Verlag *(pages 118, 122).*

Bouillard, Paul, *La Gourmandise à Bon Marché.* © 1925 by Albin Michel. Published by Éditions Albin Michel, Paris. Translated by permission of Éditions Albin Michel *(pages 86, 104, 125 and 129).*

Bourbon, Louis Auguste de, *Le Cuisinier Gascon.* Published by Les Amis du Tricastin. Reprinted by Editions Daniel Morcrette, Luzarches, 1976. Translated by permission of Editions Daniel Morcrette *(pages 100, 114).*

Bradley, Richard, *The Country Housewife and Lady's Director* (Parts 1 and 2). Published in 1727 and 1732 respectively. © Prospect Books 1980. Published by Prospect Books, London. By permission of the publisher *(page 99).*

Brazier, Eugenie, *Les Secrets de la Mère Brazier.* © Solar, 1977. Published by Solar, Paris. Translated by permission of Solar *(pages 90, 98, 110 and 120).*

Brennan, Jennifer, *Thai Cooking.* © Jennifer Brennan 1981. Originally published as The Original Thai Cookbook by Richard Marek Publishers, New York. First published by Jill Norman & Hobhouse Ltd., London 1981. By permission of Jill Norman & Hobhouse Ltd. *(pages 88, 100).*

Brissenden, Rosemary, *South East Asian Food.* © R. F. and R. L. Brissenden, 1970. Published by Penguin Books Ltd., London. By permission of Penguin Books

Ltd. *(page 143).*

Brown, Dorothy (Editor), *Symposium Fare.* © Prospect Books 1981. Published by Prospect Books, London. By permission of the publisher *(page 140).*

Brown, Helen, *Helen Brown's West Coast Cook Book.* Copyright 1952, by Helen Evans Brown. Published by Little, Brown and Company, Boston, Mass. By permission of Little, Brown and Company *(page 86, 98).*

Brunetti, Gino, *Cucina Mantovana di Principi e Popolo.* Published by the Istituto Carlo d'Arco per la Storia di Mantova, Mantova. Translated by permission of Don Costante Berselli, Mantova *(pages 8, 96).*

Caillat, A., *150 Manières d'Accomoder les Sardines.* Published by Imprimerie Colbert, Marseille, 189 *(pages 143, 144).*

Calera, Ana Maria, *Cocina Andaluza.* © Ana Maria Calera. © Editorial Everest S.A., León-España. Published by Editorial Everest, S.A. Translated by permission of Editorial Everest S. A. *(pages 96, 97).*

Calera, Ana Maria, *365 Recetas de Cocina Vasca.* © Ana Maria Calera. © Editorial Everest, S.A., León-España. Published by Editorial Everest, S.A. Translated by permission of Editorial Everest S.A. *(page 111).*

Cardona, María Dolores Camps, *Cocina Catalana.* © Editorial Ramos Majos, 1979. Published by Editorial Ramos Majos, Barcelona. Translated by permission of Editorial Ramos Majos S.A. *(page 97).*

Carter, Susannah, *The Frugal Colonial Housewife.* © 1976 by Jean McKibbin. Published by Dolphin Books, an imprint of Doubleday & Company, Inc., New York. By permission of Doubleday & Company, Inc. *(page 99, 104, 106 and 113).*

Catlin, Joan and Law, Joy (Editors), *Royal College of Art Cook Book.* © 1980 Royal College of Art. Published by the Royal College of Art, London. By permission of the Royal College of Art *(page 95).*

Chapel, Alain, *La Cuisine c'est beaucoup plus que*

des Recettes. © Éditions Robert Laffont, S.A., Paris, 1980. Published by Éditions Robert Laffont, Paris. Translated by permission of Éditions Robert Laffont *(page 150).*

Ciurana, Jaume and Torrado, Llorenç, *Els Olis de Catalunya i la Seva Cuina.* © Jaume Ciurana i Calceran per la primera part. Published by Servei Central de Publicacions de la Generalitat, Departament de la Presidència, Barcelona 1981. Translated by permission of Jaume Ciurana, Barcelona *(page 90).*

Cocina Regional Española. Published by Editorial Almena, Madrid 1963. Translated by permission of Editorial Doncel, Madrid *(pages 91, 144).*

Contour, Alfred, *Le Cuisinier Bourguignon.* Published by Laffitte Reprints, Marseille, 1978. Translated by permission of Éditions Jeanne Laffitte *(pages 155, 157).*

Craig, Elizabeth, *Court Favourites.* First published 1953 by André Deutsch Limited, London. By permission of André Deutsch Limited *(page 121).*

Croze, Austin de, *Les Plats Régionaux de France.* Published by Éditions Daniel Morcrette, Luzarches, France. Translated by permission of Éditions Daniel Morcrette *(pages 107, 117).*

Cuciniere All'Uso Moderne, Il. Published by Presso Guglielmo Piatti, Firenze, 1825 *(page 106).*

Cuisine Lyonnaise, La. Published by Éditions Gutenberg, Lyon, 1947 *(page 121).*

Cuisine Naturelle à l'Huile d'Olive, La. © 1978 Éditions De Vecchi S.A., Paris. Published by Éditions De Vecchi S.A., Paris. Translated by permission of Éditions De Vecchi S.A. *(page 128).*

Cùnsolo, Felice, *La Cucina del Piemonte.* © by Novedit Milano. Published by Novedit Milano, 1964 *(pages 100, 121).*

Daguin, André, *Le Nouveau Cuisinier Gascon.* © 1981, Éditions Stock. Published by Éditions Stock, Paris. Translated by permission of Éditions Stock *(pages 93, 109 and 129).*

Davidis, Henriette, *Pratisches Kochbuch.* Newly revised by Luise Holle. Published in Bielefeld and Leipzig, 1898 *(page 156).*

Davidson, Alan, *North Atlantic Seafood.* © Alan Davidson 1979. Published by Macmillan Publishers Ltd./Penguin Books Ltd., London. By permission of Penguin Books Ltd. *(page 130).*

Dege, Hroar, *Fra Neptuns Gaffel.* Published by H. Aschehoug & Co., Oslo, 1966. Translated by permission of H. Aschehoug & Co. (W. Nygaard) A/S. *(page 144).*

Dinnage, Paul, *The Book of Fruit and Fruit Cookery.* © 1981 Paul Dinnage. Published by Sidgwick and Jackson Limited, London, 1981. By permission of Sidgwick and Jackson Ltd. *(pages 94, 95 and 105).*

Dubois, Urbain and Bernard, Émile, *La Cuisine Classique.* Volume I, ninth edition, 1881. Published by E. Dentu, Éditeur, Palais-Royal, Paris *(pages 119, 127).*

Dubois, Urbain and Bernard, Émile, *La Cuisine Classique.* Volume II, tenth edition, 1882. Published by E. Dentu, Editeur, Palais-Royal, Paris *(page 155).*

Dumas, Alexandre, *Le Grand Dictionnaire de Cuisine.* Published by Henri Veyrier, Paris, 1973. Translated by permission of Editions Henri Veyrier *(pages 121, 128).*

Dumont, Émile, *La Bonne Cuisine Française.* Originally published in 1873. Thirtieth edition published by Victorion Frères et Cie, Editeurs, Paris 1889 *(page 101).*

Enciclopedia Salvat De La Cocina: Tomo 8. © 1972. Salvat, S.A. de Ediciones, Pamplona, y S.A., Femmes d'Aujourd'hui—Ediper. Published by Salvat S.A.

de Ediciones. Translated by permission of Salvat Editores S.A., Barcelona *(page 126).*

Favre, Joseph, *Dictionnaire Universel de Cuisine Pratique.* Published by Laffitte Reprints, Marseille, 1978. Translated by permission of Éditions Jeanne Laffitte, Marseille *(pages 94, 97, 154 and 155).*

Ferrandini, Armido, *Onestà in Cucina.* © 1976 Vallecchi Editore Firenze. Published by Vallecchi Editore. Translated by permission of Vallecchi Editore *(page 126).*

Feslikenian, Franca, *Cucina e Vini del Lazio.* © 1973 Ugo Mursia Editore, Milan. Published by Ugo Mursia Editore, Milan. Translated by permission of Ugo Mursia Editore S.p.A. *(page 151).*

Francatelli, Charles Elmé, *The Modern Cook.* Published by Richard Bentley, London 1862 *(pages 106, 111, 119 and 123).*

Franey, Pierre, *The New York Times 60-minute Gourmet.* © 1979 by The New York Times Company. Published by Times Books, a division of Quadrangle/The New York Times Book Co. Inc., New York. By permission of Times Books, a division of Quadrangle/The New York Times Book Co. Inc. *(page 142).*

Guoy, Louis P. de, *The Gold Cook Book.* © 1947, 1948, by Louis P. de Gouy. Published by Greenberg, Publisher, New York. By Permission of Chilton Book Company, Radnor, Pennsylvania *(page 156).*

Grigson, Jane, *Jane Grigson's Vegetable Book.* © 1978 by Jane Grigson. Published by Michael Joseph Limited, London. By permission of David Higham Associates Ltd., for the author *(pages 89, 150).*

Guasch, Juan Castello, *¡Bon Profit!* (*El Libro de la Cocina Ibenca*). Copyright by the author. Published by Imprenta ALFA, Palma de Mallorca, 1971. Translated by permission of the author *(page 87).*

Holleman, Ria, *Uit Grootmoeders Keuken.* © 1972 Unieboek n. v. Bussum—Holland. Published by Van Dishoeck, Bussum. Translated by permission of Unieboek B.V. *(pages 102, 116, 118 and 124).*

Horvath, Maria, *Balkan-Küche.* © 1963 Wilhelm Heyne Verlag, München. Published by Wilhelm Heyne Verlag. Translated by permission of Wilhelm Heyne Verlag *(page 111).*

Ignotus, *Culina Famulatrix Medicinae: or, Receipts in Cookery.* Published in York in 1804 *(pages 119, 120).*

Kennedy, Diana, *Cuisines of Mexico.* © 1972 by Diana Kennedy. Published by Harper & Row, Publishers, New York. By permission of Harper & Row, Publishers, Inc. *(page 87).*

Kenney-Herbert, Col. A. F. (Wyvern), *Fifty Dinners.* Published by Edward Arnold, London, 1895 *(page 133).*

Kernmayr, Hans Gustl, *So Kochte meine Mutter.* © 1976 by Mary Hahns Kochbuchverlag, Berlin-München. Published by Wilhelm Heyne Verlag, Munich. Translated by permission of Mary Hahns Kochbuchverlag, München *(pages 94, 95, 102 and 132).*

Kitchiner, Dr., *The Cook's Oracle.* Published by A. Constable & Co., Edinburgh, 1822 *(pages 96, 98, 101 and 105).*

Kramarz, Inge, *The Balkan Cookbook.* © 1972 by Crown Publishers, Inc. Published by Crown Publishers, Inc., New York. By permission of Crown Publishers, Inc. *(pages 89, 95, 105 and 111).*

Labarre, Irène, *La Cuisine des Trois B.* © Éditions Solar, 1976. Published by Solar, Paris. Translated by permission of Solar *(page 128).*

Lassalle, George, *The Adventurous Fish Cook.* © Caroline Lassalle 1976. Published by Macmillan London Limited, London and Basingstoke in association with Pan Books Limited. By permission of Macmillan

Accounts and Administration Ltd. *(page 131).*

Lazarque, E. Auricoste de, *Cuisine Messine.* Published by Sidot Frères, Libraires-Éditeurs, Nancy, 1927 *(pages 130).*

Leyel, Mrs. C. F. and Hartley, Olga, *The Gentle Art of Cookery.* © The Executors of Mrs. C. F. Leyel, 1925. Published by Chatto and Windus, London. By permission of Chatto and Windus Ltd. *(pages 112, 115).*

Lujan, Nestor and Perucho, Juan, *El Libro de la Cocina Española.* © Ediciones Danae, S.A. 1970. Published by Ediciones Danae, S.A., Barcelona. Translated by permission of Editorial Baber, S. A., Barcelona *(pages 93, 138).*

Manning, Elise W. (Editor), *Homemade Ice Cream and Cake.* © 1972 by Farm Journal, Inc. Published by Doubleday & Company, Inc., New York. By permission of Farm Journal Inc., Philadelphia *(page 154).*

Manuel Pratique De Cuisine Provençale. © Pierre Belfond, 1980. Published by Éditions Pierre Belfond, Paris *(page 123).*

Marie, Annick, *Le Grand Livre de la Cuisine Bourguignone.* © Jean-Pierre Delarge, Éditions Universitaires, 1977. Published by Jean-Pierre Delarge, Éditeur, Paris. Translated by permission of Chantel Galtier Roussel, Literary Agent, Paris *(page 156).*

Massey and Son's Comprehensive Pudding Book. Published by Massey and Son's, London, 1865 *(pages 152, 154 and 157).*

Menon, *La Cuisinière Bourgeoise.* Paris, 1803 *(pages 110, 117).*

Minchelli, Jean and Paul, *Crustacés, Poissons et Coquillages.* © 1977 Éditions Jean-Claude Lattès. Published by Éditions Jean-Claude Lattès, Paris. Translated by permission of Éditions Jean-Claude Lattès *(pages 86, 112, 125 and 145).*

Mosimann, Anton, *Cuisine à la Carte.* © Anton Mosimann 1981. Published by Northwood Books, London. By permission of Northwood Books *(pages 135, 147, 149 and 153).*

Neuner-Duttenhofer, Bernd, *Die Neue Deutsche Küche.* © 1978 by Wilhelm Heyne Verlag, München. Published by Wilhelm Heyne Verlag, Munich. Translated by permission of Wilhelm Heyne Verlag *(pages 90, 107).*

Ngô, Bach and Zimmerman, Gloria, *The Classic Cuisine of Vietnam.* © 1979 by Barron's Educational Series, Inc. Published by Barron's/Woodbury, New York. By permission of Barron's Educational Series, Inc. *(page 88).*

Nignon, E., *Éloges de la Cuisine Française.* Copyright 1933 by H. Piazza, Paris. Published by L'Édition d'Art H. Piazza. Translated by permission of Éditions Daniel Morcrette, Luzarches, France *(pages 119, 136 and 152).*

Nilson, Bee (Editor), *The WI Diamond Jubilee Cookbook.* © A. R. Nilson and National Federation of Women's Institutes 1975. Published by William Heinemann Ltd., London. By permission of William Heinemann Ltd. *(page 87).*

Nolot, Pierre, *À la Recherche des Cuisines Oubliées.* © Berger-Levrault, 1977. Published by Éditions Berger-Levrault, Paris. Translated by permission of Éditions Berger-Levrault *(page 108).*

Norwak, Mary, *The Farmhouse Kitchen.* © Mary Norwak, 1975. Published by Penguin Books Ltd., London. By permission of Penguin Books Ltd. *(page 101).*

Oberosler, Giuseppe, *Il Tesoreto della Cucina Italiana.* Published by Editore Ulrico Hoepli, Milano, 1948. Translated by permission of Ulrico Hoepli S.p.A. *(pages 118, 131, 139 and 151).*

Ochorowicz-Monatowa, Marja, *Polish Cooking.*

Translated by Jean Karsavina. © 1958 by Crown Publishers Inc. Published by André Deutsch, London. By permission of Crown Publishers, Inc., New York (*pages 113, 116*).

Ojakangas, Beatrice A., *The Finnish Cookbook.* © 1964 by Beatrice A. Ojakangas. Published by Crown Publishers, Inc., New York. By permission of Crown Publishers, Inc. (*pages 89, 114 and 126*).

Oliver, Michel, *Mes Recettes à la Télé.* © Librairie Plon, 1980. Published by Librairie Plon, Paris. Translated by permission of Librairie Plon (*pages 105, 148*).

Olney, Judith, *Summer Food.* © 1978 by Judith Olney. Published by Atheneum Publishers, Inc., New York. By permission of Atheneum Publishers, Inc. (*pages 92*).

Olney, Richard, *The French Menu Cookbook* © 1975 by Richard Olney. Published by William Collins Sons & Co., Ltd., Glasgow and London. By permission of the author, Sollies-Pont (*page 153*).

Olney, Richard, *Simple French Food.* Copyright © Richard Olney 1974. Published by Jill Norman and Hobhouse Ltd., London, 1981. By permission of Jill Norman and Hobhouse Ltd. (*page 124*).

Ortiz, Elisabeth Lambert, *The Complete Book of Mexican Cooking.* © 1967 by Elisabeth Lambert Ortiz. Published by M. Evans and Company, Inc., New York. By permission of M. Evans and Company, Inc., and the author, London (*pages 88, 96*).

Patil, Vimla (Editor), *Kashmir to Kanyakumari.* Published by Rekha Sapru for Enar Advertisers Pvt Ltd., Bombay. By permission of Enar Advertisers Pvt. Ltd. (*pages 134, 139*).

Philpot, Rosl, *Viennese Cookery.* © 1965 by Rosl Philpot. Published by Hodder and Stoughton Limited, London. By permission of Hodder and Stoughton Limited (*pages 102, 121 and 122*).

Platt, June, *June Platt's New England Cook Book.* © 1971 by June Platt. Published by Atheneum Publishers, Inc., New York. By permission of Atheneum Publishers, Inc. (*page 156*).

Pomiane, Édouard de, *Le Code de la Bonne Chère.* © Albin Michel, Paris. Published by Éditions Albin Michel, 1948. Translated by permission of Éditions Albin

Michel (*pages 108, 130*).

Puck, Wolfgang, *Wolfgang Puck's Modern French Cooking for the American Kitchen.* © 1981 by Wolfgang Puck. Published by Houghton Mifflin Company, Boston. By permission of Houghton Mifflin Company (*pages 146, 147*).

Quillet, Aristide, *La Cuisine Moderne.* Published by Librairie Aristide Quillet, Paris, 1930. Translated by permission of Librairie Aristide Quillet S.A. (*pages 86, 103 and 114*).

Ramella, Lucetto, *Ricette Tradizionali Della Liguria.* Published by Collana Tradizioni Liguri, A. Dominici Editore, Oneglia, 1978. Translated by permission of the author, Imperia (*page 132*).

Ratto, G. B., *La Cuciniera Genovese.* Published by Tipografia Pagano, Genova. Translated by permission of Industrie Grafiche Editoriali Fratelli Pagano S.p.A. (*pages 92, 93 and 100*).

Rey-Billeton, Lucette, *Les Bonnes Recettes du Soleil.* © Éditions Aubanel 1980. Published by Éditions Aubanel, Avignon. Translated by permission of Éditions Aubanel (*pages 88, 99 and 125*).

Richter, Louise and Hommer, Sophie Charlotte, *Illustrirtes Hamburger Kochbuch.* Published by B. S. Berendsohn, Hamburg, 1879 (*page 154*).

Roden, Claudia, *Picnic.* © Claudia Roden, 1981. Published by Jill Norman & Hobhouse Ltd., London. By permission of the publisher (*pages 90, 92 and 93*).

Rundell, Mrs., *Modern Domestic Cookery.* Published by Milner and Company, Limited, London, 1837 (*pages 103, 112, 113 and 124*).

Sahni, Julie, *Classic Indian Cooking.* © 1980 by Julie Sahni. Published by William Morrow and Company, Inc., New York. By permission of Jill Norman & Hobhouse Ltd., London (*pages 134, 140, 141 and 149*).

Sastre Rayo, Gabriel and Ordinas Mari, Antonia (Editors), *Llibre de Cuina de Ca'n Cames Seques.* (Cocina Mallorquina de Siempre). Published by Antigua Imprenta Soler, Palma de Mallorca, 1977. Translated by permission of Antonia Ordinas Mari, Mallorca (*page 115*).

Schlosser, Frau Rath, *Urgrossmutters Kochbuch.* ©

Insel Verlag Frankfurt am Main, 1980. Published by Insel Verlag, Frankfurt am Main. Translated by permission of Insel Verlag (*pages 116, 122*).

Senderens, Alain and Eventhia, *La Cuisine Réussie.* © 1981, Éditions Jean-Claude Lattès, Paris. Translated by permission of Éditions Jean-Claude Lattès (*pages 136, 138 and 146*).

Stan, Anisoara, *The Romanian Cook Book.* Copyright 1951 by Anisoara Stan. Published by The Citadel Press, New York. By permission of Lyle Stuart Inc. New Jersey (*pages 113, 130*).

Suzanne, Alfred, *A Book of Salads.* Published by Ward, Lock & Co., Limited, London and Melbourne (*page 98*).

Theoharous, Anne, *Cooking the Greek Way.* © 1977 by Anne Theoharous. Published by Associated Book Publishers Ltd., London. By permission of Associated Book Publishers, Ltd. (*page 91*).

Troisgros, Jean and Pierre, *The Nouvelle Cuisine of Jean and Pierre Troisgros.* © Macmillan London Ltd 1980. First published 1982 by Papermac, a division of Macmillan Publishers Limited, London and Basingstoke. Originally published by Éditions Robert Laffont S.A., Paris as "Cuisiniers à Roanne". © Éditions Robert Laffont S.A., Paris, 1977. By permission of Macmillan Publishers Limited (*pages 107, 127*).

Viard and Fouret, *Le Cuisinier Royal.* Published in Paris, 1828 (*pages 106, 108, 109 and 127*).

Watt, Alexander, *Paris Bistro Cookery.* Published by Macgibbon & Kee, London, 1957. By permission of Granada Publishing Ltd., St. Albans (*pages 132, 145 and 148*).

White, Patricia Holden, *Food as Presents.* © 1975 1982 by Patricia Holden White. Published by Penguin Books Ltd., London. By permission of Deborah Rogers Ltd., Literary Agency, London (*page 152*).

Willan, Anne and L'École de Cuisine La Varenne Paris, *French Regional Cooking.* © 1981 Marshall Editions Ltd. Text © 1981 Anne Willan and L'École de Cuisine La Varenne. Published by The Hutchinson Publishing Group, London. By permission of Marshall Editions Ltd., London (*page 142*).

Acknowledgements and Picture Credits

The Editors of this book are particularly indebted to Gail Duff, Maidstone, Kent and Ann O'Sullivan, Deya, Mallorca.

They also wish to thank the following: Danielle Adkinson, London; Alison Attenborough, Chelmsford, Essex; Josephine Bacon, Los Angeles, California; Markie Benet, London; Beverly Bernstein, London; Paul Bifulco, Bifulco's Stores Ltd., London; Nicola Blount, London; Robert Bruce, Covent Garden, London; Lesley Coates, Ilford, Essex; Emma Codrington, Richmond-upon-Thames, Surrey; Josephine Christian, Stoke St. Michael, Somerset; Mimi Errington, Screveton, Nottinghamshire; Sarah Jane Evans, London; Jay Ferguson, London; Neyla Freeman, London; Maggi Heinz, London; Hilary

Hockman, London; Lotte Keeble, Twickenham, Middlesex; Pippa Millard, London; Wendy Morris, London; Dilys Naylor, Kingston-upon-Thames, Surrey; Rosemary Oates, London; Winona O'Connor, North Fambridge, Essex; Neil Philip, Oxford; Sylvia Robertson, Surbiton, Surrey; Vicky Robinson, London; Adrian Saunders, London; Nicole Segre, London; Stephanie Thompson, London; Tina Walker, London; Rita Walters, Ilford, Essex.

Photographs by Tom Belshaw: Cover, Frontispiece, 7, 8—bottom, 9—bottom, 10 to 12, 29—bottom, 37—bottom, 40 to 53, 54—top, 55, 58, 59, 66—bottom, 67—bottom right, 74—bottom, 75—bottom, 77 to 79, 80—bottom, 81—bottom.
Other photographers (alphabetically): John Cook:

9—top right, centre right, 14, 18—bottom, 24, 25, 32—top, 33—top, 34—bottom, 35—bottom, 36—top, 37—top right, 64—top, 65—top, 80—top, 81—top, 84. Alan Duns: 9—top middle, centre left, 13, 26—top, 27, 28—bottom, 35—top right, 37—top left and middle, 39—bottom, 56, 60, 61—bottom, 63—bottom, 68, 69. Louis Klein: 2. Bob Komar: 8—top, centre, 9—top left, centre middle, 16, 17, 18—top, centre, 19 to 23, 26—bottom, 28—top, 29—top, 30, 31, 32—bottom, 33—bottom, 34—top, 35—top left and middle, 36—bottom, 38, 39—top, 54—bottom, 55—bottom, 61—top, 62, 63—top, 64—bottom, 65—bottom, 66—top, 67—top, bottom left, 70 to 73, 74—top, 75—top, 76, 82, 83.
Illustrations on page 6 by Anna Pugh. Line cuts from Mary Evans Picture Library and private sources.

Colour separations by Essex Colour Ltd.—Essex, England.
Typesetting by Camden Typesetters—London, England.
Printed and bound by Brepols S.A.—Turnhout, Belgium.